Archaeology and History in Sardinia
from the Stone Age to the Middle Ages

SHEPHERDS,
SAILORS, &
CONQUERORS

Archaeology and History in Sardinia
from the Stone Age to the Middle Ages

SHEPHERDS,
SAILORS, &
CONQUERORS

Stephen L. Dyson

Robert J. Rowland, Jr.

WITHDRAWN

University of Pennsylvania Museum of Archaeology and Anthropology
Philadelphia, PA

Library of Congress Cataloging-in-Publication Data

Dyson, Stephen L.
Archaeology and history in Sardinia from the Stone Age to the Middle Ages
: shepherds, sailors, and conquerors / Stephen L. Dyson, Robert J. Rowland.
p. cm.
Includes bibliographical references and index.
ISBN 978-1-934536-02-5 (hardcover : alk. paper)
1. Sardinia (Italy)--History--To 456. 2. Sardinia (Italy)--Antiquities.
3. Material culture--Italy--Sardinia. 4. Sardinia (Italy)--Social
conditions. 5. Sardinia (Italy)--History--456-1297. I. Rowland, Robert J.,
1938- II. Title.
DG55.S2D97 2007
937'.9--dc22
2007043192

Printed in the USA on acid-free paper.

Contents

Preface

The completion of this book has been a bittersweet experience. Bob Rowland and I enjoyed a personal and professional friendship that extended over 40 years. Our interests as students of the Roman Empire were both complementary and contiguous. Bob developed an impressive knowledge of Roman administrative, social, and economic history and of Roman provincial administration. His various interests found their focus in the study of the island of Sardinia. Long before the term *longue durée* became fashionable in classical circles, he applied the concept and approach to the long history of that island, undertaking innovative scholarship on topics that extended from prehistory to the Late Middle Ages. My own research was concerned with many of the same fields in Roman history, but with a more archaeological emphasis and with a concentration on the use of archaeological approaches such as field survey to illuminate Roman social and economic history.

Bob and I had often talked about a joint scholarly project. He stressed the under-explored archaeological resources of Sardinia, and the potential of the type of archaeological survey that was being applied increasingly on the Italian mainland. Finally in the 1980s our hopes were realized. The result was a series of productive and pleasant seasons of archaeological survey in the countryside around the west coast city of Oristano.

Bob's knowledge of Sardinia was immense, and his enthusiasm and affection for its land, people, and history was infectious. It was clear to an outsider like myself that Sardinia presented a fascinating case study for reconstructing the interaction of internal and external forces in shaping an island society over long periods of time. In the early 1990s Sardinia was relatively little known, even in Italy. There was certainly no book in English that provided an adequate historical and archaeological introduction. We decided to write such a work.

The real foundation of this book is Bob Rowland's mastery of all phases of Sardinian history and archaeology. My own role has been that of an informed outsider, adding some different perspectives and placing some of the Sardinian issues in a broader historical and especially archaeological context. Over the years we have both benefited from the thoughts and observations of the small but active body of Sardinian experts. Robert Tykot of the University of South Florida has been especially helpful, especially in the somewhat traumatic final stages of the preparation of the book. Matthew Notarian and Jennifer Kendall of the Classics Department at the University at Buffalo have been very helpful in the preparation of the illustration. Walda Metcalf, Director of Publications at the University of Pennsylvania Museum, has been a superb if exacting editor. The two Penn Museum Press external readers provided a wealth of useful commentary and criticism.

Bob Rowland was struck down by a fatal illness just as the manuscript was in the final stage of revision. He never saw the completed manuscript. Hence the published work will lack the control for accuracy and the mastery of detail that only he could have provided. However, I hope that it will fulfill the goals that both of us sought for it and will be a suitable tribute to a distinguished scholar, a most decent person, and, for me, a good and much-missed friend.

1
Approaching the Archaeology and History of Ancient and Medieval Sardinia

The larger Mediterranean islands have in recent years become a subject of increasing interest to anthropologists, historians, geographers, and archaeologists. Rather than being seen as isolated entities or historical and cultural backwaters of concern mainly to antiquarians and social anthropologists, they are now studied as complex ecological, historical, and cultural systems where local traditions and outside influences have interacted over time in diverse ways. As *Annales* history with its *longue durée* perspective has become central to historical research, the major Mediterranean islands, with their critical land and population masses, long histories, and diachronic experience of both isolation and connection, emerge as fascinating social science laboratories. This has led to comparative studies like Patton's *Islands in Time* (1996) and investigations of individual island cultures like those of Michael Herzfeld on Crete and of Christopher Smith, John Serrati, and colleagues on Sicily (Herzfeld 1991; Malone 1997; Smith and Serrati 2000).

Especially the four largest Mediterranean islands of Cyprus, Crete, Sicily, and Sardinia offer long and complex histories (Patton 1996). They are all located on long-used nautical routes in a much-traveled sea and have certainly been shaped by foreign contacts. At the same time their distance from mainland neighbors, the sporadic nature of marine contact, and their size and indigenous resources fostered the development of distinctive cultures and histories. These deep cultural histories and the dynamic of internal and external forces are among the things that make Mediterranean island research so fascinating.

Sardinia provides excellent materials for a study in Mediterranean island identity. It is the second-largest island in the Mediterranean, with more than enough land mass (the island measures 270 km on the north-south axis and 145 km east to west) resources, and ecological diversity to sustain a substantial population and foster the development of complex societies. The presence on the island of one of the few sources of obsid-

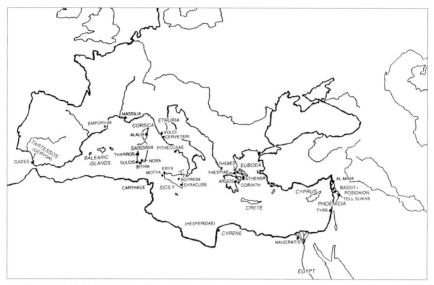

Sardinia in the Mediterranean (after Tykot and Andrews 1992).

ian in the central Mediterranean brought early contact with the outside world. Sardinia was at the edge of the Late Bronze Age trading community centered on the eastern and east-central Mediterranean. The Phoenicians early came to appreciate its strategic and commercial potential as they expanded their trade routes westward to North Africa and Spain. With the emergence of Carthage and Rome as the dominant powers in the central Mediterranean, Sardinia was incorporated into new, more complex imperial systems. Only 188 km separated the Gulf of Olbia from the coast of Roman Latium, and the distance is only 178 km from Capo Teulada to the coast of Carthaginian North Africa. Both states would eventually want to control the island.

Even in this highly competitive imperial phase in Sardinia's history, limits on the projection of both Punic and Roman imperial power and island topography fostered the survival of a strong island identity. In antiquity the passage from the mainland of both Italy and North Africa to Sardinia was never easy. Except for Elba and Corsica to the north and northeast there were no intermediate stepping stone islands that could have broken the open water voyage. Sardinia was not located at a Bronze Age or Greek colonial period crossroads like Crete, Sicily, or Cyprus. Although the establishment of Phoenician colonies in the central and western Mediterranean made Sardinia more part of the Mediterranean

Modern Sardinia.

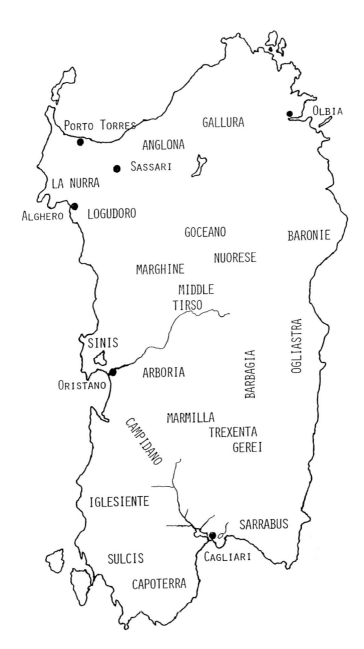

Principal regions and cities of Sardinia (after Webster 1992).

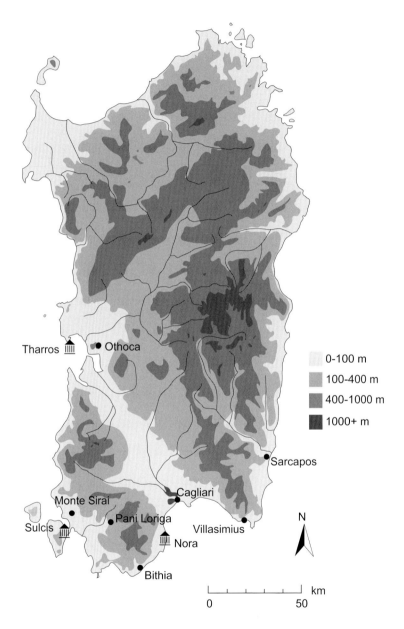

	0-100 m
	100-400 m
	400-1000 m
	1000+ m

Tharros 🏛 ● Othoca

Sarcapos ●

Monte Sirai ●
Sulcis ● 🏛
Pani Loriga ●
Cagliari
Villasimius ●
🏛 Nora
Bithia ●

N

km
0   50

The topography of Sardinia.

trading system, sailors still did not cross from the eastern Mediterranean to Iberia and south France with the frequency that they did from Greece to the Levant. Much of Sardinia's coastline, especially on the east, facing Italy, is rocky and forbidding. The rather small river valleys, especially those on the east coast, did not foster communication with the interior.

During the 8th and 7th centuries BC the Phoenicians brought Sardinia into a trading network that extended from Lebanon to the coasts of Iberia, but Phoenician settlements on the coast of Sardinia were small affairs, and their impact on indigenous cultures was limited. The Carthaginians starting in the 6th century BC were the first to make Sardinia part of an external empire, but the extent of their real control of Sardinia can easily be exaggerated. The imperial powers that dominated the Mediterranean from the Roman Empire onward treated Sardinia as a backwater to be left to its own devices. Hence for much of the time considered in this book internal forces largely shaped social and economic development on the island.

This is a study that attempts to look at archaeological and historical processes in Sardinia over long time periods. While it is traditional to discuss Sardinian prehistory in classic 19th century evolutionary terms (i.e., Paleolithic to Iron Age) and Sardinian history in relation to dominant powers in the central Mediterranean, the realities of cultural development on the island do not favor simplistic explanatory models and clear time-period divisions. Despite an often over-eager use of invasion models to explain cultural changes on the island, there appears to have been a strong continuum of insular cultural development that stretched from at least the later Neolithic of the 4th millennium BC into the Punic-Roman period toward the end of the 1st millennium BC. External influences certainly were there, but until the Carthaginian and Roman periods they were secondary to internal cultural forces. Even under the Carthaginians and Romans, the inhabitants of the island to a great extent went their own way.

Concepts such as social dynamics and cultural interaction are emphasized in part to counter Sardinian archaeologists and historians who have placed great emphasis on resistance and isolation as the shaping forces in Sardinia. That vision of island history has created a picture of static indigenous groups resisting outside forces or retreating to the inaccessible recesses of the interior. That view derives in part from the experience of early modern and modern Sardinia, when it was a marginal province in not overly progressive imperial systems. The archaeology of Sardinia from the middle Neolithic to the Punic period, however, provides considerable evidence for local initiative and creativity. This is reflected in the settlement systems, the ceremonial centers, the mortuary architecture, and the arts and crafts.

Similar internal dynamics shaped many aspects of Late Antique (4th-6th centuries) and medieval (8th-14th centuries) Sardinia, and the especially the world of the Judicate (10th-14th centuries), which recombined Byzantine and continental influences in a distinctly Sardinian way.

This study begins with the first settlement of Sardinia sometime in the Paleolithic. The starting point is easy to set, the concluding one less so. However, the final collapse of the Judicate in the 15th century and the integration of Sardinia into the Aragonese state at that time seems a good terminal point. These events marked the beginning of early modern and modern Sardinia. As is always the case with Sardinian history, those breaks with the past were less complete than often stated, but the study of Sardinia from the 15th to the 20th century is another project, well outside the expertise of the authors.

This type of *longue durée* history must draw on a variety of sources. Reliance on archaeology is great, since for much of the time period considered archaeology provides almost all of our evidence. As one moves into Iron Age and post-Iron Age Sardinia the intersections of written and material sources become more complex. The classical authors do provide much useful information, but the total body of written sources, both textual and epigraphic, is limited. Moreover, they represent a colonialist narrative, the voice of the imperialists who tried to subdue the island. If one is to understand the "other" Sardinia, the world of the indigenous peoples that formed the dynamic core of Sardinian society through much of the so-called historic period of Antiquity, one still has to rely heavily on archaeology.

With the medieval period, relative importance of the categories of evidence changes again. Literary sources, both secular and religious, exist in some numbers. Archival texts such as monastic property registers (such as the so-called *condaghi*) become available in relatively large numbers, but they too pose their own problems of interpretation. The material culture raises a whole range of problems, for the medieval archaeology of Sardinia is still in its infancy, and even the medieval architectural monuments have been less well studied than comparable monuments on the continent.

Both authors have long worked at the juncture of the "archaeological" and the "historical" and are well aware of the limits of both material and written evidence. However, we believe that a history that is not just a political and military narrative must mine judiciously all available evidence. This is especially true for a study that seeks to move beyond a focus on elites and to reconstruct the social and economic forces that shaped this island society.

A Short History of Archaeological Research

Archaeological research has played the major role in reconstructing the historical development of Sardinia for much of the period considered in the first part of this book, that is from the first settlement of the island in the paleolithic to the Roman conquest in the 3rd century BC. It has been very much of an island archaeological tradition, created either by Sards or by scholars who spent long periods on the island. At a time when historians of archaeology are increasingly interested in the intersection between dominant interpretative paradigms and the wider political, social, and intellectual world in which the archaeologists were grounded, Sardinia provides a fascinating case study of a local archaeological culture. However, the history of archaeology in Sardinia is a subject in its infancy. The most recent history of Italian archaeology (Barbanera 1998) hardly mentions Sardinia.

The rich archaeological heritage of Sardinia was long exploited for varied purposes. As early as 1365 the governor of Cagliari, Don Alberto Satrillas, purchased jewelry found in a tomb at Fordongianus and sent those treasures to the royal court in Spain. Sardinia like the rest of Europe had antiquaries interested in both classical and early Christian archaeology. By 1614 pious researchers were excavating the remains of Sardinian martyrs, keeping meticulous records that have recently proven invaluable to later researchers.

Sardinia was first "discovered" by the wider European intellectual and especially antiquarian community in the 18th century. Except for the few court centers like Cagliari the island was seen as isolated and backward (Fuos 1780). D. A. Azuni's essay on the geographical, political, and natural history of Sardinia (Mattone 1980) established a paradigm for viewing a "primitive" island that persisted into such important 20th century research as that of the French geographer Maurice Le Lannou (1979).

Early 19th century travelers and antiquarians brought Sardinia and its rich archaeology to the attention of the wider scholarly community. Among the foreigners who described the island the most important was the Piedmontese military officer Alberto La Marmora (Assorgia 1998). He traveled extensively in Sardinia, and his publications contained extensive remarks on the antiquities.

While the local collecting of artifacts dominated the archaeological scene, interest in Sardinian antiquities slowly expanded beyond the libraries of a few antiquaries. In 1802 a cabinet of curiosities that included archaeological materials was established at Cagliari, and in 1806 it was opened to the public. Gaetano Cara served as its director from 1839. He

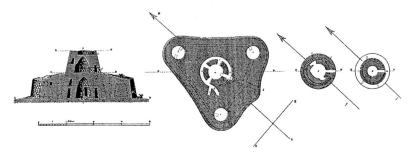

Drawings of Nuraghe Antine by Alberto La Marmora.

enriched the collections with newly discovered materials but was also taken in by forgeries such Punic-Sardinian statues. During that time excavations were started at such sites as Tharros (1841) and Olbia (1843) (Zucca 1997).

As the century advanced Romantic nationalism began to influence the Sardinians' views of their own past. Indigenous historical personages like Queen Eleanora of Arborea were turned into island heroes. That new sense of Sardinia's past promoted both the serious study of island history and a certain tendency to invent history for both historical and ideological purposes. Most important among these inventions were the "Carte d'Arborea." These began appearing on the antiquaries market in the 1840s and were accepted as genuine by most Sardinian scholars and intellectuals. They appeared to preserve precious information on the early history of the island including its Roman and pre-Roman remains. Theodor Mommsen denounced them as forgeries in the early 1870s, and after a certain resistance on the part of Sardinian scholars that sad reality was accepted (Zucca 1997).

The most important early Sardinian archaeological figure was the priest Giovanni Spano (1803-78), who played a pioneering role in recording and conserving Sardinian monuments. He had studied archaeology with the great topographer Antonio Nibby in Rome, and when he was dispatched to Cagliari in 1834, he continued his antiquarian investigations. His forte was the short, learned article, 400 of which authored by him appeared in the *Bulletino archeologico sardo*. Of his 418 publications 276 were archaeological, and they ranged in time period from prehistory to the Middle Ages. He undertook the first excavations of the amphitheater at Cagliari and conducted pioneering stratigraphic investigations at nuraghi near his home town of Ploaghe. He was the first scholar to apply the then-revolutionary "three-aged system" based on shifts from stone to bronze to iron technology to Sardinian prehistory, and advanced the study of the nuraghi from the realm of mythology to that of empirical archaeology. Through his initiative the first Sardinian archaeological journal, *Bulletino Archeologico Sardo,* started publication in 1855.

With Sardinia's incorporation into the modern Italian state continental scholars came to play a more important role in the island's archaeology, although the great majority of investigators remained Sardinian. The three most prominent figures in that next generation were Filippo Vivanet, Giovani Pinza, and Ettore Pais. Vivanet succeeded Spano as director of the Cagliari Museum. He continued the priest's active program of excavation at pre-Roman and Roman sites, and enriched the collections of the Cagliari museum. The most important contribution of Pinza (1872-1940), a non-Sardinian scholar who spent most of his career on the mainland, was the publication of *Monumenti primitivi della Sardegna,* a comprehensive collection and discussion of prehistoric sites and materials (Guidi 1988:82). Pais (1856-1939) had studied in Florence and Berlin and brought the more sophisticated continental perspective to the island's history and island. His 1923 study of Sardinia and Corsica under the Romans remains a classic (Ridley 1976; Mastino 2002).

The most important figure in Sardinian archaeology after Spano was Antonio Taramelli (1868-1939), who was appointed archaeological superintendent for the island in 1902 and held the post until his retirement in 1931 (Guidi 1988:52-54). He represented a new level of Italian archaeological professionalism, having trained with Edoardo Brizio at Bologna and Federico Halbherr on Crete. He undertook an ambitious program of field research centered especially on the island's prehistoric archaeology. His regular publications on Sardinian archaeology in *Notizie degli Scavi* brought developments on the island to the attention of a wider archaeological community.

Drawing of the nuraghe at St. Antine by Giovanni Spano.

In the middle years of the 20th century a number of distinguished Italian archaeologists such as Doro Levi, Massimo Pallottino, and Ranuccio Bianchi Bandinelli held academic and administrative positions in Sardinia (Barbanera 2003:81-88), but for them Sardinia represented a temporary appointment, while they awaited more attractive opportunities on the mainland. They had only a limited impact on the development of island archaeology.

The island academic world, especially that of the universities, has been dominated by Sardinians who have made their careers in their native land. That has led to a certain level of cultural and intellectual isolation. Since the archaeological and historical communities have always been small and power relations hierarchical, certain scholars in key positions have exercised a controlling influence. Sardinia has remained a place where a single, highly productive scholar like Giovanni Lulliu could dominate the archaeological and historical academic communities for decades. Lilliu came from Barumini, site of one of the most important nuragic complexes in Sardinia, where he would conduct some of his most important excavations. He began his career in the archaeological service, but soon moved to the university. His publications, which started in 1937, combined detailed archaeological reportage with influential syntheses of Sardinian prehistory and history. His vision of the island's history, often articulated in the popular press, has been shaped by pro-Sardinian and anti-colonialist views that emphasized the resistance of the Sardinians to outside influences and outside conquerors.

Relatively few mainland Italians not connected with the island universities or antiquities service developed a serious research interest in Sardinia. The major exception was Sebastiano Moscati and the archaeologists connected with the Istituto di Studi Fenici at the University of Rome. Moscati produced many publications on the Punic archaeology of Sardinia and organized and directed the long series of excavations at the Punic site of Monte Sirai. These studies, important as they have been, were focused more on Punic colonial archaeology than on the social and economic developments that contacts with colonial presence produced within the island's native society.

Until recently even fewer non-Italians have shown interest in the island's archaeology. The Scot, Duncan MacKenzie, who later collaborated with Arthur Evans at Knossos, did limited but important Sardinian research early in the last century (Momigliano 1999:80-83). In recent years a certain number of English, American, Dutch, and Scandinavian archaeologists have worked on the island. Key for the understanding of early Sardinian prehistory have been the excavations of David Trump at sites like Bonu Ighinu (Trump 1984). The late Miriam Balmuth played a very important role in bringing Sardinian archaeology to the attention of American scholars (Tykot and Andrews 1992). Gary Webster was one of the first field workers to attempt to apply North American processual archaeology to Sardinian prehistory (Webster 1996), while Joseph Michels and Robert Tykot have used Sardinia as a laboratory for modern obsidian studies (Michels et al. 1984; Tykot 2001). Still relatively few outside of Sardinia have appreciated the potential of its rich archaeological record and long occupation.

Dominant Paradigms

Given the conservative traditions of Sardinian archaeology, it is not surprising that the paradigms used to interpret the island's historical development are a complex combination of conservative, empirical archaeology and Sardinian identity politics. Already in the 19th century archaeology was harnessed to the cause of island identity, and strong pro-Sardinian attitudes have helped shape the scholarship of such an important contemporary figure as Giovanni Lilliu. The revolutions in archaeological theory that have transformed the process of archaeological interpretation especially in the Anglophone world since the 1960s have had little impact on Sardinia. Much of the writing on island archaeology has remained descriptive with the scholars working in what the American archaeologists Gordon Willey and Jeremy Sabloff describe as the "classificatory-historical period" and still very much driven by nineteenth models of artifact classification and historical periodization (Willey and Sabloff 1980:83-180). This has meant that the archaeologists have focused on the construction of a narrative prehistory/history based on the centrality of formal artifact typologies, period concepts like the Neolithic and the Bronze Age, and migrations and invasions.

Only recently have models of cultural development based on processual archaeology been applied to Sardinia (Webster 1996). Given the close connection between archaeological interpretation and the role played by political, ideological, and cultural concerns in shaping indigenous archaeology, Sardinia would seem to be a prime candidate for post-processual modes of archaeological interpretation, especially those related to post-colonial discourse. However, such interpretations are just beginning (Van Dommelen 1998; Blake 1997, 1997a, 2001).

Sardinians have long considered the intersection of invasion and resistance as central to the understanding of island history and prehistory. The island has indeed been invaded by many powers during its long history. For long periods Sardinia has been under the control of foreign powers. That imperial succession stretched with few breaks from the sixth century Carthaginians to the formation of the modern Piedmontese state in the eighteenth century. With that long history it is not surprising that Sardinians have tended to stress the role of outsiders in shaping island destiny.

Sardinian prehistoric and proto-historic archaeology developed at a time when invasion and mass migration models dominated the interpretation of prehistoric cultures throughout Europe. Distinctive pot forms and ax-head shapes were seen as indicators of peoples or cultures that moved through the European landscape or crossed the Mediterranean like modern imperial armies and navies. Concepts of culture change based on invasion and the rapid movement of groups into new territories provided satisfactorily simple and straightforward explanations, especially at a time when certain groups like Aryans were seen as privileged bearers of culture (Trigger 1989:152-54).

In the Mediterranean such invasion-based models merged with interpretations that regarded most major cultural innovations as originating in the eastern Mediterranean and then spreading westward. Scholars who embraced this *lux ex oriente* model embraced a variety of agents from nautical warriors to migratory priests (Renfrew 1976:34-40). Sardinia with its nuraghi, the stone towers that recalled structures like the tholos tombs of Mycenaean Greece, became prime territory for such archaeological interpretations. Scholars like Giovanni Lilliu still found the *lux ex oriente* paradigm appealing and long used it to link the origins of nuragic Sardinian to the Mycenaean world. As late as 1975 Lilliu referred to "Sardinia of the nuraghi" as an "offshoot" (*ridotto*) of Mycenaean civilization. He continued by arguing that this "oriental component ended by becoming simplified and bastardized residue of the original acquisitions from the second millennium, outside of all perspective of cultural time in an area that had lost the sense and dimension of its original values" (Lilliu 1975:180-82, 300-309).

Resistance and isolation have represented the other side of this historical and archaeological paradigm. Sardinians take great pride in their ancestors' ability to mount long-term resistance against invaders and to preserve key elements of their language and culture intact. When defeat against superior forces became inevitable, the Sards yielded the coastal lands to the invaders and retreated into the mountainous interior, where the invaders were able to impose only superficial control. An historical model of two Sardinias developed with a coastal region that had been much influenced over the centuries by foreign invaders, and the "true Sardinia" of the interior that largely resisted those outside influences and clung to its traditional culture.

Isolation and political and cultural fragmentation characterized this interior Sardinia in the early modern period. Early 19th nineteenth century travelers like La Marmora commented on the poor roads and general isolation of its impoverished communities. Max Leopold Wagner, who visited much of the island in the early years of the 20th century, observed that "travel is certainly not convenient in this still inaccessible territory (the Nuorese)" and "methods of transport were scarce and primitive, the few existing roads were in terrible condition" (quoted in Paulis 1996:22, 43). Maurice Le Lannou, the French geographer, whose 1941 classic did so much to reinforce this vision of interior Sardinia's bleak autarchy, noted as an example that "Tempio and its environs are still now so cut off that a coach has not yet been able to penetrate from outside, and all commerce takes place on horseback" (Le Lannou 1979:15). Lilliu described the island's landscape as one of "morphological chiseling" that promoted the developed of circumscribed, small- scale social and economic units (Lilliu 1967:1-11; 1988:9-15). The novels of Sardinia's Nobel Prize winner Grazia di Ledda, with their stark pictures of provincial life in the interior of Sardinia or the linguists' studies of the multiple, deep division of dialects within the Sard language, have further reinforced this view of past and present interior Sardinia (Aste 1990).

New archaeological information, especially refined and improved dating methods, and new interpretive models have forced a radical rethinking of these migration-based reconstructions of early Mediterranean prehistory. The "radiocarbon revolution," the application of recalibrated radiocarbon dates to the western Mediterranean, has dealt a fatal blow to many elements in the migration-from-the-east hypothesis. It is no longer possible to postulate a neat passage of major innovations like dry laid stone architecture from east to west, for often such developments appear to have started at the same time or earlier in the west (Renfrew 1976). More emphasis clearly has to be placed on independent invention and regional developments if we are going to understand the evolution of culture in the central Mediterranean.

Anglo-American processual archaeology also attacked this reliance on invasion as an explanatory model, but from another direction. New Archaeologists have stressed local adaptation and a systems approach that emphasizes local societal adjustments to specific environmental circumstances and downplays the impact of outside forces (Clarke 1968; Binford 1972). Local dynamics and initiatives have clearly been underestimated in explaining Sardinia's long cultural history, and the development of long lasting, slowly changing island cultures like the Neolithic Ozieri or the Bronze-Iron Age nuragic would seem best explained by such processual models. Much of the island's societal development went on with only limited outside impact.

Even Sardinia's complex history of invasion and resistance can be given more complex and subtle explanations. In recent years archaeologists and historians have increasingly integrated various strands of post-colonial theory into their research. This has allowed them to appreciate better the strength and complexity of low-level resistance to the imperial process. Students of early modern and modern imperialism have stressed the limited ability of even 18th and 19th century colonial systems to effect total change in subjected societies. Post-colonialists like James Scott have stressed the varieties of effective, non-violent resistances that indigenous groups can employ against colonial hegemony (Scott 1985). More stress has been placed on the processes of "negotiation" between colonializers and colonialized that allowed the latter to filter elements of the dominant culture that they were to accept and to retain at least some of their social and cultural systems intact.

Students of ancient empires, especially Rome, have increasingly applied these post-colonial perspectives to the ancient world (Mattingly 1997). The approach has great potential for Sardinia. Of the three major external powers that impacted Sardinia in antiquity, certainly the Phoenicians had little ability to project power and had to negotiate with the locals. The imperial success of Carthage has certainly been exaggerated, and even Roman power had its severe limits. The indigenous Sards had a long and dynamic cultural history before the colonialists came on the scene. The scholarly and ideological emphasis on retreat, resistance, and isolation has done the island peoples a disservice by underestimating their ability to react positively to the colonial process.

Another aspect of Sardinian prehistory and history worth emphasizing is that period divisions that shape historical thinking in the central and eastern Mediterranean have only limited relevance for the island. The end of the Bronze Age civilization in the late 2nd millennium BC, so important for the Aegean and the eastern Mediterranean, did not significantly affect development on the island. The transition from Antiquity to the early Middle Ages on Sardinia was again very different from what happened in either neighboring North Africa or Italy. Sardinia was impacted in only a limited manner by the Germanic and Islamic invasions, while its status as an isolated refugee island meant that the early medieval culture developed in a distinctively Sardinian manner.

2
Settling an Island
Sardinia in the Paleolithic and Neolithic

Two elements have been key for shaping the history and identity of Sardinia from the arrival of the first humans to the present day: the sea and the mountains. The coastline is long, and while the mountains often come down to the sea there are coastal plain in other areas, harbors suitable for shipping during antiquity and the Middle Ages, and a few rivers that provide access to the interior. While modern Sardinians have an ambivalent relation to the sea, it is probably anachronistic to project those attitudes too far backward in Sardinian history.

The common and sometimes dominant image of mountainous Sardinia is also a simplification of geographical reality. Only a few mountain ranges rise to over 1,000 m. Much of the island is upland rather than mountain terrain. However, it is still a rugged, divided landscape that depends on natural springs for water. The only extended coastal plain is that around Tharros on the west central coast. The other large lowland area is the valley of the Campidano that links Cagliari with modern Oristano.

Any consideration of the origins of human society in Sardinia must start with the three basic questions of "When did people first come to Sardinia?" "How did they get there?" and "What did they find when they arrived?" None of these questions allows simple, easy answers. The evidence is sparse and the interpretations often disputed. Still an attempt must be made to come to grips with the early evidence if we are to understand the foundations of Sardinian prehistory.

The Paleolithic

Occupation clearly started in the Paleolithic. Evidence has gradually accumulated that Sardinia had at least two distinct phases of early Stone Age occupation, one starting about 170,000 years ago and a second dating to the end of the paleolithic era. An understanding of this first period of settlement has been hampered by the limited archaeological in-

View of the coastline of Sardinia.

View of the interior of Sardinia.

UPPER	LOWER	CLACTONIAN ?		>150,000 BC
PALEOLITHIC	MIDDLE			
	UPPER	GROTTA CORBEDDU		15,000 – 11,000 BC
MESOLITHIC				11,000 – 6000 BC
		SU CARROPPU		6000? – 5300 BC
	EARLY	FILIESTRU – GROTTA VERDE		5300 – 4700 BC
NEOLITHIC	MIDDLE	BONU IGHINU		4700 – 4000 BC
		---------(SAN CIRIACO)---------		----------------------
	LATE	OZIERI		4000 – 3200? BC
ENEOLITHIC (COPPER AGE)	INITIAL	SUB – OZIERI FILIGOSA ABEALZU		3200? – 2700? BC
	FULL	MONTE CLARO	BEAKER A	2700? – 2200? BC
	FINAL			
	EARLY	BONNANARO A	BEAKER B	2200 – 1900 BC
	MIDDLE	BONNANARO B		1900 – 1600 BC
BRONZE AGE		NURAGIC I		1600 – 1300 BC
	LATE	NURAGIC II		1300 – 1150 BC
	FINAL	NURAGIC III		1150 – 850 BC
	GEOMETRIC			850 – 730 BC
EARLY IRON AGE	ORIENTALIZING	PHOENICIAN	NURAGIC IV	730 – 580 BC
	ARCHAIC			580 – 510 BC
	PUNIC			510 – 238 BC
LATE IRON AGE	ROMAN	REPUBLICAN	NURAGIC V	238 – 1 BC
		IMPERIAL		1 AD – 476 AD

Chronology of Sardinian archaeology and history from the Lower Paleolithic to the end of the Roman Empire.

formation and by the extreme skepticism expressed by certain influential scholars about the reality of the Sardinian palaeolithic and especially an early Sardinian occupation before the emergence of modern *homo sapiens* (Cherry 1990:175; 1992:29-30).

Such initial skepticism has often characterized paleolithic studies in the Mediterranean. The history of the discovery of the paleolithic in Greece provides an excellent case study. For a long time archaeologists denied that Greece was occupied during the paleolithic. The gradual accumulation of evidence has demonstrated that the assumption was mistaken, and scholars now acknowledge a complex history of paleolithic cultural development in Greece (Runnels and Murray 2001:9-31). The same reluctance characterized pre-neolithic archaeology on other major Mediterranean islands. However, there is now evidence for significant, sometimes very early paleolithic presences on Sicily (Leighton 2001:11-50) and Cyprus (Bunimovitz and Barkai 1996; Simmons 1996).

The evidence is mounting that hominid occupation on Sardinia goes back to the middle and possibly the Early Paleolithic. This includes material both from field surveys and stratified excavations. The finds consist

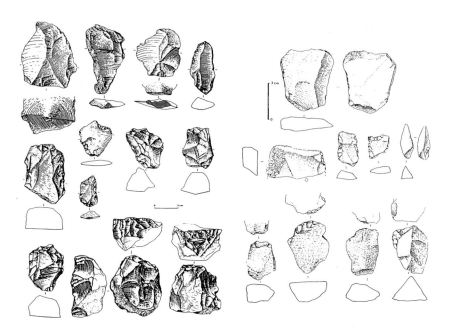

Paleolithic flints from the Clactonian period at the Sa Pedrosa-Pantalinu and the Corbeddu Cave sites (after Tykot and Andrews 1992).

mainly of stone (quartz and flint) flake and blade tools whose forms relate to the typologies of the Clactonian culture found on mainland. Two sites in the Perfugas (SS) area have yielded considerable quantities of this material, though not in sealed, stratigraphic contexts. The predominance of unstratified surface material is to be expected, since the population would have consisted of small hunting-foraging bands with mobile lifestyles (Contu 1997:28-36). The artifacts recovered suggest the presence of early hominids that came onto the island at a period, probably about 170-160,000 years ago, when the glaciation of Europe had significantly lowered sea levels. That would have allowed travel by either land bridges or by short sea voyages, with Corsica a probable intermediate stop. The early settlers apparently arrived in sufficient numbers and found on the island adequate land and marine resources to sustain their population once the rise of the sea gradually cut them off from the outside world.

Proto-humans were not the only animals that took advantage of the lowered sea levels and the temporary land bridges. At the time of the Late Pleistocene Sardinia had what scholars have described as the richest and most varied of the Mediterranean insular fauna (Vigne 1992; Schule 1993).

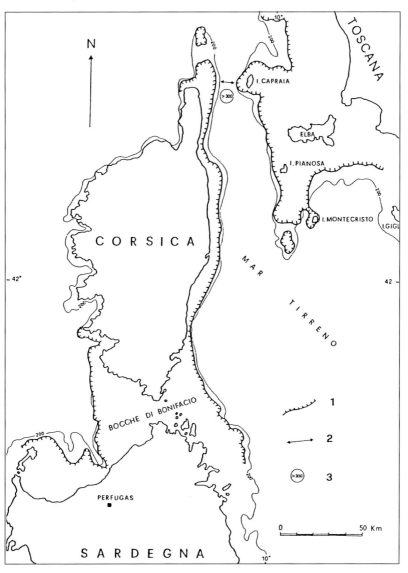

N

TOSCANA

I.CAPRAIA

(>300)

ELBA

I.PIANOSA

I.MONTECRISTO

I.GIGL

CORSICA

MAR

TIRRENO

~ 42°

42 —

200

BOCCHE DI BONIFACIO

1

2

3

200

(>300)

PERFUGAS

0   50 Km

SARDEGNA

10°

*Coastlines of Sardinia and Corsica during the last glacial periods
(after Tykot and Andrews 1992).*

As on the other major islands of the Mediterranean there is evidence for dwarfism in major mammals like elephant, pig, and hippo. In addition the *prolagus sardus,* a rabbit-like animal, *rhagomys orthodon,* a large field mouse, cervids, and other mammals as well as fish and shellfish provided protein for the population. Wild plant resources were also abundant. These first hominid populations appear to have been extinct when the first *homo sapiens* arrived on the island. It is likely that the initial populations were insufficient to sustain themselves without a regular supply of new arrivals. It is also possible that the gradual extermination of the mammalian mega-fauna produced a food crisis that led to the extinction of the proto-humans.

The last glaciation around 20,000 bp produced another significant lowering of sea levels that facilitates the arrival of *homo sapiens*. The key site for understanding this new phase is the Corbeddu Cave near Oliena (Sondar et al. 1993, 1995; Hofmeijer 1997). That is a complex stratified site, whose lowest levels have been assigned to the Upper Paleolithic. A hominid jaw fragment found there has been dated to 20,000 BP, while the main cultural horizon has been dated to 13,000 BC. While the site has not yielded stone tools, the excavators argue that some of the animal bone found in the cave shows clear human modification (Sondar, Sanges et al. 1984:29-59; Hofmeijer 1997:412-15).

The new arrivals with their broad-band sustenance strategies based on both hunting and marine/land gathering would have found an environment that was well suited to their needs. Sardinia is a large island with a variety of eco-niches. Even if many species of large game became extinct, smaller animals like the *prolagus sardus* were still abundant. The lowering of the sea levels would have increased the areas of coastal marshes with their birds and marine fauna. The warming climate would have stimulated the growth of vegetation. Upper Paleolithic Sardinia would have compared favorably with some of the richest hunting-gathering environments found in North America and could have supported a sizeable human population.

This second lowering of the Mediterranean in the period of the Upper Paleolithic provided the conditions for the last significant new population movement into the island during the prehistoric period. The retreat of the glaciers on the European continent produced a gradual rise of sea level in the Mediterranean. That process was very slow, as would have been its impact on the communities on Sardinia. As sea distances from neighboring land masses increased coastal peoples would have been stimulated to increase their mastery of the sea. However, such nascent nautical abilities should not be exaggerated. Direct contact with the Italian mainland became increasingly difficult. Corsica, which is separated from Sardinia by

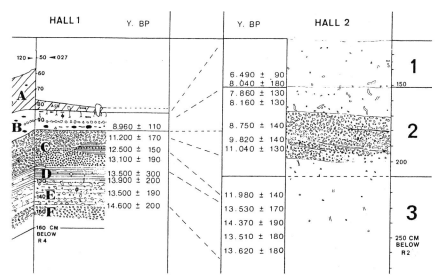

Comparative stratigraphy of two soundings in the Corbeddu Cave based on correlation of radio-carbon dates (after Tykot and Andrews 1992).

the narrow Strait of Bonifacio along with smaller islands like Elba, became Sardinia's major bridge to the outside world.

A few introductory words about Corsica are appropriate here. Similarities in cultural development between the two islands began with the Paleolithic and continued throughout the prehistoric periods (Vigne 1996), but the limits of Corsica as a neighbor connecting Sardinia to the outside world should be kept in mind. Corsica is much more rugged than Sardinia and is not capable of sustaining the population of Sardinia. Communication is limited to a narrow route along the east coast. Corsica did not have major prehistoric resources like obsidian, and it would never have attracted outsiders in any significant numbers. Furthermore, they would have made their way to Sardinia immediately, and when they did the movement probably involved very few people.

The ecological changes that characterized the end of the Pleistocene probably improved the faunal and floral resource picture on Sardinia. The warmer climate encouraged new types of vegetation, a benefit to communities heavily dependent on gathering. The rising sea levels increased the areas of coastal swamps and lagoons, with their rich marine fauna, while improved nautical skills enhanced yields from fishing. If many of the larger mammals were now extinct, a rich and diverse fauna was still to be found on the island.

European archaeologists have traditionally described this transitional period as the Mesolithic. Technologically it is generally defined by the presence of small-tool and bone-working industries which reflected the increased reliance on gathering and small-game hunting as well as the increased dependence on marine resources. As prehistorians rethink their basic premises about both the preceding Upper Paleolithic and the succeeding Neolithic, the true nature of the Mesolithic becomes increasingly ambiguous.

The Sardinian Mesolithic remains very elusive. Recently a Mesolithic site was identified at Grotta Su Coloru near Sassari. It contained four Mesolithic levels with stone artifacts dated to the early-mid 9th millennium BP. The tool repertoire was dominated by scrapers with retouched edges, although there were also small blades and retouched chips. Two major sites—Corbeddu and Filiestru—have yielded Mesolithic levels with dates going back to the early 7th millennium BC. Microlithic techniques of tool production continued in use into the Neolithic, and at least one site near Terralba has what seem to be pure microlithic deposits (Trump 1998:7-8).

The Mesolithic sample for Sardinia is therefore not large, although the evidence for that period is not extensive either on the Italian mainland or along the western Mediterranean coast in general. It can be argued that Mesolithic sites on both the mainland and the islands would have been overwhelmingly coastal sites and that most of those would have been inundated with the post-glacial sea level rise. Furthermore, such sites would usually have been very small, the seasonal habitations of small bands. Their sparse scatters of artifacts would normally have been destroyed or have escaped detection by any but the most focused archaeological investigations. Significantly the most important Mesolithic sites known in Sardinia up to the present are cave sites. It is also possible that the shifts in Sardinia material culture forced by environmental changes were not radical enough to force the development of the artifactual universe normally associated with the Mesolithic.

The most striking evidence for new developments on the island is the discovery of Sardinian obsidian in 8th millennium BP contexts on Corsica and at the early Neolithic site of Arena Candida in Liguria (Tykot 2001). Obsidian is a volcanic glass mineral much prized for its fine tool-making properties. Deposits of obsidian in the Mediterranean are rare, and geo-chemical analysis makes it possible to identify the origins of almost every obsidian piece. Evidence from sites like Franchthi cave in Greece show that long-distance trade in obsidian from the island of Melos

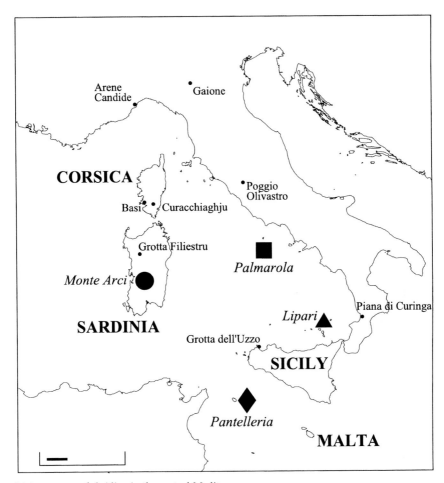

Major sources of obsidian in the central Mediterranean.

started there during the Mesolithic around 10,000 BP, another result of the increasing mastery of the sea (van Andel and Runnels 1987:58-60; Perles 1992).

The volcanic outcrops of Monte Arci on the Gulf of Oristano in west central Sardinia provided one of the very few sources of obsidian in the Mediterranean. The flows were large and quite accessible. Obsidian thus played an important role in shaping the cultures of Sardinian prehistory and in fostering the island's contact with the larger Mediterranean world. Technical studies have provided detailed maps of the distribution of Mt. Arce obsidian in the west-central Mediterranean. Less easy to reconstruct

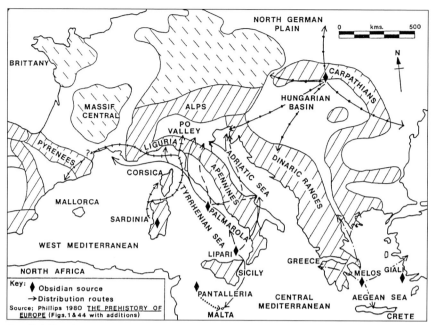

Detailed distribution patterns from main obsidian sources in the central Mediterranean (Tykot and Andrews 1992).

are the socioeconomic process that led to the extraction and distribution of that obsidian.

One model for this early obsidian exchange is based on paradigms developed in the eastern Mediterranean. It has the initiative for obsidian exploitation largely in the hands of outside maritime traders, who discovered the sources and distributed the material. For Sardinia this would imply trading parties capable of sailing over considerable distances and knowing the coasts of the island very well. However, Sardinia was not a small, sparsely inhabited island like Melos, where outsiders could easily dominate the local scene. It was a large, presumably well-populated island with the obsidian sources not readily accessible or even visible from the sea.

There is every reason to believe that it was the indigenous population who discovered the obsidian and realized its potential for tool manufacture. They then initiated its distribution over much of the island itself. The internal distribution of this precious commodity probably took place through a network of mobile bands meeting at the borders of their territories. This distribution of obsidian within the island marked the beginning of the webs of communication and exchange which were to characterize Sardinia in later epochs such as the nuragic. It was a very early counter to well-established images of Sardinia's internal isolation.

Whether those who extracted the obsidian and established the internal networks carried it across the sea themselves or met on the coast traders from the outside who exported the material cannot be determined. Probably it was a combination of both. The obsidian exchange did establish contacts with the outside world that allowed the Sardinians to import goods and ideas. Initially the networks must have been small scale and of limited geographical range. The precious stone would have gone through many hands. The island obsidian found in Liguria most probably passed from Sardinia through Corsica and Elba to the Italian coast. Still these networks meant that the island of Sardinia became one of the Mediterranean areas most exposed to innovative ideas from the outside.

Neolithic

The idea of the Neolithic Revolution has been one of the most influential concepts in Mediterranean archaeology. As original conceived by archaeologists like V. Gordon Childe for the Near East, it meant the development of the triad of agriculture, ceramics, and livestock raising that allowed for permanent settlement, greater sustainable population, and craft civilization which produced the foundations for more advanced civilizations. Childe and his disciples then argued that the Near Eastern Neolithic Revolution spread westward through the Mediterranean and northwestward up the Danube Valley into Europe (Trigger 1989:250-59).

Even though archaeologists working in the eastern Mediterranean have long questioned the coherence of what has often been described as the Neolithic package the concept of cohesive Neolithic cultures moving from east to west still has great appeal. Such Neolithic pioneers have been seen as introducing agriculture, settled village life, ceramic production, and pastoralism into Italy, France, Spain, and the islands (Whittle 1996:289-314). While crude models of migration and invasion have become less popular, archaeologists still tend often to hide behind vague diffusionist models when talking about the spread of the Neolithic both in Europe and the Mediterranean.

Sardinia poses special problems for those interested in the spread of the Neolithic in the Mediterranean. The island is not easily accessed by water. While nautical exploitation was certainly increasing and trading networks were beginning to be developed, they most likely involved small numbers of fishermen and traders. The vessels and sailing skills were not suited to the transport of large numbers of people and their increasingly complicated goods and chattels, including large domestic animals. There is the question of why the early farmers of mainland Italy would want to go to Sardinia in the first place. The east coast of Sardinia is forbidding, with little land to induce these primitive agriculturalists and pastoralists to undertake a complicated and perilous voyage. Increased reliance on agriculture limited community mobility, and there is no evidence that the areas of the coastal mainland were becoming overcrowded.

What Sardinia did have was obsidian and exchange networks both on land and sea that had long operated around that obsidian. Such networks facilitated the exchange of specialized objects, small numbers of humans and animals, and ideas. Sardinians would have wanted something in return for their obsidian. Individual elements that formed part of the Neolithic package would have met that need nicely.

Archaeologically the most visible Neolithic innovation was pottery production. Pottery scatters make sites visible in the way that flint scatters do not. While the introduction of pottery production has been regarded as the key element in defining the Neolithic, it probably was the last and least important of the three Neolithic innovations. Archaeologists in the eastern Mediterranean have long accepted the presence of a pre-pottery Neolithic. In contrast, the introduction of pottery is still central to discussions of the Neolithic in the central Mediterranean. However, the transfer of that technology to an island like Sardinia would not have been overly difficult. Pottery production is not limited by key natural resources, since clay beds are common and at that time wood supplies would have been more abundant. The forming and firing technology was not that difficult to master. Women were likely to have been the potters in those Neolithic societies, and processes of raiding and exchange could easily have brought women with ceramic skills to Sardinia in small but adequate numbers.

Domesticated plants and animals were clearly more central to the development of the larger, concentrated settlements characteristic of the Neolithic. The integration of cultivated plants into the island economy need not have been that revolutionary or produced major changes in settlement patterns or indigenous lifestyle. Paleolithic and Mesolithic groups on Sardinia had presumably become increasingly sophisticated in their exploitation of the floral environment. Seeds and information on seed cultivation brought in along the exchange networks would have complemented the resources gained from intensive gathering, but they

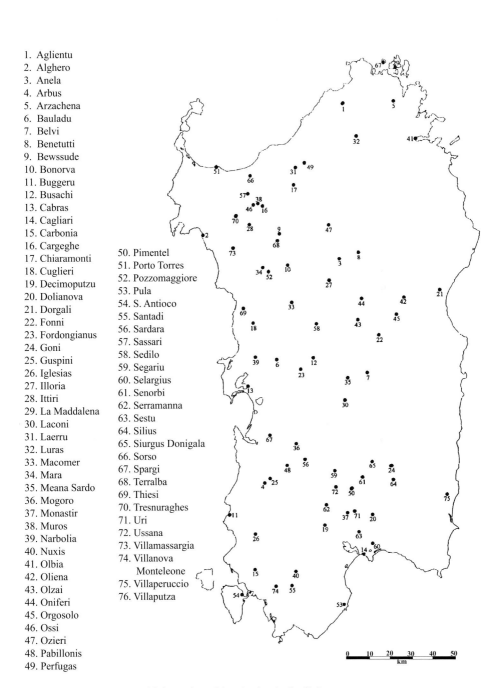

1. Aglientu
2. Alghero
3. Anela
4. Arbus
5. Arzachena
6. Bauladu
7. Belvi
8. Benetutti
9. Bewssude
10. Bonorva
11. Buggeru
12. Busachi
13. Cabras
14. Cagliari
15. Carbonia
16. Cargeghe
17. Chiaramonti
18. Cuglieri
19. Decimoputzu
20. Dolianova
21. Dorgali
22. Fonni
23. Fordongianus
24. Goni
25. Guspini
26. Iglesias
27. Illoria
28. Ittiri
29. La Maddalena
30. Laconi
31. Laerru
32. Luras
33. Macomer
34. Mara
35. Meana Sardo
36. Mogoro
37. Monastir
38. Muros
39. Narbolia
40. Nuxis
41. Olbia
42. Oliena
43. Olzai
44. Oniferi
45. Orgosolo
46. Ossi
47. Ozieri
48. Pabillonis
49. Perfugas

50. Pimentel
51. Porto Torres
52. Pozzomaggiore
53. Pula
54. S. Antioco
55. Santadi
56. Sardara
57. Sassari
58. Sedilo
59. Segariu
60. Selargius
61. Senorbi
62. Serramanna
63. Sestu
64. Silius
65. Siurgus Donigala
66. Sorso
67. Spargi
68. Terralba
69. Thiesi
70. Tresnuraghes
71. Uri
72. Ussana
73. Villamassargia
74. Villanova
    Monteleone
75. Villaperuccio
76. Villaputza

Major early prehistoric sites in Sardinia.

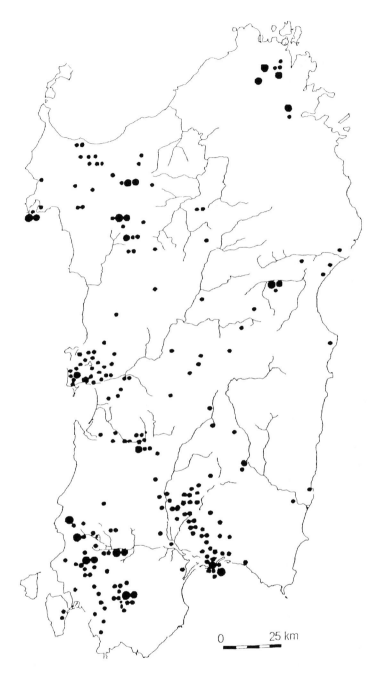

Major Neolithic sites in Sardinia.

did not produce long-term village settlements, social complexity, and all the secondary results often associated with the Neolithic.

Even more slow and complex would have been the impact of the introduction of domestic animals, especially sheep, goat, and pig. No evidence exists that the Sardinians domesticated the island species, so these animals had to have been brought in from the outside. Small numbers could have arrived through established exchange networks. Some remained attached to the communities as complementary food sources. Others went feral and enriched the meat supplies for a society that was still heavily based on hunting (Piga and Porcu 1990). These agricultural and pastoral systems evolved over long periods of time and only gradually produced major changes in economy and society. Their main initial effect was to allow the island to sustain a larger population, even as traditional meat sources were being depleted by too- intensive hunting.

Turning from theoretical models for Neolithic development in Sardinia to the archaeological record, the most important site for defining the Sardinian Neolithic is Filiestru cave located in the Bonu Ighinu Valley some 30 km south of Sassari. There the British archaeologist David Trump has documented unbroken continuity of occupation from the Neolithic through the nuragic periods, reconstructing a picture of millennia of indigenous development on the island (Trump 1984). Among the most important finds from the site were the stratified deposits of Neolithic material that allowed Trump to identify four Neolithic subphases: cardial, Filiestru, Bonu Ighinu, and Ozieri. The Filiestru cave was presumably a specialized interior hunting and pastoral site, but the presence of the cardial ware and especially Monte Arce obsidian shows that it was linked to the wider world of Sardinian interchange.

Since stratified sites like Filiestru are rare and most Neolithic sites are identified on the basis of surface scatters, archaeologists have focused on certain identifiable indicators of Neolithic presence. The most important of these for the early Neolithic has been the so-called cardial impressed ware. The name is derived from the technique of using cockle shells to incise patterns on the highly burnished surface of vessels. Early Neolithic cardial incised pottery was widespread in the central and western Mediterranean and is associated with the early Neolithic in mainland Italy, Corsica, Provence, Iberia, and North Africa (Whittle 1996:300-303, 308-10). Given the superficial similarities in the surface decoration, efforts have been made to link all of the cultures using cardial pottery and relate them all to the spread of the Neolithic in the western Mediterranean. While the decorative technique suggests some type of interaction, detailed petro-

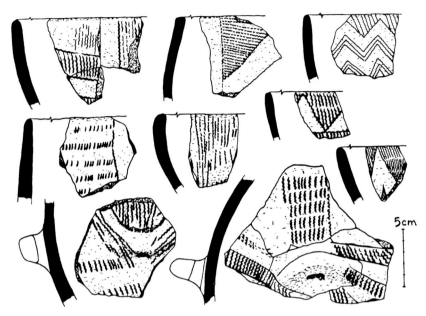

Cardial pottery from the earliest phase of the Sardinian Neolithic.

graphical studies of cardial ceramics from southwestern France showed complex, localized distribution patterns for the vessels (Barnett 1990).

Cardial pottery has been cited as the main indicator for Neolithic immigration into Sardinia. That connection must be viewed with caution. Certainly the Sardinians had increasing contact with the outside world through the obsidian trade. Cardial pots could well have been the type of prestige goods that would have been exchanged for obsidian. The arrival of a few female potters could have brought the relatively simply technology to the island. Cardial ware on Sardinia has not yet received the type of detailed petrological study that would allow the identification of local or extra-island sources, but the presence of cardial pottery should not be used to indicate the arrival of an integrated Neolithic society form the outside.

This need for caution in associating cultural change with new immigration is reinforced by a consideration of the linguistic and especially the genetic evidence. The indigenous Sard language has common features shared with other Mediterranean groups like the Basques, but that could just reflect common Mediterranean linguistic substrata and not be a result of Neolithic period population movements (Hubschmidt 1953; Blasco

Ferrer 1984:4-13). Recent research has suggested that Sardinians of different zones are much more closely linked to one another than to any groups outside the island. There is little evidence for genetic connections with nearby Corsica, let alone more distant areas such as North Africa

The current evidence for the distribution of cardial sites on the island provides further arguments against the hypothesis of Neolithic population movements. Most cardial sites have been discovered on the west and southwest of the island, well removed from the Liguria-Corsica bridge that might have facilitated the movement of significant numbers of migrants into the island. North Africa, which is closer to Sardinia, did have its own cardial pottery, but up to the present no Sardinian obsidian has been found there.

The cardial levels in Filiestru cave provide our best picture of what an early Neolithic community on Sardinia was like. Archaeologists found over a thousand fragments of ceramics associated with the cardial culture, although only 7% of those were decorated (Trump 1984:38-44). Obsidian and flints were present, although arrow points were absent. The animal bone remains were heavily weighted toward sheep, a new animal for Sardinia, with some goats and pigs. Wild deer were also present.

Cardial pottery has been found at an increasing number of types of sites both on the coast and toward the interior. The recent identification of three cardial period villages in the territory of Terralba demonstrates an interest on the part of the early Neolithic population in a zone with good foraging and agricultural potential as well as access to marine and riverine resources. It provided the type of diverse food resources required by an early Neolithic community. The presence of obsidian showed contact with Monte Arci (Atzeni 1992:36-40, 55-56). Two other cardial sites have been found at Punta Campu Sali-Arbus on the coast, just south of Marina di Arbu, and at Su Coddu 'e Santuanni-Guspini. They appear to have been positioned to facilitate exchanges along the coast between Monte Arci and the south. Different in setting was the open-air village at Ingurtosu-Arbus in the hills southeast of Montevecchio (Zucca 1987:43). The cardial sites of Grotta Maimone and Grotta Leoni are both some 40 km inland as the crow flies. Filiestru itself is also inland. It is likely that they were all seasonal hunting and foraging camps.

The identification at the Filiestru cave of two new Neolithic phases, Filiestru and Bonu Ighninu, placed between the cardial and the Ozieri cultures, provided the archaeologists with a better sense of the gradual evolution of the Neolithic in the island environment. The Filiestru pottery complex was dominated by undecorated round-bottom vessels with red ochre slips or washes and small vertical or horizontal handles. Bonu Ighinu saw the return of punched and incised decorative elements. While these stylistic distinctions allow the archaeologist to define different phases, it is worth highlighting the observation of the excavator David Trump that the overwhelming impression conveyed by the utilitarian pottery throughout the Sardinian Neolithic is one of continuity (Trump, Foschi, and Levine 1983:58-59). That also appears to be true for other aspects of the society.

The size of the known sites of the cardial and Filiestru cultures suggests small bands, perhaps no more than extended families, whose economies were based on hunting, herding, and foraging supplemented at most by the cultivation of small plots of grain and legumes. The assemblages even from interior sites included marine molluscs. Corbeddu Cave, which is about 30 km from the sea along the Cedrino River, produced quantities of snails, shell, and the remains of other maritime creatures including crabs and lobsters. Wild animals including muflone, deer, boar, and *prolagus Sardus* were more common than the domesticates such as sheep, goat, and cattle. The floral and faunal remains suggest the cyclical movement of the small bands from the coast to the interior, a progression that allowed them to exploit all aspects of their environment (Rowland 1987).

The succeeding Bonu Ighinu culture seems to have reached its apex around 4,500 BC. Bonu Ighinu sites are more common, with some such as Grotta Pitzu at Pranu-Belvi and Polu-Meano Sardo located well into the interior. They included the ritual cave site of Sa Ucca de su Tintirriolu-Mara and other caves like Grotta Filestru, Grotta Rifugio-Oliena, and Corbeddu. There were open-air villages such as Cucurro S'Arrius and Conca Illonis located on the filled lagoons around Cabras and that at Puisteris along the Mogoro River (Atzeni 1992:46-49). Significantly a number of the villages founded at this period expanded into major Ozieri sites.

The Bonu Ighinu village of Cuccuru s'Arriu consisted of a number of timber and reed huts. Associated with the village was a necropolis consisting of single-room chamber tombs cut into the sandstone. The tombs contained skeletons, pottery, and lithics. Some of the burials had polished stone bracelets and armlets and were covered with red ochre. The grave goods included obese female statuettes (Santoni et al. 1982).

These are the first attested complex burials in Sardinian prehistory. The sample for Bonu Ighinu is still quite small, but it raises several important archaeological and cultural questions. For the earlier Neolithic the archaeological record has been dominated by cave material, mainly the refuse left by daily human activity. Now we have a distinct mortuary culture with a range of objects associated only with the world of the dead.

We see here the emergence of an ideological system associated with the afterlife. It is also possible that the increased range of material goods reflects developing status differences, but one has to interpret this evidence with caution, for archaeologists have learned to be careful about reading too much into the grave deposits of any culture.

The stone statuettes found at Bonu Ighinu sites are of special interest. They are relatively small, measuring some 11.5-18 cm in height. Some have their arms folded over the belly, while others have them positioned at the side. The style is abstractly geometric with only minimal indications of anatomy. They have evoked the same range of interpretations from wife substitute to mother goddess that characterize all early female images in the Mediterranean (Lilliu 1999:12-54).

The pottery found in the Bonu Ighinu tombs represented major improvements in Sardinian ceramic technology with a fabric of relatively high quality. The favored form is a carinated bowl with the surfaces decorated with a variety of punched and linear motifs. Here as in other of its cultural manifestations Bonu Ighinu anticipates the succeeding Ozieri culture. Outside influences have been posited to explain these changes, and efforts have been made to see connections between Bonu Ighinu and mainland, Sicilian, and even Balkan pottery. Lacking precise petrological studies, however, such comparisons must be used with caution.

The appearance of the stone figurines in Bonu Ighinu burials has also been used to argue for Sardinia contacts with other parts of the Mediterranean. A wide range of parallels from as far away as Macedonia have been posited, but the use of often rather general stylistic similarities without more precise material analyses must arouse a certain degree of skepticism. Exportation of obsidian to Corsica and the continent increased, and the expanded obsidian trade could have facilitated the exchange of prestige objects like the figurines. It is also likely that the expansion of trade fostered the development of low-level hierarchies within the Bonu Ighinu communities. The burials with their status goods may well reflect that.

The Sardinian Neolithic culminated in the Ozieri culture. The name derives from the type site, the cave of San Michele at Ozieri in the north-central part of the island. The culture there was first identified early in the 20th century. The signature Ozieri artifact is a ceramic vessel with a bicolored surface slip and a complex incised surface decoration. A variety of closed and open forms were produced, including tripod vessels. The pots display a variety of decorative motifs such as zigzags, triangles, festoons, spirals, and circles, as well as representations of human figures.

Ozieri pottery is the best produced in Sardinia during the whole prehistoric period and compares well with such fine ceramic traditions as those of the Pueblos of the American Southwest (Bray 1963; Lilliu 1999:92-101, 354-75).

Lithic tools manufactured during the Ozieri period were also of high quality. The obsidian trade obviously continued to be of great importance, but other types of stones were also used. Finely chipped arrowheads indicate the continued importance of hunting, as is also reflected in the faunal record. High quality blades and polished greenstone axes were also produced. The lack of wear on the axes also suggests that they were produced for mortuary purposes or that they were objects of ritual display rather than practical use (Tykot 1999:73).

Ozieri sites have been documented throughout Sardinia. While the highest concentration is in the southwest of the island, a number are found in the interior and even along the east coast. There is a relative uniformity in the distribution of artifact types, although some regional differences are beginning to be defined. Settlement preferences can be plotted. About 40% of the known Ozieri sites are on low ridges (*cuccurus*), such as those overlooking the plains around Cagliari and the lagoon of Cabras. The latter group had outliers along the banks of the Tirso River up to Fonni and Orgosolo and around the Mogoro River just south of Monte Arci. Another 17% are in the northwestern part of the island from La Nurra to Pozzomaggiore and extending to Ozieri itself. Another 16% lie on the east coast, on the Gulf of Orosei, around the mouth of the Flumendosa River and up some of the river valleys in the area. The southwest cluster comprises about 18%.

While a few of the important Ozieri sites have yielded traces of earlier Neolithic occupation, the great majority seem to represent new foundations. This suggests a major population growth and settlement expansion during the late Neolithic. Ozieri was on the whole a society of unwalled, open-air villages, each exploiting a catchment area of about 2 km. In spite of the population expansion and a presumed increased competition for resources, the lack of defenses argues for limited tension and warfare. A small number of Ozieri sites have been found in caves, some used exclusively as habitations, some as cemeteries, others as both.

San Gemiliano-Sestu is possibly the best known Ozieri sites (Atzeni 1959-61). The village was located on an undulating ridge about 100 m above sea level. It faced onto a well-watered plain to the west and was within easy reach of a lagoon and the Gulf of Cagliari. The village consisted of at least 60 huts, most of them less than 3 m in diameter, spread out over an area of about 220 by 200 m. A range of stone tools and ceramics was found. However, since many of the huts continued to be occupied during the succeeding Monte Claro period, it was not always possible to isolate assemblages belonging to one or the other culture. As one would expect from a site so close to Monte Arci, obsidian dominated the lithic repertoire. Most of the tools were arrows, scrapers, and small, retouched blades that reflected the hunting, gathering, and sea-harvesting economy. The ceramics included both decorated and undecorated vessels, showing that the use of decorated wares was not limited to the world of the dead (Lilliu 1988:89-106). There seems to have been differences in the types of objects found in specific huts, suggesting specialized activity areas within the community. However, since the quality of documentation in the initial site publication is uneven, one has to be cautious about applying too-precise interpretations to any aspect of this archaeological record.

The economy was clearly very mixed. The faunal remains included the bones of wild animals (deer, boar, and muflon) as well as cattle, swine, and sheep. Loom weights and spindle whorls attest to the importance of weaving. Seashells were numerous. What appears to have been new varieties of grain (*triticum aestivum, triticum compactum*), barley (*hordeum vulgare nudum*), and legumes (*pisum sativum*) were recovered (Piga and Porciu 1990: 572). Since the amount of floral material reported for Neolithic Sardinia is still very small, it is premature to assume that these grains were being cultivated for the first time.

The village of Cuccuru S'Arriu, located close to the shores of both the Gulf of Oristano and the Lagoon of Cabras, was about one-third larger than San Gemiliano. Only part of the site has been excavated (Santoni 1989). Not all of the huts seem to have been occupied simultaneously, and in the current state of our knowledge it is impossible to discuss the chronological development of the village. In the Ozieri phase, remains of sea products do predominate over animal bones, suggesting a strongly maritime-based sustenance economy.

The village of Su Coddu that extended over 6 ha is the largest-known Ozieri community. Unfortunately, parts of the site had been covered by modern development so an overall picture of the community and its economy can never be recovered. The habitations ranged from simple huts to more complex structures. One of the latter had two rooms and a square portico. Another building covered some 200 m^2 and may have been a multiple family dwelling. The polylobate hut #27 yielded a white marble cruciform statuette of a type generally associated with burials. Another statuette in marble and one in terracotta were found in hut #96.

Two domus de janas *tombs in the cliff at Sant' Andrea Priu.*

Preliminary faunal studies show an abundance of shellfish and mammal remains. The bones of cows and pigs predominated over those of sheep and goats (Ugas, Lai, and Usai 1985).

The most visible and best-known monuments from the Ozieri period are the over 2,000 rock-cut hypogea known locally as *domus de janas*. They range in form from small, single-room tombs to elaborate, multi-chambered structures. The *domus de janas* probably originated as simple one-room dwellings of the dead with additional chambers added on over the course of centuries as new mortuary needs arose. Most *domus de janas* were isolated, but a few were part of extensive necropoleis with as many as 37 multi-chambered tombs clustered together. The variety of interior architectural styles is striking. Some of the burial chambers clearly reproduced the interiors of homes of the living, with roof beams, columns, and in at least one case a hearth incised in the floor (Leon Leurquin 1996:70-88).

Among the better known of the complex tombs are those of Anghelu Ruju (Levi 1952) and Santu Pedru (Contu 1964) near Alghero, Su Crucifissu Mannu-Porto Torres (Ferrarese Ceruti 1982) and S. Andrea Priu-Bonorva (Santoni 1976:3-49). Because most of the tombs were reused by subsequent generations down to the Roman period and the Middle Ages and some more recently have been converted to sheep pens, it is rare to find a *domus*

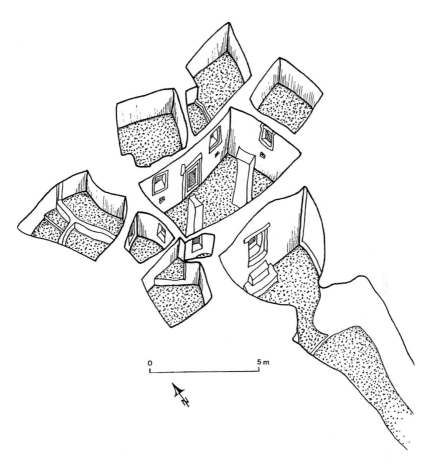

Isometric reconstruction of the domus de janas *at Santu Pedru in Alghero (after Webster 1996).*

with the initial burials undisturbed. A few of the tombs at Anghelu Ruju were still sealed when discovered, preserving the remains of offerings and funerary meals consisting mainly of lamb and shellfish in the larger cells near the entrance (Levi 1952). The small *domus de janas* at San Benedetto-Iglesias was a rare example of an Ozieri period tomb uncontaminated by any later reutilization. Within its four small cells were found 35 skulls and many scattered skeletal remains, probably from secondary burials, while flints, obsidian tools, and pottery were dispersed around the chambers. Just inside the entranceway were ash deposits, other carbonized materials, and burnt animal bones (Germanà 1995:51-52).

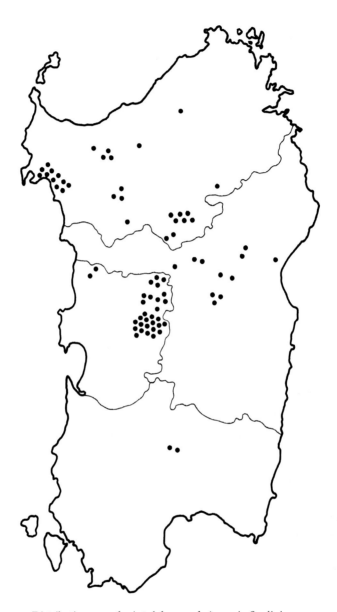

Distribution map of painted domus de janas *in Sardinia.*

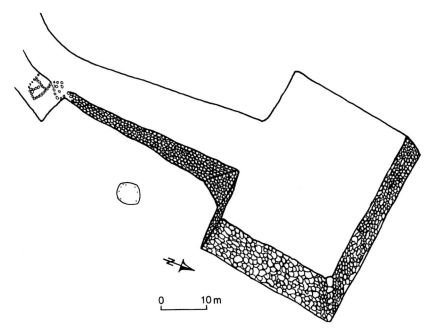

The Ozieri period ceremonial mound at Monte d'Accoddi (after Webster 1996).

Wall paintings and relief work have survived in some of the rock-cut tombs from the north and center of the island. Painted decorations were probably originally much more common, but they were more likely to perish than the carvings. Bulls' horns and spiral motifs predominate. The bulls' horns, which only appear in fewer than 5% of all *domus* are thought to be symbols of a taurine deity representing virility and regeneration, the male counterpart of the fertile mother depicted in the figurines. The chamber tombs with their bulls' horn decorations could also have been associated with an emerging local aristocracy whose power might have been based on the control of oxen and cattle.

The most extraordinary Ozieri site is the religious structure of Monte d'Accoddi-Sassari. Indeed one scholar has described it as the most singular cultic monument in the early Western Mediterranean (Guilaine 1994:338). It was a man-made high place located in the middle of an open plain. The platform which is trapezoidal in shape and measures 37.5 by 30.5 m, was built up to a height of c. 5.5 m. On its top was a rectangular structure measuring 7 by 16 m that was probably the shrine itself. The platform was approached by a 41.5 m-long access ramp. Before the construction of the high place, the site had been occupied by a late Bonu Ighinu village and then an Ozieri one. An earlier Ozieri shrine, consisting of at least one menhir and a large altar, was replaced by the later, massive Ozieri sanctuary (Contu 2000).

The construction of the high place at Monte d'Accoddi was an extraordinary accomplishment for the people of late Neolithic Sardinia, but not unusual for societies at this level of social and economic development. One thinks of early Stonehenge in England and some of the mounds of the American midwest (Emerson 1997). It documents the existence of an elite capable of marshaling the considerable human and material resources necessary for the construction of such a monument. The primacy of the cult center was apparently recognized by a number of communities. The development of this major cult center together with the lack of village fortifications suggests that local elite competitions were socially controlled during the Ozieri period and not allowed to degenerate into endemic warfare (Webster 1996:52-54).

3

Metal Technology and
the Transition to the Nuragic Period

It has been customary since the 19th century to see the introduction of metals as marking a major division in European prehistoric development. Archaeologists argued that not only did the creation of bronze tools and weapons require improved technical expertise, but it also provided the fighting and display instruments that fostered a competitive warrior society. The happy farmers of the Neolithic were replaced by a bellicose elite. The post-Neolithic prehistoric development of Sardinia has often been reconstructed in that standard farmers-to-warrior mode. Ozieri was seen as yielding to a succession of Chalcolithic and Bronze Age cultures that laid the foundations for the shepherd warriors of the Nuragic age.

What actually happened on the island appears to have been much more complex. Certainly the peoples of Sardinia early became significant players in the development of metallurgy in the central Mediterranean. The island is rich in copper and silver. Ozieri decorated ceramics demonstrated a mastery of high temperature kiln firing technology that was one of the preconditions for metal smelting. The admittedly small sample of dated finds suggests that some of the earliest metal artifacts in the central Mediterranean come from the island. It is even possible that Sardinian craftsmen pioneered certain forms of metal production, especially in silver. The transmarine connections that developed out of the obsidian trade fostered further exchanges of materials and technological innovations. The incipient social complexity of the Ozieri could have provided both the craftsmen and a market for ritual metal objects.

Evidence for early metalworking has been found at Ozieri sites. At Su Coddu-Selargius 7 of the huts produced detritus associated with copper and silver production (Giardino 1992:305). Other Ozieri sites including Cuccuru Arrius have yielded small numbers of silver and copper objects that appear to date to the 4th millennium BC (calibrated 4250-3350 BC).

While this early metallurgy is of technological interest, its social or economic importance should not be exaggerated. Metal objects would have
been few in number and would have played a very limited role in the
rituals and activities of society.

While differences in ceramic style have led archaeologists to differ-
entiate distinctive post-Ozieri cultures such as Abealzu and Filigosa, the
overall archaeological picture is one of a high degree of continuity. Certain
villages that had pottery characteristic of the successive Abealzu-Filigosa
cultures also continued Ozieri building forms and artifactual assemblages
(Lo Schiavo 1989:282-83; Contu 1997:231-34). The lithic industries showed
little change. Ritual activities still continued at Monte d'Accoddi, and the
dead were laid to rest in the *domus de janas*.

The late Ozieri and immediately post-Ozieri cultures made increased
ritual use of the standing stones known as menhirs, which become a striking feature of the Sardinian landscape. Dating of those isolated objects is
always difficult, but artistic styles employed in menhir decorations, and
their reuse in slightly later structures like Giants' Tombs and nuraghi, suggest that some of the menhirs date to the Ozieri-post Ozieri transitional
period (Contu 1965; Anati 1984:95-197).

The shape, decoration, and placement of menhirs vary considerably.
On some are carved Ozieri-style representations of the human face. Other
menhirs become abstractly carved statues representing both males and
females. One of the four statue menhirs at Genna Arrele has distinct female breasts. However, male forms predominate. Several menhirs show
representations of daggers. These weapons along with the disappearance
of the female goddess figurines suggest the strengthening of warrior male
roles in Sardinian society (Rowland 2001:26-27).

The destruction and reuse of many menhirs makes it difficult to
comment definitively about their original positioning and distribution.
Some clusters do seem to show ritual patterning. A group of seven aniconic menhirs at Corte Noa appears to have an intentional NNE-SSW
alignment, while another dozen at Su Furpini de Luxia Arrabiosa form
a zigzag pattern (Atzeni 1979-80:17-19). Some correlation seems to exist
between the concentrations of menhirs and the deposits of copper ores.
The statue menhirs at Laconi and Nurallao were less than 8 km from the
copper deposits at Funtana Raminosa, while a group recently found near
Isili, reused in a Giants' Tombs, are located in another copper-producing
region (Saba 1999).

The *domus de janas* continued to be used for burial during the Abealzu-
Filigosa periods. An important example of that is the undisturbed *domus*

Alignment of menhirs at Pranu Mutteddu-Goni.

de janas at S. Caterina di Pittinuri (Cocco and Usai 1988). The entrance had been sealed in antiquity, and the objects within were exclusively Abealzu-Filigosa in date. From the distribution of the material remains it was clear that the interior chambers had only secondary burials, while the outer cell and entrance corridor were used for mortuary rituals. Silver jewelry, other ornaments, and human bones were found in the interior. In the first chamber and the entry passage human bones were absent, but there were animal bones (mainly swine), tripods, and miniature vessels. The use of miniature vessels represents a tradition in Sardinia burial ritual that went back to Ozieri or perhaps earlier and continued into the nuragic period (Usai 1998).

While certain scholars have attempted to create for the Abealzu-Filigosa phase a complex history with minute subdivisions, the archaeological assemblages seem in reality to represent only variations in pottery styles within an ongoing Ozieri tradition (Tanda, Mura, and Pittui 1999). Some decorative motifs and ceramic forms characteristic of the Ozieri do disappear, but many ceramic shapes continue in use, and much Abealzu-Filigosa pottery can be described as undecorated variants of Ozieri. As so often happens in Sardinian prehistoric studies scholars have proposed interconnections with mainland Italy and even with southern France and Spain, but such claims have been based on little more than rather general stylistic similarities. The very general reconstructions of the historical circumstances under which such contacts might have been made do not inspire much confidence.

The presence of metal jewelry in some of the immediate post-Ozieri burials shows that the smiths were producing new types of status goods. However, metal weapons do not appear to have been common. Depictions of daggers have been found on some of the menhirs, but the daggers themselves were not well represented in the contemporary grave goods. Overall the production and use of metal objects appear still to have had a limited impact on Sardinian society outside the elite ritual sphere.

The most significant change in settlement organization was the appearance of defensive complexes at sites like S. Giuseppe and Juanne Buldu-Padria and Sa Corona-Villagreca (Anati 1984:64, 91-92). While the number of fortified sites is small, the defenses do seem to indicate increasing social tensions. They may have been caused by increasing population pressures that, in turn, generated conflicts over access to the best land and the most important mineral resources. Such competition further stimulated the development of hierarchical structures in Sardinian society.

Very important for our understanding of the transition from Ozieri to nuragic society is the cultural phase that archaeologists have designated Monte Claro (Depalmas and Melis 1989). Its relationship with the Abealzu-Filigosa culture is not clear. The limited stratigraphic evidence provides contradictory examples, with Monte Claro artifacts appearing before, contemporary with, or after Abealzu-Filagosa (Foscu-Nieddu 1998). Again the distinctive indicators are ceramic forms and decorations. Monte Claro vessels generally have rows of grooved channels or fluting incised on their surfaces. Regional styles have been identified with some of the ceramics like those of the Sulcis-Iglesiente complex lacking the fluting characteristic of Monte Claro elsewhere.

Other artifacts of the Monte Claro culture exhibit strong continuities with the Ozieri. Spear points, blades, arrowheads, scrapers, and augurs in obsidian and other stones continue the Neolithic lithic traditions (Lilliu 1988:141-42). The use of metal and especially of copper weapons seems to increase. Copper daggers, for instance, have been found in a number of burials attributed to the Monte Claro period (Usai 1998:32-34).

Sites with Monte Claro ceramics are thick on the ground. More than 80% of the known sites are located from the Gulf of Oristano southward, in the Marmilla, around Mogoro and Sardara, around the Gulf of Cagliari, and in the Campidano around the Mannu River. Interior sites are rare. Habitation sites for the first time show a clear preference for elevated, dominant positions overlooking fertile valleys, which may again reflect the rising bellicosity caused by increased population and intensified competition for the best land.

Many Monte Claro sites show continuous habitation from the Ozieri, but we also see frequent examples of post-Ozieri abandonment and new Monte Claro foundations. The newly established Monte Claro village of Corti Beccia-Sanluri expanded into a community of at least 42 structures. In the Cabras region the smaller Neolithic villages appear to have agglomerated into fewer, larger settlements. Other Monte Claro sites were equally large, but many show no expansion from the previous occupations (Rowland 2001:28).

Two northern Monte Claro villages deserve special attention. Monte Baranta-Olmedo is a fortified enclosure strategically located on a plateau above a well-watered, fertile valley (Moravetti 2000). The form of the enclosure itself anticipates structures found at proto-nuragic settlements. Located within the extensive fortified area was a village of small rectangular huts. Some of the huts were apsed. The residential area was dominated by a large (20.6 x 15.3 m) horseshoe-shaped enclosure that showed 5 successive levels of occupation, the earliest being Monte Claro. Outside the village area was a circle of menhirs 10 m in diameter that appears to have defined a ritual space.

Even larger was the Monte Claro village and high place shrine of Biriai-Oliena. This site, unlike most others, was located well into the interior on the eastern watershed of the island. Again it developed on a plateau overlooking a large, fertile valley. The Monte Claro pottery at Biriai resembles closely that found at sites in the more coastal Oristano and Mogoro areas and suggests continuing cultural contacts between the coast and the interior along the well-established obsidian trade routes.

The village at Biriai consisted of large, rectangular, apsidal huts. The numerous millstones and loom weights attest to grain preparation and wool working. The excavated huts were located in close proximity to the high place and may have been associated with its cult, serving either as dwellings for sacerdotal specialists or as temporary dwellings for pilgrims and worshipers. They may anticipate structures found in nuragic sacred areas and the modern *cumbessias* or hostels of Sardinian Christian pilgrimage sites (Castaldi 1999).

About one quarter of the known Monte Claro sites are located in caves. Around Sulcis in southwestern Sardinia the percentage rises to two-thirds. Many of those cave sites were cemeteries, but some seem to have been seasonal habitations. Most had no pre-Monte Claro occupation. The cave site of Filiestru Cava Mara produced a Monte Claro radiocarbon date of 2480+/-50 BP (Tykot 1994a:131).

The Sardinians during the Monte Claro period continued to use the *domus de janas* for burials. Sometimes they returned to tombs of the Ozieri period, while in other instances they appear to have carved out new tombs. Continuity in burial practice is well demonstrated by tomb VII at Serra Is Araus-Cabras. The entrance to the tomb was sealed with a sandstone stele whose four protuberances may represent the breasts of the fertility-funerary goddess. Within Monte Claro objects were found under Beaker-Bonnanaro material in the Ozieri period *domus de janas*.

Cist graves were also used for burials during the Monte Claro period. In some instances their structure anticipates the next stage in Sardinian mortuary architecture, the creation of the so-called Giants' Tombs. The cist grave at Su Cuadda de Nixias-Lunamatrona was later transformed into a Giants' Tomb. The Giants' Tombs of Li Lolghi, Li Muri, and Coddu Vecchiu-Arzachena were apparently constructed in two phases, the cist first and then a gallery grave with a typical Giants' Tomb entrance (Castaldi 1969).

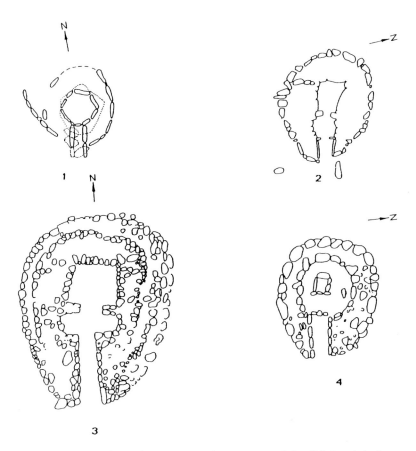

The plans of selected corridor proto-nuragic monuments (after Tykot and Andrews 1992).

During this era the increased experience with megalithic architectural techniques led to the creation of a new category of monument referred to variously as proto-nuraghi, pseudo-nuraghi, and corridor or gallery nuraghi. They were raised platforms, rectangular, circular, or ovoid in form. The platforms had stone-lined corridors or galleries built into them, often with staircases that connected to an upper level. On the top of the platforms were erected one or more huts built in stone with reed or wooden roofs.

The most important clusters of these proto-nuragic monuments are to be found in the west-central part of the island. Favored locations were

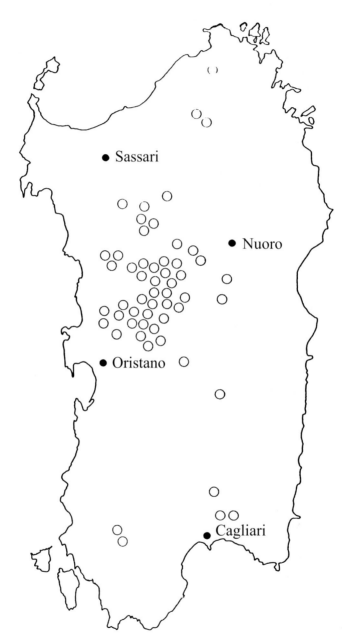

Distribution of passage proto-nuraghi
(after Tykot and Andrews 1992).

high plains and ridges that overlooked waterways and springs (Bagella 1998). The precise dates of construction are generally not clear, for the structural materials do not lend themselves to scientific dating. The best that can be hoped for is that new excavations will produce either organic remains testable by radiocarbon or artifacts like ceramics that were built into the fabric of the structures. Most proto-nuragic structures have been dated by occupation debris, but such artifacts only provide information on later site use, not necessarily the initial construction date. However, the presence of Monte Claro pottery at many proto-nuraghi strongly suggests that those developments in megalithic architecture were part of the Monte Claro cultural innovations (Lewthwaite 1986; Lilliu 1988:176-86).

The purpose of these megalithic structures is also not clear. They are often referred to as fortifications, but that hypothesis seems to have little to recommend it. The fact that some platforms had buildings on top of them suggests that they served as either shrines or residences for the elite. The raised platform would have made the house or shrine visible from a distance and enhanced its prestige. These proto-nuraghi varied considerably in size, but the largest represent major building projects. The mustering of the human and material resources for the construction of the more complex proto-nuraghi like Narocci-Arbus and Arbicci-Sardara demonstrates the increasing power of certain members of the emerging local and regional elites.

Before turning to a full discussion of the emerging nuragic culture, two other pre-nuragic archaeological phases need to be considered. The first of these is the so-called Bell Beaker culture. The name derives from the distinctive type of biconical burial vessel that appeared at many sites in western Europe during the late 3rd millennium. Archaeologists have long talked about a Beaker Folk and used the diffusion of the ceramic vessels and the associated burial rites to reconstruct major population movements throughout Europe (Trigger 1989:155). The emergence of what may be called a "post-migratory mentality" among European prehistorians has forced a rethinking of the whole Beaker phenomenon. Rather than being the signature of a distinctive culture, the Beakers should probably be seen as widely circulated prestige items without specific ethnic association (Champion 1984:155-56, 183-84, 192-95, 221-24).

Characteristic biconical Beakers have been found in Sardinia in some numbers. However, they are scattered in a variety of archaeological contexts, again probably a prestigious artifact rather than a cultural indicator (Rowland 2001:31-33). Trump has identified very early (3000 BC) comb-impressed Beaker material at Filiestru (Trump 1984), but most of the

Sardinian classic Beaker material probably dates to later periods. Another study documented 38 Beaker sites and 22 of those were at *domus de janas* (Moravetti 1980:216-22).

Beaker vessels were often associated with Ozieri and sub-Ozieri materials including figurines. In the *domus de janas* at Marinaru-Porto Torres, Beaker ceramics were mixed in with the Ozieri grave goods (Contu 1952-54:54-63). Beaker and Ozieri artifacts were found together in a *domus de janas* at Padre Jossi-Sanluri, and it appears in other period contexts. Beakers were associated with Monte Claro pottery at Monte Ossoni-Castelsardo and Monte Olladiri-Monastir and with Bonnanaro pottery at Pranu Mutteddu-Goni.

The appearance of the Beakers in Sardinia is not even associated with the creation of large, single-grave cemeteries that characterize Beaker mortuary rituals on the continent (Champion 1984:155-56, 168-69, 175-76). Current evidence strongly suggests that in Sardinia the "beaker phenomenon" represented little more than the importation of another type of prestige item along the now well-established trade networks that linked the island with the Continent. It did not represent new peoples coming in from the outside, but rather the emergence of a native Sardinian elite for whom the Beakers served as an important continental associated status symbol.

The final archaeological phase that Sardinian prehistorians see as linking the pre-nuragic and the nuragic periods is the Bonnanaro. Again it should probably be regarded as an artificial construct based mainly on ceramics. Indeed some scholars such as Lilliu regard Bonnanaro as nothing more than nuragic Phase I (Lilliu 1988:276-316). The characteristic Bonnanaro ceramics were undecorated, and in their simplicity they anticipated nuragic wares. They have been found over much of the island with the exception of the east coast. The known find spots are concentrated in the northwest and the southwest of the island and the currently accepted dates cover the period 2200-1600 BC (Tykot 1994:fig. 10).

The most characteristic Bonnanaro sites artifact assemblages are funerary, many placed in reused *domus de janas*. One hundred and 98 flexed burials of the Bonnanaro period were discovered in the *domus de janas* as the Tomb of the Warriors at Sant'Iroxi-Decimoputzu (Ugas 1990). Their grave goods included copper objects such as awls, punches, pins, daggers, and swords. Clearly this was the burial place of either a single, wealthy extended family or several connected families with warrior associations.

The Sant'Iroxi tomb was exceptional, for other Bonnanaro burials contained relatively few weapons. Reused *domus de janas* are not the only places used. Caverns, cists, *alles couvertes*, Giants' Tombs, and trench tombs were all used for internment during that period (Rowland 2001:33-34). Several Bonnanaro burials have produced skulls which show signs of tepanation, the widely used practice of cutting open of the skull of a living person to cure diseases and release evil spirits trapped within (Manunza 1998:59-105).

Recent archaeological research has provided more detailed evidence for Bonnanaro settlement patterns. Some villages were located close to nuraghi, reinforcing the notion that Bonnanaro represented the emergent phase of nuragic culture. A good example is tower A of Duos Nuraghes-Borore, where archaeologists found Bonnanaro ceramics mixed in the late pre-nuragic material (Webster and Webster 1998:188-89).

A rare example of a non-nuragic Bonnanaro settlement is the site at Stangioni-Portuscuso (Contu 1997:428). Located close to marshes, streams, and lagoons, it had a long history as an open-air station exploiting maritime and littoral resources. The cardial and Bonu Igninu Neolithic pottery documented earlier periods of occupation. The Bonnanaro phase was represented by a square structure with a threshold of small stones, pebbled flooring, and a central hearth.

The Bonnanaro culture has taken us to the threshold of the island's defining epoch, the nuragic and to the middle of the 2nd millennium BC. Island archaeologists for cultural and even ideological reasons have emphasized the supreme importance of that era. Certainly the nuragic centuries saw important cultural changes, but the foundations in village life, production technologies, and even extra-island contacts had been laid in the periods and cultures described in this and previous chapters.

4

The Emergence of the Nuraghi

The mid 2nd millennium BC saw the appearance of the nuragic culture that has dominated the study of the later prehistory of Sardinia and shaped the island's self-identity. For many Sardinian archaeologists this is a defining moment in Sardinian history, when a culture very distinctive to the island emerged and provided an archaeological unity and identity. The most characteristic development of this period was the construction of large numbers of the circular towers known as nuraghi. Even after thousands of years of monument destruction, the nuraghi remain ubiquitous presences in the Sardinian landscape. Archaeologists estimate that some 7,000-8,000 still exist and as many as 5,000 may have been destroyed, especially around major population centers like Cagliari. Archaeological pioneers like Angius and Taramelli reported the ongoing destruction of many towers in the 19th century, but new fieldwork continuously documents previously unknown nuraghi.

The almost obsessive claims of the modern Sards for nuragic originality have been countered by efforts of non-native archaeologists to credit non-Sardinian groups with the invention, development, and importation of the towered form. In the 18th and 19th centuries Greeks, Phoenicians, Pelasgians, Egyptians, Iberians, Canaanites, even the giant sons of Adam- all found their advocates as nuragic inventors (Spano 1867:43-49; Lilliu 1962:255-76; Leighton 1989:195). Similar if more sophisticated models of external influence were posited well into in the 20th century. Many of those interpretations grew out of the *lux ex oriente* paradigm of diffusionism that long dominated Mediterranean archaeology. Its advocates claimed that innovations like nuragic construction started in the eastern Mediterranean and were carried west by traders and missionary priests (Trigger 1989:150-55).

The Mycenaeans were recently touted as the innovators who brought the key architectural developments associated with nuragic culture to the island. Giovanni Lilliu, the dean of Sardinian archaeologists, long held that

1. Abbasanta
2. Aidomaggiore
3. Ala dei Sardi
4. Alghero
5. Antas
6. Arbus
7. Arzachena
8. Arzana
9. Austis
10. Ballao
11. Barisardo
12. Barumini
13. Bauladu
14. Baunei
15. Berchidda
16. Birori
17. Bitti
18. Bonarcado
19. Bono
20. Bonorva
21. Borore
22. Cabras
23. Cagliari
24. Calangianus
25. Cuglieri
26. Decimoputza
27. Dolianova
28. Domunsovas Canales
29. Dorgali
30. Elmas
31. Esporlatu
32. Esterzili
33. Fonni
34. Furtei
35. Galtelli
36. Genoni
37. Gesico
38. Gesturi
39. Ghilarza
40. Goni
41. Gonnosno
42. Guamaggiore
43. Guspini
44. Isili
45. Ittireddu
46. Ittiri
47. Laconi
48. Laerru
49. Loceri
50. Loiri
51. Lunamatrona
52. Macomer
53. Mara
54. Maracalagonis
55. Mogoro
56. Monastir
57. Mores
58. Muravera
59. Norbello
60. Nulvi
61. Nuoro
62. Nuragus
63. Nurallao
64. Nurri
65. Olbia
66. Oliena
67. Olmedo
68. Oniferi
69. Orani
70. Orgosolo
71. Oristano
72. Orroli
73. Orune
74. Ossi
75. Ottana
76. Ozieri
77. Padria
78. Palau
79. Pattada
80. Pauli Arbarei
81. Paulilatino
82. Perdasdefogu
83. Perfugas
84. Ploaghe
85. Pompu
86. Posada
87. Pozzomaggiore
88. Quartucciu
89. S. Basilio
90. S. Caterina di Pittinuri
91. S. Gavino
92. S. Giovanni Suergiu
93. S. Pantaleo
94. Samassi
95. Samatzai
96. Samugheo
97. San Sperate
98. Santadi
99. Sardara
100. Sarule
101. Sedilo
102. Selargius
103. Senorbi
104. Serramanna
105. Serrenti
106. Serri
107. Sestu
108. Settimo S. Pietro
109. Siddi
110. Siniscola
111. Sisini
112. Siurgus Donigala
113. Sorgono
114. Sorso
115. Suelli
116. Tergu
117. Tertenia
118. Teti
119. Thiesi
120. Tinnura
121. Tonara
122. Turri
123. Usellus
124. Villacidro
125. Villagrande Strisaili
126. Villamassargia
127. Villanovaforru
128. Villanovafranca
129. Villaputza
130. Villasor
131. Villaspeciosa

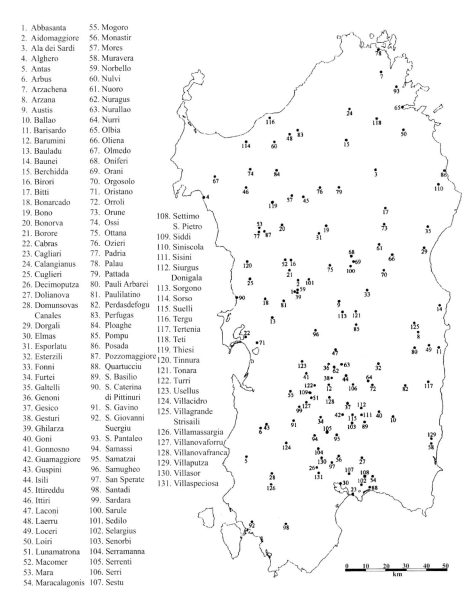

Major nuragic sites in Sardinia.

Single-towered nuraghe.

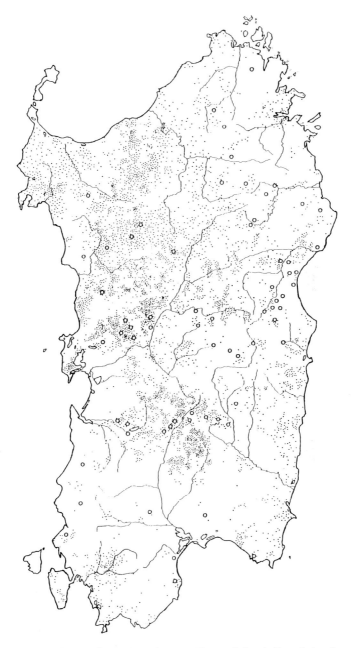

Distribution of nuragic settlements. The small dots indicate isolated nuraghi and the larger circles indicate villages (after Tykot and Andrews 1992).

the Mycenaeans were the only people capable of instructing the Sardinians in the techniques for creating such sophisticated stone structures as the nuraghi (Lilliu 1967:160-63, 181). The recalibration of radiocarbon dates in Europe and the Mediterranean has undermined the validity of such models of east-to-west cultural movement. Architectural inventions that were thought to have originated in the eastern Mediterranean have now been found to have been employed at the same time or earlier in the west. This radiocarbon revolution has forced scholars such as Lilliu to acknowledge that the process of nuragic architectural innovation and development was to a large degree an indigenous one (Renfrew 1973; Lilliu 1988:315).

The reconstruction of the evolution of the nuragic culture has proved very difficult, especially for the architectural history of the tower themselves. Efforts have been made to reconstruct the historical development of the nuraghi based on detailed structural analyses, but such architectural histories are heavily dependent on generalized evolutionary typologies and do not sufficiently consider questions of regional variation and local conservatism. Well-controlled stratigraphic excavations at nuraghi are still relatively rare. Even the best of those provide more information on occupational than on building history. It is still difficult to date precisely the initial construction phase of most single towered nuraghi or to chronicle the structural changes that led to more complex buildings.

Some tower sites do provide evidence for continuity of occupation from proto-nuragic to nuragic settlements, but they seldom yield firm dates for that process. The Nuraghe Albucciu-Arzachena in northern Sardinia, for example, preserved traces of a proto-nuragic phase in the fabric of its later tholos. A date of 3770+/-250 BP provided by material from a fireplace at the site only documents a certain occupation phase and certainly postdates the initial tower construction by several centuries (Antona, Ruju, and Ferrarese Ceruti 1992:37-56). Nuraghe Monte Asinu-Siurgus Donigala in south central Sardinia also combines elements of both proto and classic nuragic structures. However, surface pottery at the site cannot be dated earlier than the Middle Bronze Age (Costa 1984).

Certainly the experience gained in constructing the proto-nuraghi and especially the skills acquired in selecting and moving the hard stones of Sardinia and using them to build corbelled vaults were applied later to the creation of the classic nuraghi. It is generally difficult to see any significant continuity in form or function between the two types of monuments. The proto-nuraghi were most likely designed as platforms to enhance the display of structures such as shrines or elite housing. The nuraghi would seem to have been designed for defense

Interior vault of the nuraghe Is Paras at Isili (NU) (after Lilliu 1999).

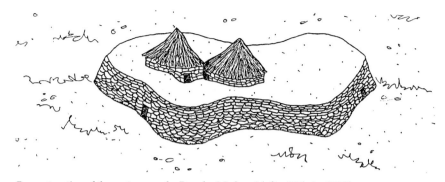

Reconstruction of the proto-nuraghe Brunku Madugui (after Webster 1996).

and habitation. They had single low doors, interior stairways, and a fighting platform at the top. The nuraghi also served as territorial markers. Placed at highly visible locations, they asserted a group's claim to a particular area.

Dating the emergence of the mature nuragic culture of which the towers are the identifying monument is made more difficult both by the limited number of radiocarbon dates and by the problems often associated with the interpretation of those dates, but the radio-carbon sample is expanding, and some patterns of information are emerging. The central tower of the complex Nuraghe Su Nuraxi-Barumini has yielded a C-14 date of 3420 BP+/-200, the fully developed tower at Ortu Comidu-Sardara 3310 BP+/-50; that at Pizinnu-Posada 3350 BP+/-50; and that at Noeddos-Mara 3360 BP+/-70 (Tykot 1994:131). The still small sample suggests that nuragic emerged in the mid-late 2nd millennium BC.

Nuragic settlements developed most frequently in the intermediate level highlands, where a combination of decent soil and adequate water provided the best preconditions for agriculture, pastoralism, and hunting. Water from springs, streams, and rainfall was more abundant, more potable, and more dependable than in the lowland zones. Wild animals (deer, boar, hare, and, prior to its being hunted to extinction, *prolagus Sardus* were abundant, while eel and other fish would have been found in the rivers and streams (Rowland 1987). The large stands of oak (*quercus ilex)* in the uplands would have provided supplies of acorns for livestock feed and for bread dough. While the farming plots would generally have been small, their agricultural potential was probably comparable to that of the lowlands. Barley was the basic grain crop, requiring a shorter growing season than wheat and having a higher yield.

The uplands of Sardinia where the nuraghi were concentrated are often described as marginal for farming. This is not totally accurate as can be seen from a combination of recent archaeological and geomorphological research and 19th century studies of population and agricultural productivity. Field surveys by Lenore Gallin in the territory of Sedilo in the uplands southeast of Macomer have documented a dense nuragic settlement pattern with 55 documented nuraghi. That relatively large prehistoric population inhabited a "well-watered basalt plateau surrounded by rich alluvial lowlands; each nuraghe was located near optimal farmland and was supported by some 500 ha of land, sufficient to provide for eight to ten families in a mixed agro-pastoral regime" (Gallin 1989:224). More than 35 springs watered the territory. In 1846 the same territory had a population of 2,326 persons, of whom 450 were farmers and 218 were shepherds with some of the latter engaged in cultivation.

Other areas with high concentrations of nuraghi have been equally well populated and productive in more recent times. During the 19th century 330 farmers and 240 shepherds lived in the nuragic rich territory of Sorgono in the central uplands. Crop yields ranged were 7-fold for grain and 14-fold for barley. There were 12,000 nut trees, 120 horses, 1,050 cows, 2,300 pigs, 3,500 goats, and 16,000 sheep (Angius 1833-56:287-89).

These 19th century statistics support those who argue for a successful mixed nuragic pastoral-agricultural economy in the Sardinian uplands, and they contradict the picture of pure nuragic pastoralism that has dominated much of recent Sardinian scholarship. It fits well with Benadetto Meloni's description of traditional agricultural practice around Austis in the central highlands: "What is important to note is that itinerant pastoralism accompanies agriculture and that the two activities exchange resources, which guarantees a complete ecological equilibrium. The practice of cereal culture on arable lands, associated with a system of rotation, guarantees that the soil will be cleared of weeds and other infestations, consequently improving the quality of the pastures" (as cited in Rowland 2001:38).

The nuragic cultural system seems to have spread from its original upland core into the more marginal highland and lowland zones. This secondary distribution was uneven. The relative lack of nuraghi in fertile lowland zones like the Campidano has long puzzled scholars. Some have argued that this void reflects a history of tower destruction and the recycling of nuragic stone in these more intensely populated and cultivated areas, a process that started in the Roman period and continued into modern times. Other explanations are also plausible. It is possible that nuraghi are not found in the lowlands because the environment was not conducive to the success of the nuragic sustenance systems. The modern agricultural exploitation of those areas is the result of the introduction of an intensive, cash-crop economy that employs heavy agricultural equipment. The heavy soils would have had less appeal for more traditional farmers. Other aspects of the lowland areas may have inhibited nuragic development. Famine, poverty, disease, and early death were the constant companions of those who farmed these areas until quite recently. Vittorio Angius, who traveled the Campidano in the 1830s to the 1850s, commented on the bad air, bad water, terrible heat, and the swamps and marshes. Springs were rare, and the rivers carried no water in summer. Cereals depended on rains coming at the right time, and their failure led to famine (Rowland 2001:37). It was a marginal land that would have had very little attraction for most prehistoric settlers of the island.

The Rise of Nuragic Complexity

During the course of the later 2nd millennium, the elites of some nuraghi were able to amass considerable wealth and power. This led to the building of more complex nuragic compounds and the accumulation of a richer and more varied material culture. These phenomena were certainly the outgrowth of increased social and economic stratification. Chieftains and dominant families used the enlarged monumental complexes as power bases to overawe and subdue their neighbors and to engage in regional rivalries. These elites also benefited from and probably encouraged increased craft production that fed into trade networks that extended throughout the island and to lands beyond the sea.

The complex nuraghi have attracted a great deal of archaeological research, although of uneven quality. Some large and important sites like Barumini have been extensively excavated. Investigations there and at other similar sites has provided a reasonably full picture of the physical world of the complex nuraghi at the height of their power and prosperity. Reconstructing the social and economic processes that led to that complexity has not proven to be so easy. Such research has been further limited by gaps in our chronological information. The paucity of secure dates makes it difficult to determine when a nuraghe reached certain stages of its structural and cultural development.

A plausible developmental history can be reconstructed for certain of the more famous complex nuraghi. One early sign of emerging complexity was the building of a walled courtyard in front of a tower such as hap-

Aerial photograph of the nuragic complex at Losa (Abbasanta) (after Lilliu 1999).

pened at Giba 'e Skorka-Barisardo near the east coast (Lilliu 1988:502-503). Slightly more sophisticated were nuraghi with walled courtyards and second towers like Nargius-Bonarcado north of Oristano (Anati 1984:65). The final phase in the conversion of relatively simple nuraghi into nuragic fortresses with multiple-towered and interconnected external bastions seems to have occurred between the mid-late 2nd and early 1st millennium BC (Santoni and Sebis 1984). Some of the complex multi-bastioned structures were apparently the product of a single building program,

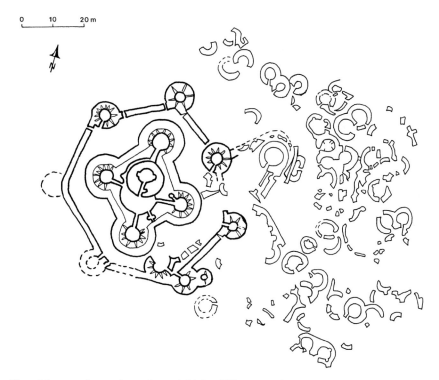

0   10   20 m

Plan of the nuragic complex at Barumini (after Webster 1996).

while others developed gradually, reaching their most fully developed state only after several intermediate stages (Santoni 1993:15-17). In certain instances such as nuraghe Losa-Abbasanta northeast of Oristano the last phase of the outer defensive perimeter seems to have been constructed in haste (Santoni 1993:17-20).

The most famous and impressive of these complex nuraghi is Su Nuraxi-Barumini. It started as a single tower probably in the late 2nd millennium BC. The central nuraghe was first reinforced by a bastion with four towers at the angles and then by an outer fortification wall with eight defensive towers. This whole process was probably completed by the 8th-7th century BC. An extensive village grew up around the central fortification, whose inhabitants would have exploited the fertile plain of the Marmilla. The complex appears to have been sacked by the Carthaginians in the 6th century BC (Webster 1996:162-64).

The large complex at Nuraghe Santu Antine-Torralba southeast of Sassari has been described as one of the most impressive products

View of the nuragic complex at Barumini with village in foreground.

of nuragic architecture. It was the first nuraghe actually illustrated in a publication, appearing in the 1774 work of Francesco Cetti (Contu 1988). The core was a three-storied central tower that originally stood some 21 m high. That was enclosed within a two-storied triangular bastion with three towers interconnected by a basalt wall. There were two wells within the bastion. Among the great range of artifacts found at S. Antine were metal-working tongs, bun ingots, and a large number of bronze objects. Clearly part of the community's power and prosperity was based on its metal productions. From a later period of occupation came Iberian and Phoenician pottery of the 8th-7th century BC as well as evidence for contact with the Villanovans of Etruria. The site also had an important Roman phase (Contu 1988:243-71, 273-304, 397-441).

Nuraghe Losa-Abbasanta, located on an exposed plain between Oristano and Macomer, had a structural history as long and complex as Barumini. The core was a single nuragic tower that was later reinforced by a triangular bastion. A straight wall flanked by two circular towers was then added on the northwest side. The outer perimeter was defended by a wall with at least four towers that enclosed 39,000 m² of potential settlement area. The village at the site continued to be occupied into the Roman

Aerial view of nuraghe S. Antine.

period with the dwellings retaining the circular plans characteristic of the nuragic period.

Nuraghe Arrubiu-Orroli, located on the basaltic high plain on the upper reaches of the Flumendosa River, was even more complex than S. Antine but is less well preserved. The core was again a three-storied central tower, which originally stood 25-30 m high. To this was added a five towered bastion covering some 3,000 m^2, an area 1.67 times larger than Losa. The complex was in the final stage surrounded by a seven-towered fortification wall (Lo Schiavo and Sanges 1994). A hoard of metal, mostly lead, was found under the surface of the courtyard, and the archaeologists unearthed a large number of storage jars. The bones of deer, muflon, boar, rabbits, hare, *prolagus Sardus*, ovicaprids, bovines, and swine were recovered, indicating that the meat of both wild and domestic animals were part of the diet. They were supplemented by quantities of shellfish, especially mussels, showing regular contact with the coast.

The development of these complex nuraghi required considerable advances in both the organization and direction of a large structured workforce engaged in quarrying, transporting, and working enormous masses of stone. Territorial power was evidently being concentrated in the hands of an ever more powerful elite, and a more complicated political hierarchy was being created. It is quite likely that in Sardinia, as happened with the British hillforts "gradually in each of the natural territories one centre gained supremacy over the rest and outlived them to become the natural focus of the region" (Cunliffe 1978:260).

While the occupation history of individual nuraghi can seldom be reconstructed in the detail modern archaeologists would like, enough evidence has been recovered to make some generalizations. It appears that the development of the complex nuraghi did not mean the abandonment of many of the smaller towers. The complex nuraghi, and especially those less formidable than at Barumini, seem to have served as a central place for the smaller nuraghi clustered in the neighboring territory. Nuraghe Attentu-Ploage east of Sassari with its two-towered bastion, had within a 3 km radius 14 nuraghi. Nuraghe Orolo-Bortigali near Macomer, a complex nuraghe of similar plan but located in more mountainous terrain, had 9 nuraghi within 2 km to the north, south, and east. Nuraghe Piricu-Santulussurgiu, north of Oristano, placed on a ridge above the confluence of two streams, had 20 presumably dependent nuraghi within 2 km (Lilliu 1984:66, fig. 59 #3).

It is natural to see in these clusters of simple nuraghi arranged around a complex structure evidence for the emergence of a chieftain-level society, where a lord commanded the allegiance of segments of the surrounding warrior population. Joseph Michels and Gary Webster identified ten such "subregional level polities" in the Margine alone (Michels and Webster 1987:5-10). Spacial studies around Monte Acuto have divided the adjacent territory into eight distinctive regions, each with its complex nuraghe (Basoli and Foschi Nieddu 1991:23-40).

Attempts have even been made to see in the interactive distribution of simple and complex nuraghi the beginnings of social and political structures that survived into later eras. The Romans may have based their administrative subdivisions on territories defined by these complex nuraghi (Solmi 1917:102-21). One such nuragic territorial unit formed the basis of the *territorium* of the Roman city of *Neapolis* and the medieval *curatoria* of Bonorzili. The original nuragic polity likely had a "a central authority of regal type" with a political and economic organization that fostered the foundation of villages and the construction of fortresses to consolidate and possibly expand the tribe's territory (Ugas 1998:537-540).

The World of the Nuragic Villages

At the base of these socioeconomic hierarchies stood the villages. Many of those huddled at the bases of the nuragic towers, but others developed in the open countryside, apparently unconnected to any fortification. Sardinian archaeologists have long focused their research on nuraghi and on religious sites like sacred wells with the result that the villages, and especially the villages not attached to nuraghi, have been inadequately investigated. That situation is beginning to change. While comprehensive excavations of villages are still relatively rare, the cumulative evidence from many smaller investigations is providing a composite picture of the structures and histories of these village communities (Webster and Webster 1998).

Some of the larger complex nuraghi such as Barumini were surrounded by large villages that suggest a substantial dependent community, but there was not always a close correlation between the size of the nuraghe and the extent of the village. Nuraghe Sa Mandra 'e sa Giua-Ossi just south of Sassari is a stumpy little single tower, but its village was revealed by excavation to have been large, and the accumulation of bronze objects suggests that it was wealthy as well.

Survey archaeology has played a major role in expanding our knowledge of the distribution of nuragic villages. Indeed, the majority of the villages not associated with nuragic towers are known only from surface scatters. The villages without nuraghi are proving to be abundant. In the territory of Dorgali near the coast east of Nuoro, 67 of 78 known nuragic period villages had no associated tower (Fadda 1985a:111). The territory of Oliena just east of Nuoro also had a large number of villages without nuraghi, many of which were quite large (Contu 1997:546). Increasing numbers of towerless nuragic villages have been found in the hinterland of the Gulf of Cagliari, in the Sinis area, in the Oristanese, in Marmilla, in Marghine-Planargia, and in the territory of Olbia (Rowland 2001:40). While most of the villages have been found at altitudes ranging from 200 to 700 m, some such as Arvu-Calagonone-Dorgali were at sea level and other at higher elevations. The large village of Ruinas-Arzana on the eastern edge of the Gennargentu was located 1,197 m above sea level (Ferreli 1999).

Aerial view of the nuragic village of Serra Orios (after Lilliu 1999).

The growing evidence for these unprotected villages provides an important corrective to the impression of nuragic bellicosity suggested by the towers and by the representation of warrior activities on nuragic *bronzetti*. Clearly large sectors of the populace had little to fear either from their neighbors or from raiders coming from a greater distance either by land or sea. Moreover, the increasing number of these documented villages forces an upward estimate of the population of nuragic Sardinia. While precise demographic reconstruction is impossible, the combination of towers, tower villages, and open villages argues for a densely inhabited island. One scholar has hazarded an estimate of 450,000-600,000 for the population of Sardinia at the height of the Later Bronze Age (E. Usai 1995:257).

House construction was simple. Many of the village huts had stone lower walls, which would have supported thatched, wooden, or even stone roofs such as one finds today in shepherds' *pinnettas*. There is also evidence for some mud brick construction. The interior diameters ranged from 5 to 8 m. Interior walls were chinked with cork, baked clay, or other materials and covered with mud. Some huts had flooring and most had hearths either in the center or on the perimeter. Many had niches built into the walls. In the huts at S'Urbale–Teti, a village in the mountains southwest of Olbia, a large number of domestic objects were left in those niches (Angioni and Sanna 1996). In some instances several huts were interconnected, suggesting a single domicile for an extended family. At a later date groups of interconnected huts were built around a courtyard, each group remaining separated from its neighbors (Ugas 1987).

The villages also contained specialized buildings that probably were used for ceremonial functions. A hearth in the apse of one structure in the village of Sa Tumba-Serrenti on the eastern edge of the Campidano northeast of Serramanna yielded traces of a burnt incense-like substance (Fadda 1995). At S'Arcu is Forras-Villagrande Strisali on the eastern flank of the Gennargentu a large (17 m length) megaron structure with an interior divided into four chambers was located just outside the village. Part of a model nuraghe, pieces of votive swords and fragments of lead found in front of it suggested its ceremonial function (Webster 1996:146-47).

Most important among the special structures within the nuragic villages were the so-called meeting areas. These were open courts lined with benches and often graced with a ceremonial structure in the center. A small village near Dore-Orani in the Barbagia southwest of Nuoro has provided the earliest known nuragic meeting area. It had space for about ten people, a central altar on a circular base, and three small pools that probably served the needs of water cults (Foschi Nieddu 1995). Much more impressive was the meeting hall at Nuraghe Palmavera-Alghero near Alghero. It was the largest structure on the site, measuring 12 m in diameter. In the center was a model of a nuraghe in stone set on a platform. A large quantity of animal and bird bones as well as shellfish was found in the room suggesting that it was used for ceremonial meals (Moravetti 1992:83-107). These meeting rooms with their distinctive furnishings imply that these communities were organized around some sort of headman-council structure with the nuraghi themselves assuming a place in collective worship.

Evidence for food processing and diet in the nuragic villages is still limited. Large numbers of grinding implements and storage vessels and some remains of grain, barley, grapes, and almonds have been identified. Wild olive found at a nuragic site in the territory of Sarule in the Barbagia southwest of Nuoro is dated to 1000 BC. Almost every village excavation has produced objects related to wool processing and cheese making. Faunal

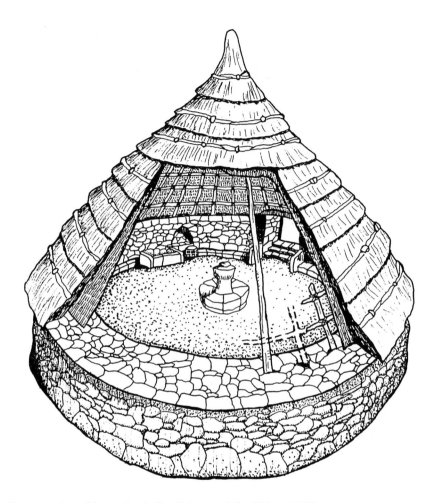

Reconstruction of the meeting hall at Palmavera (after Webster 1996).

remains attest to the importance of both stock raising and hunting. The prominence of young sheep / goat bones evident in the samples from earlier periods continues (Webster and Webster 1998:191). At Nuraghe S. Barbara-Bauladu northeast of Oristano the repertoire consisted of 37.96% sheep/goat/muflon, 18.84% pig/boar, 2.97% *prolagus Sardus*, 0.99% deer, 0.14% porcupine, 1.42% birds, and 0.71% fish (Gallin and Fonzo 1992). The sample from tower A of nuraghe Duos-Nuraghes-Borore south of Macomer yielded among the wild animals 13% deer, 5% rabbit/hare, and 2% bird. *Prolagus Sardus* and deer appear in a number of other sites (Rowland 1987).

By the later 2nd millennium BC, the construction of the nuraghi and the development of their distinctive communities had transformed the visual landscape and probably the social structures of the island. Virtually every high place had one of these towers that probably served both to distinguish territory and link a society. This age also saw changes in the economy, technology, ideology, and outside contacts of Sardinian society.

5
Technology, Commerce, and Ideology in Nuragic Society

The nuragic period saw the full entry of Sardinia into the Age of Metals. By the mid-late 2nd millennium BC, bronze working had become a very important activity throughout Sardinia, best documented by the large number of stone molds for the casting of metal objects found all over the island. Another good indicator of the increased availability of metals is the employment of lead strips to repair large ceramic vessels. Apparently the labor and materials costs of metal repairs had become less than that of producing large ceramic pots.

New excavations at both nuraghi and nuragic villages have markedly increased our information on copper and bronze production. A few examples should suffice. In the territory of Bauladu near Oristano the field work at nuraghi S. Barbara and Zinnuri produced evidence for small scale metal production (Gallin and Tykot 1993; Dyson and Rowland 1988:133). Bronze foundries were found at the sites of Puddialvu-Calangianus in the north of the island near Tempio Pausanio and at S'Urbale (*Notizie degli Scavi* 1889:92-93; *Notizie degli Scavi* 1931:69-70). Masses of slag were unearthed at nuraghe Nieddu-Nurallao located in the mountains east of Oristano (Lilliu 1988:466). Several hammers suitable for metal working as well as a bronze hoard and quantities of ash and charcoal were found at a nuraghe on Monte Sa Idda-Decimoputzu northwest of Cagliari.

The quest for metal ores increasingly shaped settlement location. The concentration of nuraghi in the metal-rich area of Montevecchio, along with evidence for the processing of ores at some of those sites, shows the vitality of the metal-based economy in the southwestern part of Sardinia. Similar combinations of metalworking artifacts have been found at other places on the island (Gras 1985:66-70; Giardino 1987: Webster 1996:136).

The social and economic forces shaping this newly increased metal production can only be tentatively reconstructed. The ruling elites certainly provided an important stimulus as the finds at towers and bastions demonstrate. At Su Nuraxi-Barumini most of the bronze finds came from

Small bronze statuette of nuragic warrior.

*Small bronze statuette of an archer-Cagliari, Museo Archeologico Nazionale
(after Lilliu 1999).*

the bastion area, with only a small amount from the village (Lilliu 1952-54:269-70, 282-300). Ox-hide ingots were found under the floors of nuraghi at Ozieri and Nuragus. The industry was not totally in the hands of the nuraghi-based elite. A number of villages have provided evidence of metalworking activities (Bernardini 1993:37-38).

A very important product of this new bronze industry was the *bronzetti* or small cast-bronze figurines, whose abstract forms and primitive stylistic vigor have long fascinated archaeologists and have recently attracted the attention of art collectors. A lack of archaeological context makes the dating of most of them difficult, but the most recent evidence places the probable start of production at least as early as the 10th century and possibly as far back as the 12th or 13th centuries BC (Lilliu 1966:26-32, 1997a:331-46; Gras 1985:136-40). The subjects portrayed were impressively varied. Very common were statuettes of warriors and archers, and those have been used to argue for the bellicose nature of Sardinian society during the Bronze Age. Other representations apparently had religious or mythological meanings. Figurines interpreted as priests, priestesses, and ordinary people making offerings appear with musicians and ithyphallic dancers. *Bronzetti* of women holding children or a warrior on their laps presumably take us into the realm of religious myth, as do the warriors depicted with four arms and four eyes and a bull with a human bust. Some statuettes depict yoked oxen, probably a reference to agricultural productivity. Another important type is the bronze boat, sometimes depicted with crew or cargo (Lilliu 1966).

Many efforts have been made to relate the *bronzetti* to Sardinian folk traditions and to see them as evidence of a *longue durée* continuity of custom and belief into post-nuragic times (Rowland 2001:69-70). Such interpretations should be viewed with caution. We have in fact little idea about what meaning those small bronzes had for the people who made and used them. Their frequent appearance at sacred sites, especially wells, suggests that they were often offerings made in the fulfillment of vows (Pinza 1901:150-56; Lilliu 1966), but they are also found in mortuary and domestic contexts (Desantis and Lo Schiavo 1982; Ferrarese Ceruti 1985). Our problems with interpreting the *bronzetti* are compounded by the lack of recorded context. Many belong to poorly provenanced antiquarian and museum collections or have appeared mysteriously on the antiquities market. The increased popularity of the *bronzetti* among collectors has led to the massive looting of nuragic sites to supply the art market. It has probably also contributed to an increase in the production of forgeries (Lilliu 1995:111-14, 127-30).

*Small bronze statuette of seated mother and child from Santa Vittoria di Serri
(after Lilliu 1999).*

Small bronze of mythical figure with four eyes and four arms from Teti Albini (NU) (after Lilliu 1999).

Certainly the over-all picture that emerges from the study of the small bronzes is of an artisan class of considerable inventiveness and technical skill and of outward-looking, creative nuragic aristocracies. The heyday of the nuragic bronze production coincided with the most extensive inter-connections between Sardinia and the wider Mediterranean world since the great days of the Stone Age obsidian trade. The striking small statu-ettes stand as a challenge to any notion of Sardinia as an inward-looking, non-creative society oriented toward its mountains and away from the seas that surround its shores.

Nuragic Mortuary Ritual

The period that saw the significant shifts in settlement structures and social organization and craft production represented by the rise of the nuraghi also experienced changes in mortuary ritual. The characteristic burial monument of the nuragic age is the so-called Giants' Tomb. The core structure of the Giants' Tomb was a slab-lined, rectangular funerary chamber enclosed in a long apsidal mound of earth. While most were single chambered, there is at least one example of a tomb with two inter-connecting burial chambers. The chamber and tumulus often formed a monument of considerable size. That at Su Crastu Covocadu-Tinnura near the coast west of Macomer measured some 30 m in length. The shape and building techniques of the tombs were certainly influenced by the older *alles couvertes* (cover passage tombs) and in some cases there was a con-tinuity of construction and use history. In the tomb at Li-Lolghi-Li-muri the older *alles couvertes* of Bonnanaro date was later expanded into a much larger Giants' Tomb (Castaldi 1969).

Giants' Tombs were generally fronted by large, stone- lined, semicir-cular entrance courts. A forecourt like that at Maddu II-Fonni in the moun-tains south of Nuoro could measure as much as 24 m in diameter. A large stele with its lower section pierced by a porthole was often placed at the entrance to the tomb itself. Those entrance partitions showed considerable variation. In some instances the stele consisted of a rectangular lower slab onto which was fitted a semicircular gable. In others the stele was replaced by a stone wall pierced by a porthole that provided access to the interior of the tomb. S'Orku-Quartucciu near Cagliari and Bidistili-Fonni are good examples of the latter design. The courtyards sometimes incorporated other features, such as benches placed around the entranceway.

Menhirs and smaller standing stones known as betyls have been found at certain Giants' Tombs. They are generally phallic in form, but a

Interior corridor of a Giants' Tomb.

Entrance stela from the Giants' Tomb at Coddu Vecchiu.

few have what appear to be female breasts. One from S. Pietro di Golgo-Baunei on the coast southeast of Nuoro had a human face carved on it (Lilliu 1995b). Even smaller stones, referred to as *betelini*, have also been unearthed at a certain number of mortuary sites. Such standing stones long remained features of the Sardinian landscape with some being cited as boundary markers in medieval documents.

The funerary rituals associated with the Giants' Tombs can only be imperfectly reconstructed from the scattered, fragmentary artifacts found in and around the tombs. Skeletal remains and intact funerary deposits within the tombs are rare. Features like basins and votive pots from the tomb forecourts suggest ongoing ritual activities involving family and clan. A basalt basin, presumably for funerary libations was, found next to the stele porthole at Domu 'e S'Orku-Siddi in the Marmilla near S. Gavino Monreale. Votive hearths were discovered in front of the exedra at the Giants' Tomb at Barnavu Mannu-Santadi in the uplands southeast of Carbonia (Bittichesu 1998). The largest of the Giants' Tombs at Madau-Fonni had a hearth with quantities of ash and carbon placed before the port hole (Lilliu 1995:337).

Given their size and limited number the Giants' Tombs were prob-ably only burial places for the elite. The mortuary chambers were not large, and not every nuraghe had an associated Giants' Tomb. Around La Nurra only 8 Giants' Tombs have been identified in a territory with 276 nuraghi. Intensive survey in the Marghine and Planargis regions plot-ted 332 nuraghi but only 88 Giants' Tombs. Even though some Giants' Tombs have been destroyed the evidence strongly suggests that they were limited to the elite with the ordinary inhabitants being interred elsewhere (Rowland 2001:45). The inter-visibility between the tombs and certain nuraghi suggest that the two types of monuments shared a ritual land-scape dominated by the hegemonic landscape of the elite (Blake 2001).

Anthropological and folkloric interpretations of these tombs abound. Some would see in the tomb form itself the representation of a boat that conveyed the deceased to the afterlife. For others the curvature of the back wall recalls the horns of a bull, while the actual tomb chamber represents its head or body. Such bovine symbolism would represent continuity with the taurine motifs found in the walls of the *domus de janas* (Lilliu 1995:349, 361-72). The ample forecourts permitted more complex rituals than were possible in the restricted antechambers of the *domus de janas*. A rite of heal-ing by incubation related to a hero cult might have taken place at those tombs. Rituals associated with ancestors or heroes are suggested by the presence of later materials in the tombs (Lantenari 1954-55:17-19; M. Perra

1997:787-93). The Giants' Tombs at Brunceu Espis di Fontanazzu and Su Monte de s'Ape-Loiri showed unbroken continuity of activity into the Roman Imperial period. Sa Ena'e Thomes-Dorgali was even reutilized in the Middle Ages (Rowland 1981:14, 58; Pulacchini 1998:43). The associations of these Sardinian tombs with later hero cults have their parallels in Iron Age Greece (Antonaccio 1995).

The Giants' Tombs are not found everywhere in Sardinia. In the Gallura and Igliesente regions the nuragic inhabitants used natural cavities in the granite bedrock for burial. Dry stone compartments were constructed within caves to form the burial chambers, and the entranceways were sealed with rock (Ferrarese Ceruti 1968). It is not certain whether those tombs represented regional and ethnic differences or were the response to different geological conditions. *Domus de janas* also continued to be reused during the nuragic period. In the limestone and Miocene sediment areas of the northwest where basalt building materials were lacking, a number of rock-cut tombs were modified to imitate Giants' Tombs.

Water Cults

The nuragic period saw the increase in the importance of cults related to water. Life in the uplands, where the nuragic settlements were concentrated, depended on the continued flow of natural springs and fountains, especially in the long months of the annual summer drought. Concerns about water have shaped Sardinian folklore and popular religion from the nuragic period to the present. The sacred well near nuraghe Santu Millanu-Nuragus was rebuilt twice during the Roman period. Some 9 kilos of Roman bronze coins of the 1st and 2nd centuries AD were unearthed at the well at S. Antine-Genoni, a testament to decades of modest devotion (Guido 1933). It is not an accident that many sacred wells bear the names of Christian saints or even, as at S. Anastasia-Sardara and S. Salvatore-Cabras, incorporated the cult places into the Christian structures. The power of divinity to control hydrological resources was not overlooked by early missionaries and clerics (Lilliu 1998a).

Such associations have continued into modern times. The custom of dunking a human skull in water at the time of the new moon was practiced well into the last century. During Holy Week water was often sprinkled in the wells and springs to assure an abundant reserve of water during the summer season. At Nurallao the statue of St. Peter was carried in procession to a well, lowered into it, and the saint asked whether there would be rain or not. At Perdasdefogu during times of drought, the images of S.

The Water Sanctuary at Su Tempiescu (after Fadda 1988).

Isidoro and the Madonna of the Graces were carried in procession to the river, where their feet were bathed, while priest and parishioners recited propitiatory prayers (Rowland 2001:46-47).

The evidence for water cults begins before the full nuragic period. Votive offerings at the site of Abini-Teti date to the early Bonnannaro period around 2000 BC, while those at the spring of Sos Malavidos-Orani can be placed in the later Bonnannaro. In their most fully developed forms the water cults focused on sacred wells. Many of those came to serve as the religious centers for tribes and confederations, a custom that appears to have persisted into the Roman period. The increasing prosperity and the growing social complexity of the later 2nd millennium BC stimulated

Aerial view of the sacred precinct and well at Santa Cristina.

architectural elaboration. Elite patronage is further demonstrated by the presence of quantities of luxury goods among the votive offerings.

The shrines were self-contained complexes set within an enclosure that was sometimes marked by betyls. The sacred wells and springs were enclosed within underground or largely underground nuragic towers that were approached by stairways. The heights of such towers varied. The structure in the sacred well at Mitza de Nieddinu-Guspini was 2.75 m high, that at S. Anastasia-Sardara 5.05 m, and that at S. Cristina-Paulilatino more than 7 m. The over-all height of the pozzo Milis-Golfo degli Aranci exceeded 13 m. The stairs into the wells were fronted by a vestibule similar to a Giants' Tomb forecourt.

One of the smallest, but also the best-preserved of the well sites was that at Su Tempiesu-Orune. A landslide dated to the 9th century covered the site and preserved the remains of the sacred well largely intact. Su Tempiesu was constructed of large stones that had to be transported from at least 10 km away. The water from the spring gushing from the rock face was channeled into the main chamber then out into a smaller pool. The complex had a rectangular vestibule and stone paving. The walls of the main chamber were angled inward to form a triangular roof into the top of which were inserted 20 votive swords. The smaller pool also yielded numerous bronze votive offerings. At the base of the entrance wall were stone benches, and the entire complex was surrounded by a curved stone wall. On both sides of the temple area were separate structures, each of which contained votive offerings (Webster 1996:182).

The most elegant of the surviving sacred wells is that at Santa Cristina-Paulilatino. It has a vestibule, a stairway, and a chamber-fountain area. The well was built of fine ashlar masonry, some of the best in Sardinia. A large village grew up around the sanctuary. Phoenician and Punic imports were found at the site and large numbers of molded terracotta fragments related to the cult of Ceres and Demeter dating to the late Punic period were also discovered there (Webster 1996:184-88). They testify to its long-lasting importance for the local rural population.

The most imposing of the nuragic shrines is the complex at S. Vittoria-Serri. The sanctuary was built on a small plateau with a commanding view of the surrounding countryside. At S. Vittoria the sacred well was only one element in a much larger ritual complex. Only 3 m of what may have been a 12 m high well chamber survive. The sacred well was approached by a keyhole-shaped, paved vestibule, and 13 steps led down to the well itself. Originally a large basin stood between the exterior wall and the left wing of the vestibule. On the right side of the basin an opening connected to a channel leading away from the well-chamber. There were benches alongside the vestibule. The complex of features suggests a variety of cultic functions associated not only with water but also with animal fertility and social and political cohesion.

A 50-m long street connected the sacred well with another rectangular building 5.8 x 4.8 m in size. Inside that latter structure were two altars and a betyl. Votive objects in bronze, silver, gold, ivory, and amber were discovered inside. Underneath the floor were numerous remains of animal bones and seashells, presumably representing the remains of ritual meals.

Entrance to the sacred well at Santa Cristina.

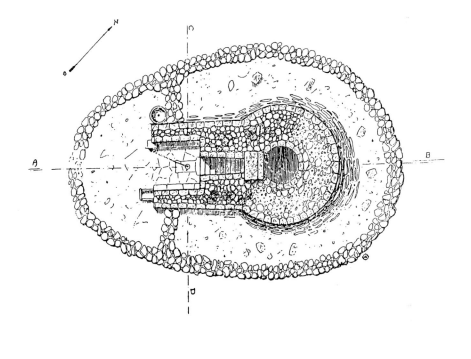

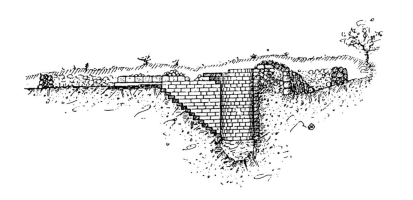

Plan and section of the sacred well at Santa Vittoria di Serri.

Two other circular structures flanked that building. The street continued another 8 m, ending in a large (11.5 m dia) circular structure with a stone bench along the inside wall. A block of stone in the center might have supported a model of a nuraghe in the manner of Palmavera.

North of this main sanctuary stood a building known as the chief's dwelling. It was a reused single tower nuraghe with a keyhole vestibule more than 5 m long. The nuragic period occupation level in the chief's dwelling produced pig, cow, and sheep bones along with pottery, fragments of bronze objects, a crucible and some slag. East of this was the so-called festival enclosure, a stone lined ellipse with an interior courtyard measuring 50 x 40 m. A number of stalls, perhaps facilities for a market, opened onto the courtyard. With its surrounding rooms the complex recalls the modern Sardinian *cumbessias* or *mursitensis* that provided shelter for worshippers at Christian shrines. Perhaps this is an example of continuity of cult from the nuragic into the modern period. Porticos that could have served as communal dining halls opened onto the courtyard. An attached cooking area produced large quantities of ash and food refuse.

At the easternmost part of the S. Vittoria-Serri complex was the so-called meeting hall, a circular structure some 14 m in diameter and outfitted with an interior bench. Several basins, an altar and a betyl were found inside the meeting hall. A thick layer of ash with animal bones and pottery fragments surrounded the betyl and altar (Contu 1999).

The ritual complex at S. Vittoria-Serri also provided important evidence for exchange contacts between Sardinia and the wider Mediterranean world and for the continuity of island cult practices well beyond the high nuragic period. Among the votives found there were objects imported from Proto-Villanovan and Etruscan Italy. Punic material was found in the well as were other objects showing that religious activities continued at the sanctuary into the 2nd-1st centuries BC. A destruction level of that date may be related to a Roman attack on the shrine. The adjoining nuraghe was converted by the Romans into a shrine of the goddess Victory. However, worshippers apparently returned to the nuragic sanctuary, for later Roman material was found there (Zucca 1988).

A religious complex of such size and complexity demonstrates sophisticated political and social interactions among the late 2nd, early 1st millennium nuragic groups. While the prime function of Santa Vittoria would have been religious, the array of different buildings shows that a range of political, social, and economic activities took place there. It clearly drew individuals and groups from a large catchment area. The investment in

Aerial view of the "festival closure" at Santa Vittoria di Serri (after Zucca 1988).

permanent structures and the long time range represented by the votive objects are striking. The sanctuary at St. Vittoria-Serri provides insight into a world very different from that of small, isolated, xenophobic groups that is often seen as the core world of nuragic Sardinia.

Other Cult Centers

Other cult places were also frequented by nuragic worshippers. An important recent addition to our knowledge of nuragic religion was provided by the discovery of the megaron temple at S'Arcu'e is Forras-Villagrande Strisali, high in the mountains of Ogliastra. The complex included a temple surrounded by a *temenos* wall, a nuraghe with three rounded projecting towers, and a large village (Webster 1996: 146-47). The temple megaron was 17 m long and divided internally into four chambers. Various objects of bronze including votive swords were found inside the megaron. Fragments of a model nuraghe and votive swords were also found in front of the temple. The large quantity of scrap metal found at the site suggests metal-working activity associated with the temple and the village.

Two other types of religious gathering places were represented by Orulu-Orgosolo, which was a sanctuary without well or fountain, and Sa Domu's s'Ossu-Dolianova. The first site yielded miniature nuragic pots, bronze model boats, and silver and bronze vessels along with evidence for cultic activity that extended down into the Roman period. Both shrines produced enormous quantities of animal bone, votive objects, and a sequence of Punic and Roman coins that extended down to the reign of Julian in the 4th century AD (Salvi 1989:17-21).

Miniature vessels such as those found at Orulo-Orogsolo played an important role in nuragic worship. A private collection in Oristano has some 175 miniature vessels dating from the final Bronze Age into the early Iron Age. All were found in a shrine associated with the complex nuraghe Sianeddu on the Sinis peninsula. The Middle Bronze Age levels of the Giants' Tomb at Moru-Arzachena also yielded miniature vessel as did tower C of nuraghe Arrubiu Orroli (Lo Schiavo and Sanges 1994:48, 61).

The nuraghi themselves sometimes became the objects of religious devotion, a means of creating symbolic and ritual cohesion in the community. The presence of stone models of nuraghi in the village assembly rooms has already been mentioned and bronze models are also known. Some abandoned nuraghi seem to have become cult centers as was apparently the case for nuraghe Su Mulinu-Villanovafranca. Occupation in the nuraghe itself appears to have ended by the 11th century BC. However, the tower continued to be used as a cult place from the end of the 10th-early 9th century BC into the 2nd century AD with a hiatus in the 5th-4th centuries BC. Two hearths were unearthed, one preserving traces of the burning of some type of aromatic substances, while the other yielding quantities of bones of young animals, mainly piglets with some lambs and calves. Offerings from the 10th-8th centuries included amber, gold, rock crystal, ivory, copper, and bronze. Hundreds of lamps, mainly in pottery, along with plates and cups were unearthed. Central to cult practice from the 8th century onward was a stone carving of a nuragic tower (Ugas and Paderi 1990). The abandoned nuraghe S'Aneri-Pauli Arbarei had a similar

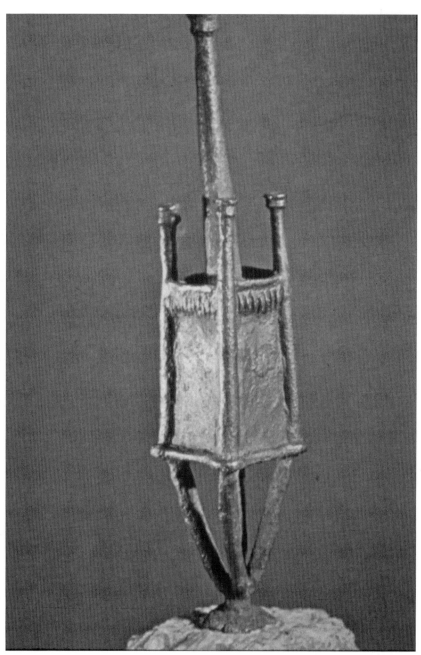

Bronze model nuraghe from a sacred well at Olmedo-Sassari, Museo Nazionale Archeologico.

Head fragment from sculpture from Monte Prama.

history of cult activity with offerings extending from the 9th century BC to the Roman period (A. Usai 1987).

An important new insight into nuragic religious practices and social organization was provided by the discovery in 1974 of a hoard of large stone statues at Monte Prama-Cabras (Webster 1996:179-81). The statues lay shattered at the base of a complex nuraghi. Seventeen of the 25 statues represented warriors, portrayed in a style that clearly derived from the nuragic bronzes. Eight of the warriors wore various types of armor and weapons, and 18 are of a type designated as "boxers," depicted bare chested with a folded belt around their waists. Their left arms held shields that were raised over their heads. The sculptures had all been broken into fragments. It has been suggested that this destruction was caused an attack by the Phoenicians from nearby Tharros, an assault designed to demonstrate the power of the colonists over the indigenous elites. Given what is known about Phoenician-nuragic power relations such an aggressive action on the part of the colonists does not seem too likely. Such aggressive behavior might better be associated with nuragic rivals.

The statues were part of a funerary complex with at least 33 graves, 30 of which were aligned in a long row. The deceased were buried in crouched seated positions. Only a few personal items were buried with the bodies. The mortuary population consisted of 23 adults and 5 youths. Fourteen to 20 of the adults were male and 23 females. The oldest individual was c. 50 years old at time of death and the youngest 14-15. About half of the dead were under 25. Only a few personal objects were buried with the bodies (Tronchetti et al. 1991:119-31).

The complex seems to have flourished during the 7th century BC. While other scattered finds of large stone sculpture have been reported from Sardinia, the size and complexity of this sculpture group remains unique. Whatever the cause of its ultimate destruction, the establishment of such an impressive mortuary cult place and its later development must be related to the proximity of the recently established settlement at Tharros. The family or clan that ruled the nuragic territory close to Tharros must have developed into what anthropologists call a gateway community that controlled interchanges between the coastal Phoenicians and the tribes of the interior. Key to the success of such gateway communities were the diplomatic skills of certain elite individuals, the so-called big men of anthropological parlance. Such big men often converted their situations into positions of wealth and power for their families (Gibson and Geselowitz 1988:22-24; Holloway 2001). The Mediterranean and Western European Iron Ages provide several apparent examples of this phenom-

0   50   100 cm

Reconstruction of two monumental statues from Monte Prama (after Webster 1996).

enon. Parallels for the sudden appearance of large-scale stone sculpture at a similar stage of social development can be found in Iron Age Iberia and La Tene Gaul (MacKendrick 1972:28-31; Dominguez 2002). The Picenum region of mainland Italy provides some interesting examples including the Capestrano warrior (*Eroi e Regine* 2001:104-09). Who the sculptors were is unclear, since neither the nuragic peoples nor the Phoenicians had much experience in the carving of large-scale sculptures. Cyprus, where a stone sculpture tradition developed early, provides a possible source of craftsmen, especially since what appears to be a late 7th century Cypriot object was found in one of the Monte Prama graves (Sismondo Ridgway 1986:63).

Nuragic Culture and the Outside World

The era of nuragic florescence saw Sardinia again enter into the wider Mediterranean world. The obsidian trade had early opened up Sardinia to Corsica, northwest Italy, and the southern coast of France. While the mechanisms of that exchange were complicated and not easy to reconstruct at this distance in time, there is no question that ideas as well as materials and objects traveled along the complicated trade networks.

The decline of the obsidian trade that resulted from the increased use of metals probably led to decreased extra-island contacts. The period of relative isolation was short lived, and by the 15th century BC Sardinia was again part of the Mediterranean trading community. The island is rich in metals, especially copper. It may also have had small but significant supplies of that rare metal, tin. Casserite, the ore from which tin is extracted, was present in southwestern and southeastern Sardinia, and some casserite debris has been found at nuragic sites (*Notizie degli Scavi* 1911:301; *Monumenti Antichi* 1915/16:413). The tin used in nuragic bronzes most likely came from the island. Whether enough tin was available in Sardinia to have made it an important export commodity is another question.

Significant technical differences distinguish the archaeological efforts to reconstruct the trade in metals from that in obsidian. Obsidian can be sourced with great precision, and detailed patterns of exchange can be reconstructed. While copper and tin also have identifiable trace elements, those became masked as metals were cast and recast.

However, reasonably reliable source tests can be conducted on raw copper found in archaeological contexts. Such scientific analyses have produced surprising information about the patterns of Late Bronze Age

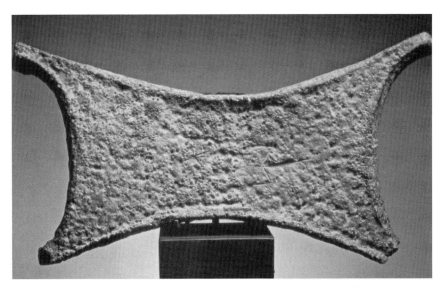

Copper ingot found at Serra Ilixi (NU).

Mediterranean exchange and have stimulated a fundamental rethinking of the nature of culture contact during that period. The so-called Sardinian oxhide copper ingots provide a good case in point. Large metal ingots cast in the shape of an oxhide have been known from Sardinia since 1857. They have also been found in considerable numbers in other parts of the Mediterranean, including on wrecks on the seabed. It had long been assumed that they were produced from raw copper that was mined in Sardinia and exported to places like Cyprus. Cypro-Minoan signs found on some of them have reinforced that hypothesis. The trade in copper ingots has been reconstructed as a classic example of the center periphery colonialist model, with Sardinia playing the role of the peripheral-colonized culture, exporting raw materials and importing finished goods (Rowlands, Larsens, and Kristiansen 1987).

That paradigm had to be modified when isotope analyses conducted on ingots found in Sardinia demonstrated to the satisfaction of many experts that the copper in them was Cypriot in origin (Lo Schiavo and D'Oriano 1990; Atzeni et al. 1998; Stos-Gale et al. 1998), suggesting that nuragic Sardinia was importing metal for its own craftsmen rather than just exporting raw materials to the more industrial societies in the eastern Mediterranean. Other evidence reinforces this picture of a very complex Sardinian bronze craft tradition. The oxhide ingots had a wide distribution within Sardinia. They are well represented at coastal sites, but have also been found in considerable numbers in the interior as well. They document an island-wide procurement and production network linking both coast and interior with the extra-island world (Lo Schiavo 1998a, 1999). The high demand for metal is also evidenced by the presence of plano-convex ingots, the form apparently indicative of another copper production system on Sardinia (Stos-Gale and Gale 1992).

This information forces a reconsideration not only of the patterns of trade between Sardinia and the eastern Mediterranean but also of the peripheral nature of the Sardinian economy in the Bronze Age. The Sardinian demand for metals was apparently so high and the production centers so active that local metallic resources were not sufficient. The islanders needed to import raw copper from the eastern Mediterranean. The presence of large ingots of Cypriot copper at interior sites demonstrates the existence of complex exchange networks that hardly fit with the isolated, inward-looking Sardinia of popular perception.

The second half of the 2nd millennium saw the development of a trading system originating in the Minoan-Mycenaean centers of the Greek mainland, but expanding outward to include Cyprus, Syria, and Sicily. Type artifacts like Late Helladic pottery document this developing trade, and excavations on both land and sea have provided abundant evidence for this first major Mediterranean interaction sphere.

Discoveries starting during the 1970s have demonstrated that Sardinia was part of this world. In 1976 Mycenaean pottery was discovered in a clandestine dig on the shore of the Gulf of Orosei in east-central Sardinia. That chance find was quickly followed by the recovery of stratified Mycenaean material at nuraghe Antigori-Sarroch southwest of Cagliari and then at other sites. Antigori, the site of what seems to have been a nuragic emporion or trading center, yielded pottery of Mycenaean III B (1340-1210 BC) and III C (1200-1100 BC) types in association with nuragic pottery (Ferrarese, Vagnetti, and Lo Schiavo 1987).

There is now a considerable body of material found in Sardinia that can be associated with the Mycenaean world. A limited amount of this seems datable to Late Helladic III A-B with a Mycenaean jar, apparently produced in the Peloponnesos found at nuraghe Arrubiu-Orroli on the Sarcapos River Late Helladic III A2 (1375-1300 BC). An ivory plaque with the depiction of the head of a warrior with a boar-tusk helmet found at Mitza Purdia-Decimoputzu has been dated to Late Helladic III A. The nuragic habitations at Monte Zara-Monastir have yielded a few pieces of Mycenaean III B pottery. Faience beads found in a Giants' Tomb at San Cosimo-Gonnosfanadiga are similar to examples from the Lipari Islands

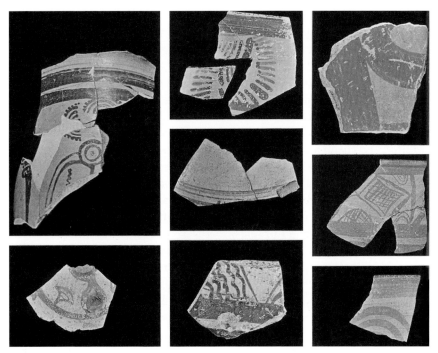

Mycenaean sherds from Nuraghe Antigori (after Lilliu 1999).

and Thapsos (Rowland 2001:56). With the LH IIIC (1190-1050 BC) the number of Sardinian sites with Mycenaean material increases. While most finds are coastal, some imported items found their way into the interior (Knapp 1990:126-28; Webster 1996:140).

Sardinian interactions with the eastern Mediterranean were more than just a marginal Mycenaean connection. The complexity of those contacts can be appreciated from a consideration of the island's relations with Cyprus. Cypriot metal objects have turned up at nuragic sites, and there is some evidence for Cypriot influences on nuragic craft techniques (Webster 1996:140-42). The two islands shared certain traits in their metal-working traditions including the use of heavy-duty metal-working instruments like shovels that were not part of the craft repertoire in other Mycenaean controlled areas like Crete.

This Cypriot trade connection peaked around 1200 BC but continued down to the turn of the millennium and even beyond. At Muru Mannu-Tharros Cypro-Mycenaean pottery was found in levels dated to the 11th-9th centuries, while ingots and objects of Cypriot production or at least reflecting Cypriot influence have appeared in Iron Age contexts (Bernardini 1991a). Some of these objects may have been heirlooms, but it seems increasingly likely that the Sardinian-Eastern Mediterranean connection was never broken at the end of the Bronze Age.

One important and still unanswered question was what the Sardinians exchanged for those raw materials and finished goods. Certainly pastoral products such as wool and hides were exported. Pottery that appears to be Sardinian has been found at Kommos on Crete, but it was almost certainly from containers used for transporting other products. Sardinia may have had tin, and it is possible that Sardinian iron was extracted early. In tower C of nuraghe Antigori-Sarroch a piece of worked iron was found in a stratified context with 13th century BC Cypriot pottery. Iron was reported together with amber and nuragic bronzes at Forraxi Nioi-Nuragus and at Perda'e Floris-Lanusei. There also appears to be evidence for early iron working in the hinterland behind Nora (Vagnetti and Lo Schiavo 1989; Botto and Rendelli: 1998:726-27).

The mechanisms of exchange were complicated and are hard to reconstruct with the limited evidence currently at hand. A site like Antigori seems to have served as an emporion with resident traders and perhaps even craftsmen from the Mycenaean and Cypriot worlds (Cline 1994:92-93), but, one should not exaggerate the impact of this Mycenaean trade on the development of nuragic society. While the quantity of Mycenaean material known from nuragic sites has increased markedly since 1980, it is currently not sufficiently abundant to suggest anything more than a marginal Mycenaean influence on Sardinian society. One should avoid the colonialist trap and not assume that a few Mycenaean traders with beads and trinkets would have altered the dynamics of a society as vigorous and well integrated as that of Late Bronze Age Sardinia.

Nor need it be presumed that this was a one-way process in which only traders from the outside came to Sardinia. While island folk tradition claims that "the Sardinians have in their blood a mysterious repugnance to the sea," the large number of miniature ships among the nuragic bronzes suggests otherwise (Webster 1996:178). It appears likely that from the days of the obsidian trade the Sardinians were sailors who explored the central Mediterranean. The presence on the Lipari islands of nuragic pottery dated 1125-850 BC, material that would not have had great external trade value, suggests Sardinians may have traveled there (Kollund 1996). Sardinian objects have also been documented from the graves at Pontecagnano south of Naples (Lo Schiavo 1994). Islanders themselves probably transported some of the Sardinian material found on the coast of Tuscany (Camporeale 1969:94-97).

Nuragic bronze boat model-Cagliari, Museo Nazionale Archeologico (after Lilliu 1999).

Much of the seaborne trade undertaken by the Sardinians would have focused on neighboring islands and on the west coast of Italy, but the depiction of what appears to be a nuragic boat on a LH III C stirrup jar from Skyros raises the possibility that the islanders could have been in trade across the Mediterranean (Gras 1985:108). The nuragic pottery found at Kommos has already been mentioned. Archaeologists working at the short-lived site (cc. 1220-1120 BC) of el-Ahwat near Megiddo in Israel claim to have documented a Sardinian presence (Zertal 1997, 1998).

The best-known if the most debated evidence for Sardinians in the eastern Mediterranean is the case of the Sherden who appear among the sea peoples invading Egypt during the 19th Dynasty (1349-1197 BC). Their depiction on New Kingdom Egyptian monuments has been cited to support a variety of historical reconstructions. At one time the Sherden were seen as a people who were repulsed from Egypt and then moved westward to establish the nuragic culture in Sardinia. That view has lost most supporters (Sandars 1978: 161, 198-299; Drews 1993:69-72, 152-55, 217-18). If there is a connection at all between Sardinia and the invaders of the Nile delta, it probably took the form of small numbers of nuragic seamen who joined a mixed group of invaders who attacked Egypt (Drews 1993:50, 54).

6

The Transition to the Iron Age and the Phoenician Connection

Sardinia differed from the Mycenaean core areas of the northeast Mediterranean in that it experienced little or no break in east-west contacts between the end of the Bronze Age and the establishment of the Iron Age. The nuragic culture itself continued unbroken from the Mycenaean to the Phoenician periods without the Dark Ages that followed the end of the Mycenaean Greek world. Since trade objects dated to the turn of the millennium are rare the documentation of continuity in outside contact is difficult, but eastern Mediterranean bronzes that seem to date to around 1000 BC have been found at nuragic sites (Cross 1984; Barreca 1986a). The discovery of an anthropomorphic sarcophagus of Philistine type at Neapolis suggests settlers arriving from the Levant in Sardinia sometime shortly after 1100 BC (Bartolini 1997).

At present there is no evidence for permanent Phoenician settlements on Sardinia at so early a date. Some pre-colonial Phoenician material has been discovered along the coast or in the river valleys. Such sporadic finds probably document the presence of traders who used the nuragic coastal settlements as ports of call on their way to and from the Iberian peninsula. Their return voyages may be documented by examples of Iberian metal-work found in Sardinia such as the bronze sword found in the Monte Sa Idda hoard (Lo Schiavo and D'Oriano 1990:105-15; Cruz Fernandez Castro 1995:135-47).

Nuragic interactions with the outside world during this transitional era were not limited to the Phoenician orbit. Villanovan material has been found at a number of sites in different parts of Sardinia. Nuragic artifacts have also appeared among the grave goods at Cerveteri, Populonia, Vetuolonia, Vulci, and Tarquinia. The inhabitants of Vetulonia and Populonia located in the heart of the Etruscan metal-producing districts seem to have been especially receptive to works of Sardinian artisans. These contacts continued into the Etruscan period. David Ridgway has argued that "it seems increasingly possible that the earliest external and

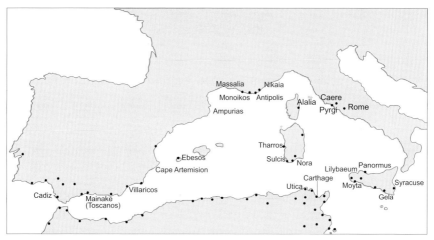

Punic sites in the central and western Mediterranean (after Von Dommelen 1998).

mutually beneficial assessment of the metallurgical potential of Villanovan Etruria was not planned in the Aegean or the East, but in the West itself and no further away than Sardinia" (Ridgway 1988:496).

The Foundation of the First Phoenician Settlements

In the period 750-650 BC and possibly earlier a series of Phoenician settlements was established along the south and southwest coasts of Sardinia. These foundations were usually situated on islands and promontories that provided maximum natural protection to the insecure colonists. Phoenician settlements like Cagliari, Sulcis, Nora, and Tharros not only became the major urban centers of Punic Sardinia but continued as important Roman cities. While their general history is known, detailed reconstruction of their development during the early years is difficult. Some cities like Nora, Bithia, Tharros, and Bosa were continuously occupied through the Roman period, while others like Cagliari and Sulcis/San Antioco remain major centers today. A good portion of ancient Nora is now under water. Documenting the thin layers associated with the earliest Phoenician settlements at such places has always proved difficult, but recent archaeological research has provided much new information and raised important questions about this first Phoenician phase.

Several Phoenician settlements were established at the sites of previously existing nuraghic communities. While some of the nuraghi were probably occupied when the Phoenicians arrived, others had been deserted for many years. The nuragic community at Tharros had been abandoned several centuries before the Phoenicians arrived in the later 8th century BC. The Phoenician settlement at Ozieri was built over the remains of an Ozieri village with no apparent intervening occupation.

In other cases the relation between nuragic and Phoenician settlement cannot be so easily determined. The Punic original settlement of Othoca was the site of an extensive nuragic village (Zucca 1998). At Nora the archaeologists have not been able to determine if the indigenous center was still functioning at the time of the Phoenicians' arrival. However, there are some indications of interaction between nuragic folk and Phoenicians after the establishment of the Punic city (Pesce 1972:48-51, 102; Bernardini 1993a:58). At Monte Sirai the Phoenicians partially dismantled the complex nuraghe Sirai located at the foot of the citadel. A portion of the nuraghe may also have been turned into a shrine of Astarte. The Phoenicians also established their necropolis at the site of a nuragic village. Several nuragic sites have been found in the area of later Cagliari, but the extensive rebuilding that has taken place there over the centuries does not allow archaeologists to determine their relation to the earliest Phoenician settlements (Tronchetti 1990:20, 35-36).

An important if very controversial document related to the first Phoenician settlements on Sardinia is the Punic language inscription from Nora, the ancient settlement southwest of Cagliari. The stone was found in 1773 in a vineyard near the city. Both the meaning of the Phoenician text and the date remain a source of considerable dispute. One scholar sees it as memorializing the dedication of a temple to Pumay, a deity usually linked with Cyprus. Another interprets it as a monument erected by a general named Pummay (i.e., Pygmalion) to commemorate his victory over a community called Tarsis, presumably Nora or another place in the vicinity. A third, very different reading of the text interprets it as the record of a Sardinian victory set up by "MLKTN, son of SBN, PNY's general." All of those were Phoenician names, suggesting a Punic victory over locals (Rowland 2001:60-61).

The dates assigned to the inscription also vary widely. The most accepted current view is that it belongs to the late 9th century BC, roughly the same period as the foundation of Carthage, but well before any archaeological evidence for the first Phoenician settlement at Nora. The earliest post-Mycenaean ceramics from Nora appear to date only to the 8th century BC, a century after the generally accepted date for the inscription (Finocchi 2000).

The Punic inscription from Nora.

The settlement histories of the other major Phoenician centers in southwestern Sardinia must be reconstructed solely from the archaeological evidence. At Sulcis the first Phoenician occupation began in the period 750-740 BC, and it had become a well-organized community by the end of the 8th century BC. Traces of an early fortification system suggest conflicts either with nuragic neighbors or with other Phoenician settlements (Barecca 1983:296). Sulcis's connection with the Euboean settlement at Pithekoussai on the island of Ischia has been documented from the late 8th-early 7th century. Euboean, Protocorinthian, and Ischian pottery has been found in considerable quantities in the lowest levels of both the settlement and the tophet or child burial cemetery at Sulcis. The inhabitants of Sulcis seem also to have had significant contacts with Phoenician Iberia (Bartolini 1998a: 91-110). The oldest Phoenician pottery at Bithia dates to the last quarter of the 8th century. That relatively late date suggests that Bithia might have been a secondary foundation from another Phoenician settlement, most likely Nora that was located some 30 km to the north (Bartolini 1998). Some of these earliest Phoenician settlements did not survive to grow into major centers. At San Giorgio-Portoscuso on the southwest coast a Phoenician incineration cemetery of the 8th century BC documents the short history of such a transitory community (Bernardini 2000).

The Phoenicians gradually extended their hegemony into the hinterland immediately behind their coastal settlements. The most important of these close-by interior settlements was Monte Sirai-Carbonia, whose foundation dates to the mid 8th century (Moscati 1993:85-91). It probably served both as an agricultural center to supply food for Sulcis and as a military fort to secure control over the routes leading to the mining centers of the Cixerri Valley. Other smaller outposts of this era have been discovered in the interior. Their earliest archaeological levels have yielded a mixture of nuragic and Phoenician pottery, suggesting relatively peaceful interaction.

The nature of these early settlements and their relation to the indigenous peoples around them can only be tentatively reconstructed from the present evidence. One reading of the Nora inscription has it as a dedication set up after a Phoenician victory over Sardinians. There is some evidence for an early defensive wall at Nora, and the early Punic graves contain weapons, especially daggers (Moscati 1995:210). On the other hand, indigenous material appears in graves at Nora, Bithia, Tharros, Sulcis, and Othoca, and in the tophet at Sulcis, documents of peaceful interaction. At Bithia the combination of what seems on the basis of skeletal evidence to

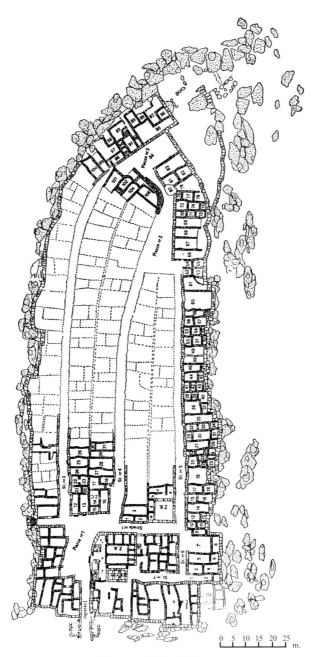

The plan of Monte Sirai.

be indigenous people and native weapons suggests the possibility of native mercenaries serving with the Phoenicians (Bartolini 1983a: 59-60).

The evidence from the nuraghi themselves is equally ambiguous. An apparent burnt layer with 8th century BC Phoenician pottery at nuraghe Nurazzou-Gonnoscodina and the clear late 8th century burnt layer which marked the end of the village of Palmavera-Alghero might document Phoenician aggression (Moravetti 1992:121). They might also be evidence for plundering raids by one native group against another.

A much more complicated picture of Phoenician-indigenous interaction comes from the excavation at Sant'Imbenia-Alghero, the later Roman *Portus Nympharum*. The village that grew up adjacent to the nuraghe had habitations built around courtyards and some communal areas with benches. Imported materials found there included Phoenician amphoras of the 8th-7th centuries along with locally made imitations and a variety of Euboean drinking vessels (Bafico and Rossi 1988). Items such as Levantine cooking pots found within the village strongly suggest a peaceful interaction between the Phoenicians and the local nuragic inhabitants.

An important basis for such peaceful interaction may well have been the extraction, processing, and trade in metals. Sant'Imbenia, located close to the metal-rich Argenteria, was a major center for bronze production. Two metal hoards weighing in total 87 kg were found there. One was in a Phoenician amphora, the other in an imitation of the same amphora type. Graffiti on the two vessels included a Phoenician and possibly a Philistine name (Bafico and Rossi 1988:52-53). Phoenician objects, especially metal weapons and tools and quality ceramics, circulated widely among the nuraghic settlements, as can be seen in the luxury bronzes found at nuraghe S'Uraki-S. Vero Milis, at Tadsuni, and at the sanctuaries of S. Vittoria-Serri and S. Anastasia-Sardara (Tore and Stiglitz 1987).

The Phoenicians seem to have undertaken some cautious explorations up the east coast, as 6th-5th century anchors and pottery have been found in the waters off eastern Sardinia (Lo Schiavo 1996). Some 7th-6th century pottery has been excavated at Olbia, and there is a 7th century Phoenician seal in a private Olbian collection (D'Oriano 1996; Filigheddu 1996). This limited Phoenician penetration did not seem to have impacted the dynamics of local nuragic development or nuragic contacts with the other parts Mediterranean. Trade with Etruria remained very important. For the period 620-540 there is considerable evidence for Etruscan goods at nuragic sites and nuragic objects in Etruria. Fibulae of Etruscan origin have been found in Sardinia (Tronchetti 2000). The presence of three Sardinian bronzes in the Cavalupo tomb at Vulci may document a marriage alliance between Sardinian and Etruscan aristo-crats (Lo Schiavo 1994:77-79).

Contacts with the Phoenicians and the Etruscans certainly reinforced the position of certain big men within nuragic society. This phenomenon has already been discussed in the case of the Monte Prama tomb and sculpture complex. Another example might be the tomb at Sa Costa-Sardara near S. Anastasia. It was a variation of a Giants' Tomb in which a number of bodies had been interred. One individual had been placed on a large sheet of bronze, something like a bed of honor. Among the many objects placed with the grave goods were two figurines of archers, copper ingots (including oxhide ingots weighing 22 kg), and 193 kg of lead. The date of the tomb is debated, but the *bronzetti* would seem to place it in late 9th-early 8th centuries at the earliest, the moment of initial Phoenician contact (Ugas and Usai 1987).

A major challenge facing the archaeologist who studies the Phoenician period in Sardinia is differentiating the changes that took place in both co-lonial and indigenous society during the three or more centuries from the earliest external settlements to the beginning of Carthaginian hegemony. A combination of archaeological specialization with Punic and nuragic scholars working in their separate spheres and historical ideology, especially on the part of Sardinian scholars, has led to an emphasis on contrast and conflict. However, it is likely in an historical situation with this type of cultural contact that a gray zone of cultural contact developed, especially places where there was a weak colonial presence and a dynamic indigenous society.

Such a nuanced picture emerges from the study of early Tharros. The original 8th century settlement developed at two places-the abandoned, sand-covered nuragic village of Su Muru Mannu on the hill north of the later town and the plateau to the south above Capo S.Marco in the area of nuraghe Baboe Cabizza (Zucca 1998a). Each settlement had its own cemetery. By the late 8th-early 7th century a tophet was established at the Muru Mannu site and by the 7th-6th centuries a rectangular, three-celled temple had been built at the southern site.

Tharros also provides evidence for a cautious development of the hin-terland on the part of the Phoenicians as well as the emergence of multi-cultural settlements close to the city. The late 8th-early 7th century incin-eration cemetery found at Su Padrigheddu-S. Vero Milis near the nuraghe S'Uraki probably documents the presence of a small Phoenician emporion in what was still nuragic territory (Tore 1991).

The role played by the citizens of Tharros in trade with the natives of the interior is documented by the development of the jewelry industry

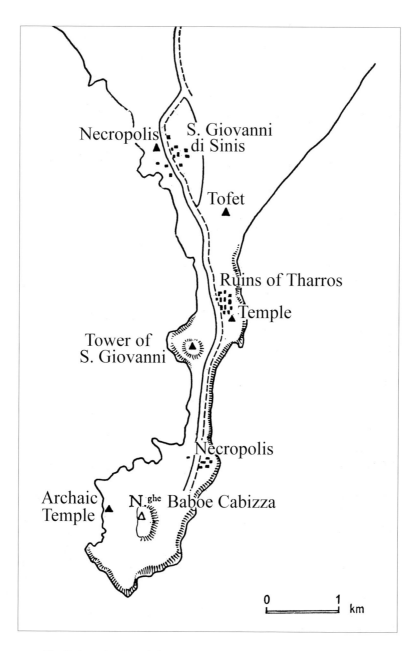

Necropolis S. Giovanni
di Sinis

Tofet

Ruins of Tharros

Temple

Tower of
S. Giovanni

Necropolis

Archaic   N.ghe Baboe Cabizza
Temple

0   1
                     km

The Sinis peninsula and the major sites at Tharros (after Acquaro 1979).

at Tharros during the 7th-6th centuries (*BM Tharros* 1987). The graves of Tharros crudely plundered in the 19th century produced massive evidence for local Egyptianizing such as scarabs, jewelry that presumably was used as valuable trade items in the Phoenician interactions with the nuragic natives.

Despite their limited abilty to project power the Phoenicians did have a major impact on the island. For the first time permanent colonial settlements linked the coast and interior of Sardinia with the wider Mediterranean world on a regular basis. In some cultural areas like urban development the Phoenicians were certainly more advanced than the indigenous peoples. However, their settlements were always small and their military power limited. They could only survive by developing a high degree of accommodation with the natives. In this respect they were very much like the French settlers of North America.

7

The Arrival of the Carthaginians

The power dynamics within Sardinia changed dramatically with the arrival of the Carthaginians on the island. By the 6th century BC contacts between North Africa and the Phoenician mother settlements of the eastern Mediterranean had been disrupted, and the city of Carthage had emerged as the hegemonic power in the western Punic world. Shortly after the middle of the 6th century BC the Carthaginians dispatched to Sardinia an expeditionary force under a general called either Malco or Maleus. This military undertaking was certainly a reaction to the new Greek colonial aggressiveness in the northwest Mediterranean. The Greeks attempted to found a settlement at Alalia in Corsica, leading in 535 BC to a sea battle off Corsica between the Greeks and the combined fleets of the Carthaginians and the Etruscans. The Greeks apparently prevailed, but they made no more colonial foundations on the islands (Bernardini et al. 1999). Despite their alliance of convenience with the Etruscans the Carthaginians were also concerned about such rising powers as Caere and even Etruscan dominated Rome (Cornell 1995:210-214). They saw in Sardinia an important power base in the west-central Mediterranean and a potential source of minerals, grain, and mercenaries.

Malco had been a successful general in Sicily, and the Carthaginians expected him to repeat his winning performance in Sardinia. However, his expedition was defeated. The sparse written sources do not allow us to determine whether it was the Phoenicians, the native Sardinians, or a combination of both that destroyed the Carthaginian armies. A decade was to pass before the Carthaginians returned again to Sardinia. One result of the disaster was the installation of the family of the Magonids in a position of power at Carthage, who were to use that political power base to advance their agenda of dominating Sardinia (Lilliu 1992).

In the mid-520s two Magonids brothers, Hasdrubal and Hamilcar, mounted a new expedition against the island. Opposition was again fierce. Hasdrubal was mortally wounded in battle, but his brother achieved some

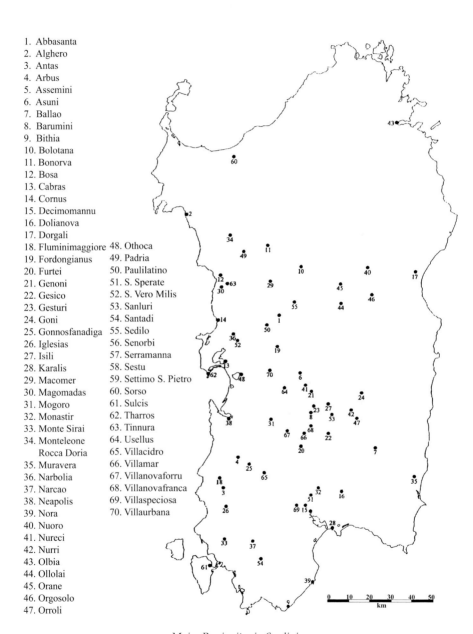

1. Abbasanta
2. Alghero
3. Antas
4. Arbus
5. Assemini
6. Asuni
7. Ballao
8. Barumini
9. Bithia
10. Bolotana
11. Bonorva
12. Bosa
13. Cabras
14. Cornus
15. Decimomannu
16. Dolianova
17. Dorgali
18. Fluminimaggiore
19. Fordongianus
20. Furtei
21. Genoni
22. Gesico
23. Gesturi
24. Goni
25. Gonnosfanadiga
26. Iglesias
27. Isili
28. Karalis
29. Macomer
30. Magomadas
31. Mogoro
32. Monastir
33. Monte Sirai
34. Monteleone
    Rocca Doria
35. Muravera
36. Narbolia
37. Narcao
38. Neapolis
39. Nora
40. Nuoro
41. Nureci
42. Nurri
43. Olbia
44. Ollolai
45. Orane
46. Orgosolo
47. Orroli
48. Othoca
49. Padria
50. Paulilatino
51. S. Sperate
52. S. Vero Milis
53. Sanluri
54. Santadi
55. Sedilo
56. Senorbi
57. Serramanna
58. Sestu
59. Settimo S. Pietro
60. Sorso
61. Sulcis
62. Tharros
63. Tinnura
64. Usellus
65. Villacidro
66. Villamar
67. Villanovaforru
68. Villanovafranca
69. Villaspeciosa
70. Villaurbana

Major Punic sites in Sardinia.

success. Archaeological evidence of sacking and destruction shows that the old Phoenician centers on Sardinia resisted the Carthaginian advance (Tronchetti 1988:88-89). Over the next century the Carthaginians pursued a vigorous imperialism in Sardinia that led to at least their nominal control of the old Phoenician settlements and of considerable portions of the interior (Tronchetti 1988:101-11; Perra 1997).

One aim of this activist Carthaginian policy was to limit access to the island by other powers in the Mediterranean. The Greeks were never able to establish settlements there. Most of the Greek goods found on Sardinia were probably imported by Punic traders. The Carthaginans were equally suspicious of former allies in Italy. In the years after their arrival in force in Sardinia, evidence for Etruscan trade diminishes sharply. The treaty of 509 BC between a newly autonomous Rome and Carthage asserted Punic control over external trade with Sardinia (Scardigli 1991:47-87).

Controlling the entire island proved more complicated. Historians and archaeologists have tended to reconstruct the Carthaginian empire building in Sardinia as a complex process that involved a significant military presence, the construction of a system of border fortifications that resembled a Roman-style frontier line or *limes*, and the foundation of a number of rural estates and settlements (Barreca 1986:31-40). The arguments and evidence for all of those policy initiatives should be treated with caution. Much is known about Carthaginian military activities in both Iberia and Sicily. One thing that is very clear from those other imperial examples is the limited Punic ability to project military or demographic power. Their armies were always heavily dependent on mercenaries, many of them recruited locally, and they were not always well suited for garrison duty. Unlike the Greeks or the Romans they did not have a large surplus peasant population to export to new lands.

It is also important to remember that the Carthaginian occupation like the Phoenician extended over 300 years during a period of complex changes in power relations in the central Mediterranean. The Punic rulers in Sardinia must have experienced the same ebbs and flows of power as happened to the Carthaginians in both Sicily and Iberia. The Carthaginians were able to filter external influences, but they were not able to exclude them totally. Likewise, the indigenous inhabitants of the island should not be seen as passive, victim societies, ever in physical and cultural retreat. Rather, their history during those centuries was one of continuing, complex interaction with the Carthaginians and among themselves. Punic and nuragic archaeologies operate often with rigid and exclusive agendas. Combined with the lack of chronological refinement in the analysis of much material culture that has meant that we are only just beginning to understand the processes of imperial-indigenous interaction on the island.

The older Phoenician centers appear to have been the first to suffer from the new Carthaginian aggression. They were accustomed to their own independence and felt only limited ethnic kinship with the North Africans. They resented the new imperial power and offered stiff resistance. The Phoenician settlement on Mount Sirai was attacked and sacked. At Bithia there is an almost total lack of 5th and early 4th century material in the necropolis. The tophet temporarily went out of use. Sulcis also suffered in the wake of the Carthaginian arrival (Moscati, Bartolini, and Bondi 1997:71).

The Sards also were not spared. Indigenous settlements near the coast were especially vulnerable to attack. A destruction level at Cuccureddus-Villasimasius dated to c. 525 BC suggests the nuragic center had become a victim of Carthaginian expansion. The assault may have been linked to the Carthaginians efforts to strengthen their settlement at Cagliari and eliminate a rival indigenous maritime center (Moscati 1989:200-201).

Research on Carthaginian imperialism in Sardinia has focused the Punic development of an intensive agricultural export economy based on a combination of agricultural villages and plantations. The Carthaginians have been credited with the initial development of the system of *latifundia* or large, slave based estates that was later imported and refind by the Romans. The southwest of Sardinia and especially the valley of the Campidano northwest of Cagliari have been seen as one of the areas where the Carthaginians pioneered that system (Bondi 1987:191-95). Such intensive and extensive agriculture would have required a much more aggressive exploitation of the interior than the Phoenicians had undertaken, and it also would have required the creation of frontier defenses to protect these farming settlements from the still-unconquered warriors of the interior.

In the 1970s Ferruccio Barreca identified a series of Punic fortifications in Sardinia that he argued were elements in an interior defense line designed to keep the indigenous population at bay. That *limes* that he reconstructed as being in place by the mid-5th century BC ran roughly northwest to southeast from Padria (Barreca 1978:115-27; 1986:31-40, 87-88, 279-325; Rowland 1982). The idea of a well developed Punic frontier system appealed to scholars like Lilliu, who saw it as a barrier instrumental in the historical development of two Sardinias, one servile and collaborationist and the other free and resistant (Lilliu 1995:19-20).

This vision of a Punic *limes* dividing Sardinia raises a host of problems. The Punic frontier model developed by Barreca and others clearly is based on the Roman system, but the Roman *limes* was a complicated defensive system sustained by a semi-bureaucratic officer class, a professional garrison army, solid control of the territory behind the *limes*, a complex network beyond, and a good communication network. It is by no means clear that the Carthaginians could have developed any of those components and certainly not all. Their military leaders were often adventurers, who were minimally under the control of the home government. Their army was heavily dependent on restless mercenaries, not the best troops to be placed in isolated garrison positions. The Punic hold on even those lands that lay within the frontier was tenuous, and there is very limited evidence for a developed Carthaginian communication network (Barecca 1986:89-90).

Subsequence archaeological research has led to the questioning of significant parts of Barecca's hypothesis. Most of the fort sites on the so-called *limes* lack Punic military artifacts and Punic inscriptions. The presence of Punic ceramics or coins tells us little about the ethnic origins of the occupants, since these artifacts were part of the Punic-native trade network. The identification of the forts as Punic garrisons had been based largely on their utilization of construction techniques associated with Punic building traditions, but regular masonry construction appears at a number of nuragic sites that were not part of the frontier line. The use of such building technology can more plausibly be connected to the military and architectural acculturation of the locals than to the presence of Punic engineers. Indeed the *limes* concept might be reversed, and the more sophisticated forts seen as nuragic reactions to the new Carthaginian aggressiveness (Lilliu 1988:475-77).

It would be better to see Carthaginian policies in Sardinia as based on a desire to reinforce the Phoenician coastal urban network and advance a more vigorous but still limited policy of gaining control of more of the hinterland. Representative of urban reinforcement was the program of city wall rebuilding. The old Phoenician wall at Nora was rebuilt after the Carthaginian conquest. The fortifications of the citadel at Karalis have been dated to the 4th-3rd centuries BC. The walls at Monte Sirai were rebuilt around 360 BC (Moscati, Bartolini, and Bondi 1997:76).

The Carthaginians were especially interested in the development of the Tharros region both for its agricultural potential and for the trade networks that extended up the Tirso Valley into the interior. The old Phoenician settlement became one of their major points of control

(Acquaro and Mezzolani 1996:13-14). Tharros had already become a major commercial and production center in the Phoenician period, as witnessed by the many imported objects found in its tombs. The vast numbers of finds in the burials dating to the period of Carthaginian occupation show that the prosperity continued. Uncontrolled excavations in these cemeteries during a mid 19th century looting frenzy produced more than 4000 scarabs, even more jewels and at least 10,000 rings as well as enormous amounts of glass and pottery (Zucca 1998b:9-15).

To the south of the Gulf of Oristano a new settlement was established at Neapolis toward the end of the 6th century BC. The presence of even earlier imported pottery in the area suggests commercial contact with the nuragic natives who controlled the complex nuraghe at Sedda is Benas (Zucca 1987). By the 4th century BC, Neapolis had achieved a high level of urban organization and boasted its own wall. The large quantities of Attic pottery found there document a well-developed network of contacts outside of the narrow Punic commercial orbit (Zucca 1987:51-52, 99-100, 191). Farmsteads began to be established in the hinterland of Neapolis by the late 6th century. This suggests a program of colonialization on the Greek and Roman model that was rare in the Punic world. However, one has to be cautious in assigning all such rural sites to the Carthaginians, for it is as likely that some could have been occupied by acculturated natives drawn into the Punic orbit of Neapolis (Van Dommelen 1997).

The most isolated and innovative new Carthaginian urban foundation was Olbia on the northeast coast of the island. The city was established in an area that historically had seen little Phoenician or Carthaginian presence. While there may have been a small Punic settlement at an earlier date at Olbia, a true urban center seems only to have developed in the middle years of the 4th century (Antona et al. 1991:53-60). The large defensive walls of granite were probably built after the greater settlement was established. Within the walls the town was laid out on an orthogonal plan. On the acropolis a temple of the Punic deity Melqart was built. Artifacts from the town cemeteries and from other parts of the site document active trade with Etruria, Latium, Marseilles, South Italy, Attica, and Carthage. The new center was certainly a collection point for the agricultural and pastoral products of the interior and the coastal market from which imported goods were made available to the indigenous settlements. It was also a military/naval outpost that could keep an eye on the west coast of Italy and the rising power of Rome (Rowland 2001:73).

All the Punic coastal cities served as gathering points for pastoral and agricultural products that were shipped to the homeland in North

Africa and as the launching places for the trade networks that extended into the interior. They were also production centers. At Tharros iron had been smelted in the area of the tophet from at least the 5th century BC. Green jasper scarabs were also produced at Tharros. Most of the amulets found in the tophet at Sulcis were probably locally made. Many of the settlements must have also been centers of pottery production (Bartolini 1973; Tronchetti 1995).

The Carthaginian impact on the countryside was more complicated and has been the subject of considerable historical and archaeological debate. It has already been noted that Carthaginian power in North Africa was based in part on large agricultural estates. It has often been argued that the Carthaginian conquest of Sardinia was marked by the widespread destruction of native settlements and their replacement by a combination of latifundia and peasant settlements. Evidence for such radical rural policies has been seen in references to a Carthaginian prohibition on the planting of fruit trees. Even if such a policy was actually promulgated the Carthaginian colonial administrators were not in a position to enforce such draconian measures (Marasco 1988:188; Brizzi 1989:83).

Many of such ancient and modern reconstructions of rural policy have been simplifications of much more complex realities. Some ancient authors asserted that the Sardinian natives took refuge in the mountains. Lilliu claimed that the Carthaginians expropriated two-thirds of the island and talked about "the collaborators, subject to the Punic colonizers, and the resistant 'maquis' barricaded and incarcerated in the deep 'Indian reservation' of the Barbagia" (Lilliu 1988:418-19; 1995:19-20). However, logic, studies in comparative colonialism, and the archaeological evidence from Sardinia suggest that all of these are simplifications.

The Carthaginian military had an ability to extract tribute and taxation from the indigenous communities in a way that the Phoenicians had not. The limited literary evidence suggests that grain was a major part of that extractive economy. Sardinian peasants had long been practicing a mixed agriculture that included significant grain production. In a landscape like that of Sardinia the most effective way to increase grain yield within the available technology would have been to force intensification of production by the small farms that already existed rather than create large, slave-based estates. Instead of positing the massive development of a colonialist agriculture that drove the natives back into the uplands one might better see the countryside right up to the edge of the towns sprinkled with new settlements and estates but dominated by indigenous settlements in various degrees of culture change.

The strongest evidence for Punic settlement in the countryside comes from the cemeteries. That at Villamar at the edge of the Campidano consisted of chamber tombs, including one with a symbol of the Punic deity Tanit scratched on a wall and 21 infant burials that hint at the Carthaginian custom of child sacrifice. While a nearby site has been interpreted as a fortified Punic settlement, the archaeological material suggests a native community (Paderi, Ugas, and Siddu 1993). Isolated rural burial places might have been the resting places of members of a Punic elite that controlled a nearby estates. However, the graves could also have belonged to members of the acculturated native ruling class.

Punic trade goods have been found at many sites both mortuary and domestic. Some may document Punic settlers, but the total repertoire of material from many such sites suggests that they were inhabited mainly by indigenous peoples who embraced certain aspects of the Carthaginian material world. Carthaginian objects in the Giants' Tombs at Fontanazza-Arbus and Bruncu Espris-Arbus most likely documents the practice of natives taking prestige imports to the afterlife rather than any Carthaginians reusing native burial places (*Notizie degli Scavi* 1927:360-66). The large quantity of Punic material found at nuraghe S. Antine-Torralba was certainly the product of indigenous trade connections rather than Punic colonization (Bafico and Rossi 1988). At nuraghe Ortu Comidu-Sardara the mixture of nuragic and Punic materials provide in the words of the excavator "a glimpse into the domestic life and the peaceful integration of the nuragic and Punic people of the nuraghe" (*Notizie degli Scavi* 1983:384). So-called Punic sites in the territory of Sanluri such as Bia'e Collanos, Brunk e' Cresia and Brunku Predi Poddi are more likely to have been indigenous villages trading with the Carthaginians (Paderi 1982).

The imported material that survives in the archaeological record is overwhelmingly ceramic, consisting of a mixture of Punic and Greek wares. Striking throughout this period is the increasing number of Greek imports, a reflection of the increased productive power of Greek centers, especially Athens, and the increasing cultural Hellenization of the Punic world. The number of amphorae and drinking cups found on the island show that the Sardinian elites like those of Iron Age Europe were engaged in formalized, collective drinking rituals designed to enhance their power and prestige (Rowland 2001:83).

The complexity of the interactions between Carthaginians and natives in rural Sardinia is well illustrated by the country shrines. In many instances those cult places were water shrines with deep roots in the nuragic and even pre-nuragic past. The indigenous identity of the sacred place remained intact. At the same time certain cult items, especially the votive terracottas, clearly reflected contacts with the Punic and Greek world and the adoption of an outside religious iconography. Many of the small votive terracottas served the Greek cult of Ceres and Demeter that itself had been exported from the Greek to the Punic world, probably through Sicily. With its emphasis on fertility Ceres and Demeter worship represented the type of religious practice that moved easily from one peasant culture to another. The Sardinians could have adopted the cult from the Carthaginians or acquired it directly through the experience of military service in Sicily. Greek-inspired figurines were not limited to the sanctuaries but have been found in both the nuraghi and in the native tombs (Van Dommelen 1996-97:314-15).

The cultural complexity of these religious interactions can be better appreciated through a more detailed discussion of the archaeology of specific religious centers. At Narbolia in the hinterland of Tharros a nuragic well continued to be a center of worship after Carthaginian occupation. Votive figurines of Punic manufacture replaced offerings of indigenous production (Moscati 1968). The nuragic spring shrine at Terreseu-Narcao continued in use during the Punic period, but the votives came to reflect the influence of the cult of Demeter. The same thing happened at the sacred well of Cuccuru S'Arriu-Cabras (Moscati 1992:87-89). The excavations at the shrine of nuraghe Lugherras-Paulilatino have produced Ceres figurines and Punic coins, as well as matrices used in the production of those votives. The cult practice continued after the Roman conquest (Regoli 1991).

The complexity of these religious developments in the countryside can be further appreciated by a consideration of the early history of what was later to become the very important, but also isolated sanctuary of Sardus Pater at Antas in southwest Sardinia. Around 500 BC a small shrine was built adjacent to a nuragic burial ground and sacred place. Two centuries later three rooms were added to the cult building, and it was now adorned with Doric columns and Egyptianizing architectural mouldings (Garbati 1999:151-66). The shrine was probably already associated with the Punic Sid Babai and the cult used as a means of promoting indigenous loyalty and submission.

The religious history and associations of that cult of Sid Babai may have had deeper roots in island religion. A bronze figure of a nude hunter-warrior holding a lance in his left hand and with his right hand raised as if in benediction was found in a nuragic tomb at nearby Antas. It has been identified as an archaic image of Sid Babai (Rowland 2001:87). Two bronze figurines in the Cagliari Museum, one a 5th-4th century BC statuette possibly from Ogliastra and the other a 4th-3rd century piece from Gesturi, seem also to represent Sid-Pater.

There is no denying that the shrine had particular importance for Carthaginian worshippers, which we can deduce from the large number of Punic dedications, including those made during the 4th and 3rd centuries BC by high officials of Karalis and Sulcis. However, this sacred place was in an isolated location, well removed from the Carthaginian centers of power. The deity worshiped there seems to have had nuragic as well as Punic identities. Rather than being an exercise in colonialist religion, the cult center at Antas may well have represented an effort to develop a shrine that integrated Punic and native worship (Minutula 1976-77:399-438; Zucca 1989:36-38).

An important indicator of the limits of Carthaginian influence in the countryside is the relatively few Punic words that found their way into the Sardinian language. The Sard words *mitza* and *mitzixedda* seem to derive from the Punic *mitsa* for spring. A few other words related to topography and natural history are of Punic origin. Considering that Punic was the language of much of the ruling elite in Sardinia for some seven centuries, its impact on the indigenous vocabulary was surprisingly small (Paulis 1996).

An aspect of Punic imperial policy that has not received sufficient attention was the recruitment of Sardinian warriors for mercenary service in various Carthaginian wars and the roles returning mercenaries played in changing island society. Sardinians are documented as fighting for Carthage against Syracuse as early as the 5th century BC (Pais 1881:326-28). The discovery of a 4th century BC Syracusan coin at Planu Guventu-Barumini and bronze arrow points of Sicilian type in the territory of Ittireddu and elsewhere suggest the presence of returned mercenaries. Repatriated warriors with their pay packets and loot would have become big men in their communities and the foci of interaction between Carthage and the nuraghi. Such interactions were not always peaceful. Sardinian mercenaries were involved in the island revolt against Carthage of 379 BC.

Nuragic chieftains who were involved in trade and official interactions with the Carthaginian administrators, and leaders among the returned Sardinian military veterans formed the basis of an expanding Punicized native elite. We meet such an individual in Hampsicora, the national hero celebrated in Sardinia for leading early resistance to Rome (Dyson 1985:252-255; Zucca 1986). He had wealth, large land holdings, and an extended network of clients in the lowlands. He was also an acculturated native leader who served as an intermediary between the Carthaginians and the *Sardi pelliti* the less Punicized natives of the interior.

One signature development of the Carthaginian period in Sardinia was the increased importance placed on the tophets at the major Punic centers. These were extensive cemeteries composed of infant burials. At Tharros most of the deceased were not more than six months of age. Their bodies were cremated and deposited in urns. A relatively small percentage of the urn burials (300 out of 5,000) was marked by stele (Moscati 1995:302-303). While tophets have long been associated with human sacrifice, current thinking is that most of the infants interred were stillborns or the victims of high infant mortality (Fedele 1983; Ribichini 1989).

Most of the tophets in Sardinia have been poorly excavated, and that creates major problems when one wants to reconstruct their developmental history. A few do seem to have had Phoenician origins. Burials at the S.Antioco tophet started in the late 8th century BC, and there is an early one at Tharros that can be dated to the 8th-7th centuries BC. That at Bithia probably began in the late 7th or early 6th century BC (Tronchetti 1979:201-05; Acquaro and Mezzolani 1996:46-81; C. Perra 1998:157-62).

Most tophets, however, saw their maximum use in the period of Carthaginian urbanism. The first tophet stelae at Tharros date to the mid-6th century BC, and the cemetery was restructured in the 4th century BC. At Karalis a tophet associated with the S. Gilla settlement has been dated to the 6th century BC (Acquaro 1989:15; Usai & Zucca 1986:158-65, 171-72). The tophet cemetery at Monte Sirai only started in the 4th century BC, three centuries after the establishment of the Phoenician settlement. It has been suggested that the late tophet at Monte Sirai marked that settlement's transition from a military outpost to an independent urban center (Aubet 1993:216).

We have only limited information on Punic sacred architecture during the long period of Carthaginian occupation. The foundation dates of many shrines cannot be determined with any precision while their continued use in the Roman period destroyed many traces of their earlier history. A number of Sardo-Punic temples seem to date to the late 4th or early 3rd centuries BC. At Monte Sirai the castle keep was transformed into a temple complex with courtyard and four altars during that period. Also at Monte Sirai a small shrine with central vestibule and rooms on the side and rear was built on the slope above the tophet (Fantar 1973; Bondi 1995; Perra 1998). The so-called monolithic temple at Tharros, one decorated with Doric columns and Egyptianizing molding, seems to date to the late 4th or early 3rd century BC (C. Perra 1998:165-72).

Stela from Sulcis depicting a woman holding an ankh *symbol (after Moscati 1993).*

The diversity of cultural and artistic influences operating in Sardinia during the Carthaginian period can best be appreciated by studying the sculpted stelae. Nora and Sulcis have provided the greatest selection. The stelae from Nora dated to the 6th-4th centuries BC are closely related to those from Carthage. Many are aniconic with decorations showing Egyptianizing influence but little contact with Greek art (Moscati 1992a:39).

The production of stelae had a longer history at Sulcis, and the iconography was much more complex. The earliest stones most likely date to the mid-6th century BC and the latest to the 1st century BC. Distinctive to the Sulcis stelae are representations of figures clad in long gowns with a stole hanging from the left shoulder and an Egyptian *ankh* symbol in the right hand. Female figures holding a disk to the chest are also common. In the long Sulcis series one can see changes from Punic-Egyptian to Greek styles especially during the Hellenistic period (Moscati 1992a:41-51). Not surprisingly the stelae from M. Sirai are strongly influenced by those of Sulcis, located a mere 13 km away, but they tend toward a greater schematization of the human form and a simplification of architectural representations (Garbini 1966; Moscati 1992:45-51). The rather morbid fascination with the Punic tophets makes one forget that they were intended as specialized infant and child cemeteries and that during the Carthaginian era adults and even children were buried in a variety of other ways. While the Phoenicians had generally practiced cremation, the Carthaginians until the 3rd century preferred inhumation. After that cremation again became more common. Chamber tombs were very common at urban centers like Cagliari. The Tuvixeddu cemetery at Cagliari that started in the 6th century had inhumation burials that were mainly set in shaft graves (Bartolini 1981; Stiglitz 1999). In late Punic times burials inside storage vessels, usually amphorae, appear sporadically, and the practice continued into the late Roman period (Paderi, Ugas, and Siddu 1993:123-43).

The other Punic sites provide a diverse picture of adult burial practices. At Settimo S. Pietro and S. Sperate, two early foundations of Karalis, the dominant burial practice was inhumation in large stone cists. At Nora the inhumations were placed in shaft graves and stone lined pits. At Bithia inhumations in stone cists prevailed from the mid-6th century to the late Punic period. The necropolis at Sulcis had burials in shaft graves and in chambers with an entrance corridor and two or more mortuary rooms. From the late 6th century onward the predominant burial custom at Tharros was inhumation in pits, shafts, or chambers. Shaft, trench, and

Stela of female figure making an offering (after (Moscati 1993).

chamber tombs were common at Cornus, but some families deposited their dead in the ancient *domus de janas*. That may well document a strong indigenous presence in the population of Cornus (Bartolini 1981; Barreca 1986:279-325).

The stelae and the often architecturally impressive tombs indicate that the honoring of the dead was an important concern in Punic society. Reconstructing the non-archaeological details of mortuary ritual is more difficult, given the limited literary sources and the often poor quality of cemetery excavations. Cicero mentions that in his time the population of Nora had the custom of gathering at the cemetery on a fixed day to honor the dead (Cicero *Pro Scauro* 11). Some cemetery altars where sacrifices or libations could have been offered have been found. The ritual breaking of vessels at the tomb and the provision of offerings of food and drink for the dead have been documented. The dead went into the afterlife provided with personal possessions such as amulets, scarabs, razors, and decorated ostrich eggs, but we have no clear picture of what they believed happened to the deceased once they passed over to the great beyond.

8
Conquest, Resistance, and Continuity in Republican Sardinia

Punic Sardinia appears to have remained relatively peaceful and prosperous throughout the later 5th, 4th and early 3rd centuries. Carthage tried to regulate contacts with the outside world, but the process was one of filtration, not of total isolation. Carthage itself was experiencing the impact of many aspects of Greek culture (Moscati 1993). The flavor of the coastal cities remained predominantly Punic, but the picture in the interior was more complex. Rather than hypothesizing some stark political and cultural frontier that divided Carthaginians and the nuragic peoples, we must see a complex world of social, economic, and cultural interaction. There is no reason to think that the indigenous peoples of Sardinia who had displayed such cultural dynamism over the previous millennia suddenly collapsed in the face of the limited forces of Carthaginian imperialism. Some nuragic natives did become totally Punized, and no doubt some Carthaginians went native. In most instances the Sards borrowed selectively from the colonial power, keeping much of their culture intact. Unfortunately for the student of both Punic and Roman Sardinia the material borrowings are easily documented in the archaeological record, while persistent customs and folkways are not.

Meanwhile the Romans were extending their hegemony over the Italian peninsula. It was just a matter of time before the neighboring islands would attract their attention. The image of Rome as a non-commercial, non-maritime power and the interpretation of the treaties between Rome and Carthage as instruments designed to limit Roman access to Sardinia have led to an underestimation of Rome's interest in the offshore islands, but as early as the 4th century BC the Romans apparently attempted to found a colony in Sardinia. This was the *Pheronia polis* mentioned by Ptolemy, probably located near the mouth of the Posada River on the east coast of the island. The name of the settlement seems to derive from the Italic deity Feronia (Torelli 1981; D'Oriano 1985; Marasco 1988:51-52). The effort was not successful, but it raised anxieties in Carthage that probably led to the 348 BC revision of the Rome-Carthage treaty with more stringent provisions about Roman trade with Sardinia (Scardigli 1991:89-127).

While this new treaty tried to restrict Roman trade with Sardinia, the Carthaginian ability to enforce such a policy was surely very limited. The archaeological evidence suggests that the flow of goods from the mainland to the island was considerable. Such trade with the west coast of Italy was very likely in the hands of Romans or their Latin or Italic allies. Black-glazed pottery, some with Latin graffiti, has been found at both Punic and nuragic sites (Rowland 1981:44-45, 58). A 3rd century BC wreck loaded with Greco-Italic amphora and black- glazed pottery found off Villasimius was more likely to have been a vessel trading with the island than a ship headed elsewhere that was blown off course (Bartolini and Marras 1989).

With the outbreak of war with Carthage in 264 BC the Romans were forced to establish their maritime hegemony in the central Mediterranean. The immediate impact on Sardinia was limited. While the Romans appear definitely to have captured Aleria in Corsica, the reality of their attack on Olbia and the nature and extent of their other actions in Sardinian waters are more open to historical dispute. Sardinia was not mentioned in the treaty of 241 BC that ended the First Punic War. The island remained Carthaginian territory with Carthaginian garrisons in place (Scardigli 1991:205-43).

That situation changed quickly. By 239 BC the mercenary revolt had broken out in North Africa, followed in 238 BC by mercenary rebellions in Sardinia. Our sources unfortunately say little about the parties involved in that latter uprising. Initially hesitant to become involved, Rome soon changed its mind and in 238-37 BC sent a fleet to seize the island. The Carthaginians protested diplomatically but were helpless to intervene militarily. In the end they were forced to acknowledge Roman hegemony and as a further humiliation were compelled to pay new indemnities to Rome.

The interwar seizure of Sardinia by the Romans was regarded in antiquity as one of the acts of hubris that ultimately produced the nemesis of the Hannibalic War. The action, however, had a clear justification in *Realpolitik*. The island was less than 100 nautical miles from the mouth of the Tiber and was of greater strategic importance to Rome than was Sicily. The demonstrated weaknesses in Carthaginian military control posed serious security problems in that unstable mercenary bands could quickly turn to piracy and make raids on the sea lanes serving Rome and the Italian coast. The grain fields of the Campidano were more accessible to Rome wiits expanding, dependant population than those recently acquired in eastern Sicily (Dyson 1985:246).

The initial Roman campaigns in Sardinia, most likely focused on gaining control of the Punic coastal centers, went smoothly, but the Romans soon found that pacifying and controlling the interior was going to be far less easy. Their forces quickly became engaged in major wars, especially in the northeast part of the island. Single consular campaigns are documented in Sardinia for every year between 236 and 231 BC. In 232 and 231 BC both of the consuls were dispatched there (Dyson 1985:245-251; Meloni 1990:43-52), and in those years Roman generals were three times awarded triumphs by the senate for thir victories in Sardinia.

By 227 BC the Romans felt sufficiently secure in their hold on the island to regularize its administration with the appointment of a *praetor* or *propraetor*. This administrative transformation and especially the new fiscal impositions that went with it produced further rebellions. A consular army of two legions, some ten thousand soldiers, led by C. Atilius Regulus was sent to the island in 225 BC. His military actions appear to have produced relative peace on the island, and that calm lasted until the outbreak of the Second Punic War in 264 BC (Meloni 1990:52-53).

With the resumption of Roman-Carthaginian hostilities at the outset of the Second Punic War the Carthaginians were bound to try to use Sardinia as a theater of operations against Rome. The Romans moved early to keep the Carthaginians out of the island. A large Roman fleet under Cnaeus Servilius blocked attempts by the Carthaginian navy to use Sardinia as a base, and in spite of increased demands on Roman military resources the *praetor* Aulus Cornelius Mammula was assigned a legion to maintain peace in Sardinia. The Carthaginian victory at Cannae in 216 BC dramatically changed the situation. The Roman central government could not even adequately provision Mammula, and he was forced to turn to the Sardinian communities for supplies. Their initial response to the Roman request was generous, but continued exactions produced increasing resentments. That and the real possibility of Carthaginan victory led the indigenous elite to reestablish contacts with their former Punic colonizers. In 215 the Punicized Sardinian leader Hampsicora organized a delegation of leading citizens who went to Carthage, where they informed the Carthaginians that the Sardinians had grown weary of Rome's harsh and greedy rule and especially of the oppressive tribute and the unjust requisitions of grain. The island was clearly ripe for rebellion (Zucca 1986).

The Carthaginians quickly seized this new opportunity to make trouble for the overextended Roman forces. One of their first actions may have been to issue a new series of coins to help finance Sardinian revolts against Rome. Two unique series of coins, one with the head of a young woman on the obverse and a standing bull on the reverse, the other with a diademed male head on the obverse and a standing bull and an ear of grain on the reverse are dated to about 216 BC and seem best associated with the planned rebellion (Acquaro 1974:105-107; Zucca 1988a; Manfredi 1995:200).

The Carthaginians dispatched to Sardinia a military force under Hasdrubal the Bald. Unfortunately, a storm diverted his fleet to the Balearic islands, and the Punic reinforcements did not arrive in Sardinia until after the first battle between native rebels and the Romans. Meanwhile their leader Hampsicora had gone to the interior to gather support among the indigenous tribesmen, the *Sardi pellitii*. In his absence his son Hostus moved rashly against the Romans. The *propraetor* Titus Manlius Torquatus, a grizzled veteran of earlier Sardinian wars, defeated the young man in battle, and the Sardinians fled back toward Cornus. At that point the Carthaginian forces finally arrived and rallied the Sardinians. The Romans retreated toward Cagliari, allowing the advancing Sardo-Punic forces to devastate the rich lands of the Campidano. Finally the Romans turned to challenge them. In a battle that probably took place near modern Sanluri Torquatus soundly defeated the combined indigenous-Carthaginian forces (Dyson 1985:252-54).

Once more the Sardinian-Carthaginian army retreated toward Cornus with the army of Torquatus hot on their heels. The Romans then besieged and captured the city. Those communities that had supported Hampsicora surrendered to the Romans and gave hostages. Tribute in cash and grain was extracted from each center in proportion to their resources and their disloyalty. Torquatus returned to Rome and announced that Sardinia had been subdued. A garrison of two legions was maintained in the island until 206 BC (Meloni 1990:63-65).

Sardinia saw relatively little military action during the rest of the Second Punic War. In 210 BC a small Carthaginian fleet raided both Olbia and Cagliari but without major effect. No other major raids are reported. Sardinia instead became a major supply source for the Roman war machine with grain the major item provided. During the years 204-202 BC the Sardinian praetors sent large quantities of grain either to Rome or to Roman armies in the field. In 202 BC grain from Sardinia and Sicily was so abundant at Rome that the price collapsed. In addition the Romans received minerals, wool, cloth, cheese, horses, and timber from the island (Livy 28.5; 29.36.1; 30.3.2, 30.24.5; 36.2).

Roman military activity in Sardinia between the end of the econd Punic War and 181 is poorly documented. Livy noted that the legion sta-

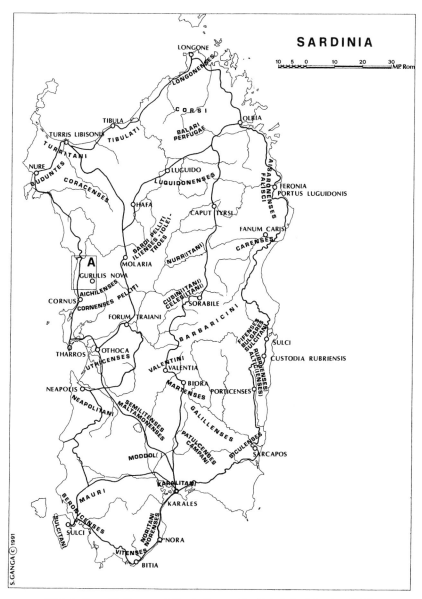

Distribution of indigenous tribes in Roman Sardinia (after Mastino 1993).

tioned in Sardinia during the war was dismissed, but a force of 5,000 Latins was enrolled to meet military needs on the island (Livy 31.8.10). Tensions undoubtedly continued. In 198 BC M. Porcius Cato, a rising senator with an already established reputation for probity, was appointed *praetor* on Sardinia. He focused on reducing Roman administrative expenses and curbing the activities of the moneylenders (Dyson 1985:255).

The administrative reforms did not prove adequate to quell native discontent, and new military actions had to be undertaken. The *Sardi pelliti* who had supported Hampsicora needed to be subdued and the Roman control of the interior strengthened. Related to such campaigns may have been the burial of the hoard of Republican *denarii* that was found at Burgos northeast of Macomer. The latest coin in the deposit was a *denarius* of 195 BC in nearly mint condition. The find spot suggests that that the Romans launched one of their first attacks from Cornus through Marghine and Goceano toward the headwaters of the Tirso River (Rowland 1985:104).

A new round of hostilities began in 181, when the *praetor* Marcus Pinarius Rusca was forced to repel an attack of the Ilienses. In 178 the *praetor* Titus Aebutius informed the Senate there that had been a great uprising in Sardinia. The Ilienses with the aid of the Balares had invaded the pacified parts of the island, and the Roman army, weakened by pestilence, had been unable to mount an effective resistance. The impact of that dire report by Aebutius was reinforced by the arrival of envoys from the Sardinian towns who lamented the damage their country holdings had suffered from raids launched by groups from the interior and begged for increased protection. Clearly the Roman hold on the supposedly pacified parts of rural Sardinia was threatened (Dyson 1985:255-56).

The Senate appreciated the seriousness of the growing threat and dispatched to Sardinia Ti. Sempronius Gracchus, the *consul* of 177 and one of the most capable commanders of his generation. He was supplied with an army of two legions, supported by auxiliaries and naval forces. After two years of successful campaigning Sempronius reported that he had pacified his province, and he was awarded a triumph. One of the special features of his triumphal procession was a map of Sardinia with the locations of the campaigns indicated on it. Sempronius claimed that he had killed or captured more than 80,000 Sardinians (Dyson 1985:256-57). If true the figure is astonishing, for it would have represented one-quarter of the later population in 1728 and nearly one-eighth of that in 1881 (Corridore 1902:133; Pardi 1925:116-17).

Even if the figures are exaggerated, the campaigns of Gracchus decimated the native populations of the border regions and of much of the

Painting in the viceregal Palace in Cagliari showing Roman combat against the Iliensi.

interior. The Roman commander clearly felt that a scorched-earth policy was necessary, and it indeed seems to have been effective. For decades there was relative calm in Sardinia. Sempronius was forced to return to Sardinia in 163-162 BC, but his actions at that time did not warrant a second triumph.

The next Sardinian triumph did not come until 122 BC, after the prolonged but poorly documented campaigns of Lucius Aurelius Orestes. Only one other Sardinian triumph was celebrated during the Republic, that of Marcus Caecilius Metellus in 111 BC. Since he had first gone to Sardinia in 115 BC, we can assume that his campaigns were extensive (Broughton 1968:541). Unfortunately the only other information that we have on his actions in Sardinia is an inscription from Esterzili referring to his mediation of disputes between the Galilenses and the Patulcenses Campani (Mastino et al. 1993). We can assume that all was not quiet on the Sardinian frontier during those years, but the level of hostilities was not such as to produce the level of enemy casualties that would justify a triumph.

Sardinia remained an important source of grain for Rome during the later Republic. Cato maintained the grain tribute and Gracchus even increased it. That action was probably designed both to punish disloyal communities and to encourage settled agriculture (Livy 41.17.2-3). The post-Sullan revolutionary Marcus Aemilius Lepidus fled to Sardinia in the hopes of cutting off Rome's grain supply. Cicero, speaking in the early 60s in support of Pompey's special command against the pirates, described Sardinia as one of the three bulwarks of the Roman grain supply (Cicero *De Lege Manilia* 34). Varro commented ironically that "nowadays, almost all heads of families have crept within the city walls, abandoning their plows and sickles, and prefer to occupy their hands in the theater and circus rather than in the grain fields and vineyards, so we hire people to bring to us from Africa and Sardinia the grain to fill our bellies" (Varro *RR* 2.1.3). The advantage of controlling a major source of grain so close to the capital made Sardinia a key point of contention between Sextus Pompey and Octavian during the Civil Wars of the late 40s and early 30s BC.

With the final triumph of Augustus in 31 BC the place of Sardinia within the food supply system for the city began to change. Two Augustan writers still commented on Sardinia's wheat productivity. It has been calculated that with optimal productivity Augustan Sardinia could have supplied subsistence-level grain for about 300,000 people (Rowland 1990). However, the emperor could now call upon the surpluses of Egypt and the intensified production of North Africa to supply the bulk of the Roman subsidized grain.

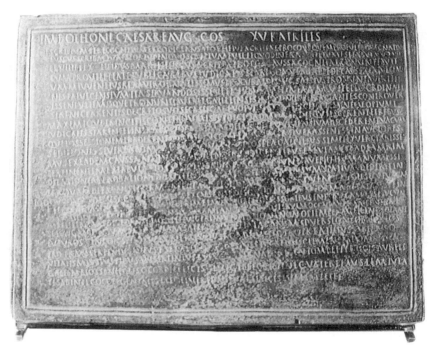

Bronze tablet from Esterzili dealing with indigenous land disputes (after Mastino 1993a).

Scholars of the Roman grain supply like Geoffrey Rickman have argued that Sardinian grain became relatively unimportant for the city during the high empire (Rickman 1980:106-107). Pliny does mention Sardinian grain with other grain in the context of weights and measures, so that the decline in production may have only been relative (Pliny, *Natural History* 18.12.63). With the transfer of the capital to Constantinople in the early 4th century and the shifting of the Egyptian grain supply there, Sardinia resumed its importance as a provider for Rome. The poet Prudentius writing in the late 4th century AD mentioned the extraordinary quantity of grain transported from Sardinia to fill the granaries of Rome (Pais 1923:2.508).

Ancient accounts of the abundant grain surpluses provided by Sardinia to the Romans came to play an important role in much later debates on the agricultural potential of the island. Early modern historians contrasted the supposed fertility of Roman Sardinia with their impoverished contemporary agricultural scene and used the ancient evidence in the ongoing debate about agrarian improvement in Sardinia. A Spanish cleric wrote in 1611 that "all writers, ancient as well as modern, who mention Sardinia, call it fertile and abundant; experience shows this to be so, and if it were cultivated (most of it is not), it would provide grain for all the nearby realms" (Plaisant 1970:80). That supposed golden age of Romano-Sardinian grain production inspired Francesco Gemelli, emeritus professor of Latin eloquence at the Royal University of Sassari, to publish in 1776 three volumes devoted to schemes for improving the productivity of Sardinia's lands (Gemelli 1776).

Nostalgia for the fertility of the Roman era was set against grim contemporary reality. The Jesuits of Cagliari recorded years during the late 1500s "of such hunger and so sterile that the majority of the people could sustain life only with wild ferns and other weeds" (Manconi 1982:56). During the terrible famine of 1680, some 80,000 people out of a total of 250,000 on the island were said to have died and entire villages were devastated (Manconi 1982:61). The central cause was the dreadfully low level of crop returns (Manconi 1982:65-66).

These catastrophes were partly the result of deficiencies in social and economic organization of the countryside of early modern Sardinia, but they may also have been caused by deterioration in the micro-climate of Europe. The early modern period was the time of the Little Ice Age, when yields would be expected to have been lower. Only with the middle of the 19th century did the climate return to conditions similar to those of Roman times (Lamb 1981; Fagan 1999:181-201). Since then sporadic droughts and famines have occurred, but on the whole farmers using technologies that were not that much changed from the Roman period produced much higher yields. In the territory of Sassari that in Roman times would have provided a substantial portion of the grain shipped from Turris Libysonis to Ostia the land produced yields of twenty times the seed sown. Even in the uplands a community like Gavoi produced yields of seven to one for grain and ten to one for barley. The average grain yield for the 264 villages for which Angius provided data in his early 19th century survey was nearly ten to one (Rowland 1990:18). All of this 19th century evidence supports the Roman testimony that Sardinia had the potential to be a significant grain producer.

A fundamental issue for the student of Roman Sardinia is how the rural economy was organized. The standard assumption has been that the Romans inherited a system of slave-based estate or *latifundia* production from the Carthaginians, and that they then expanded and refined that system. It has been further asserted that the extensive slaving that was a byproduct of the brutal campaigns like those of Sempronius Gracchus in the early 2nd century BC provided the indigenous servile labor supply that allowed the expansion of the *latifundia*.

The estate model of late Republican grain production in Sardinia has many problems. In spite of a popular myth slave based estate agriculture was not well suited to the production of large grain surpluses, especially in the landscape of Sardinia. For that village/farmstead production units were much more successful (Dyson 1992:32-34). On the island only the Capidano region had the terrain suitable for any type of estate agriculture, but the area has provided little evidence for the large rural villas that would have formed the central nodes of such slave-based estates (Rowland 2001:124-25, 183-87). In much of the rest of the island the arable land divided naturally into relatively small plots that were best worked by individual farmers. The nuragic natives had long exploited such limited resources effectively and provided agricultural tribute to the Carthaginians. The archaeological evidence increasingly indicates that many of the small nuragic sites continued to be inhabited in the Roman period. It is likely that the Romans continued to skim off their own tribute from these small production centers.

Punic Continuity and Roman Innovation in Urban Life

The archaeological evidence for urban life during the Roman occupation is much more abundant than that for the Phoenician and Carthaginian eras, but the interpretation of that evidence poses its own special problems. The archaeological focus on urban life in Punic and then on imperial Roman Sardinia has meant that the important transitional period of the Roman Republic has been neglected. This has led to an exaggerated picture of urban decline in the late Republic and early Empire.

Tharros provides a good case study. It has been argued that the city went into a serious decline after the Roman conquest, only to revive in the 2nd and 3rd centuries AD (Meloni 1990:288). That decline was related to the loss of administrative connections with Carthage and the Romans' lack of interest in a major west coast island port. However, the Romans even more than the Carthaginians imported Sardinian agricultural products, and Tharros was the most important outlet for one of Sardinia's richest agricultural areas. While the archaeological evidence from Tharros for this time period has not been well studied, it does suggest considerable urban activity. A *horreum* (granary) built at San Salvatore-Cabras near Tharros around 200-180 BC was very likely intended as a storage center for grain collected from the interior (Donati and Zucca 1992:18-19). A 3rd-2nd century BC tombstone of two Greeks from Massilia found at

Tharros attests to its ongoing role as a Mediterranean-wide commercial center (Manganaro 1994:262-63). The continued use and even enlargement of the Punic-period temples and the addition of a shrine of Saturn at the tophet during the 2nd century BC document the continued presence of the local Punic elite (Zucca 1984a:54-58; Acquaro and Mezzolani 1996:36-38).

The evidence from other communities reinforces that picture of urban continuity after the Roman occuaption. The temple of Melqart at Olbia was restructured soon after the Roman conquest in the late second-early third century BC (D'Oriano 1994). At Sulcis a temple was dedicated to the Punic god Elat in the 1st century BC, and numerous inscriptions from that site attest to the continued use of the Punic language throughout the Republic. Burials continued in the tophet (Cecchini 1969:93; Bondi 1987a:187-89). At Bithia the history of the temple of Bes attests to even stronger Punic continuity. The first temple appears to date to the 4th century BC. Roman Republican activity is attested by the presence of a large number of votive terracottas dated to the 3rd-1st centuries BC. These were deposited by sick suppliants who were seeking cures at the shrine, mirroring the popularity of such medical votives in Roman Republican Italy (Pesce 1965; Uberti 1973; Agus 1983:41-47; Moscati 1992a:75-83). Some of the dedications consist of figurines pointing to the affected part of the body. Others are miniatures of the afflicted parts themselves. Representations of limbs and genitalia are especially common (Galeazzi 1986, 1991).

The final rebuilding of the Bes temple of Bithia took place in the late 2nd or early 3rd centuries AD. A Neo-Punic inscription records that the reconstruction was undertaken by the assembly of Bithia and the head magistrates who still bore the Punic title of *sufetes*. Cults of Bes were popular in Sardinia, with attestations at Fordongianus, Olbia, Carales, Maracalagonis, and Turris. They represented continuity with Punic practices, but they also reflected Roman Imperial interest in Egyptian cults (Agus 1983). The ongoing use of the Punic office of the sufetes is attested at other centers like Karalis. Late Republican, early Imperial Neo-Punic inscriptions are common. Indeed the latest attestation of the Neo-Punic language is a Constantinian-period graffito from S. Salvatore Cabras (Zucca 2000:1130).

This same continuity with Punic Sardinia can be seen in urial practices. The Tuvixeddu cemetery at Karalis, where burials started in the 6th century BC, continued in use until the early empire (Angliolillo 2000; Salvi 2000). The cemeteries around Olbia that date from the late 4th/early 3rd centuries BC to the early Empire manifest a high level of Punic conservatism. In many cases the tomb can be identified as Roman period only by the coins included among the mortuary material, since the ceramics and burial mode reflect Punic traditions. Only slowly did inhumation yield to cremation (Rowland 2001:110-11).

A useful if biased Roman perspective on Late Republican Sardinia is provided by Cicero's speech in defense of Marcus Aemilius Scaurus, governor of the island in 55 BC (Broughton II 1968:217-18). He places special emphasis in the surviving Punic elements in the island elite, since it was the Punic aristocracy who had spearheaded the prosecution of Scaurus. The Punic-Sards Aris and Bostar of Nora were the objects of special attention from Scaurus's defense attorney. Cicero certainly played on Roman ethnic prejudices, but behind his exaggerated rhetoric lay the reality of strong Carthaginian continuity in the cities of Sardinia.

The survival of many elements of Punic culture especially in the cities did not mean that Late Republican Sardinia was totally isolated from the larger Roman world. The administrative hand might have been light, but in the wake of the officials came traders and tax farmers both Roman and Italian, who were looking for opportunities in the province. By the 2nd century BC we have evidence of *Falesce quei in Sardinia sunt* (*ILLRP* 192). Reference to *Sodales Buduntini, Buduntinenses* or *Budentes* in northwestern Sardinia suggests connections with Butuntum in Apulia (*AE* 1985: 486). These Romans and Italians began to create their own communities and their own built environment, especially in the sacred sphere. At Sulcis a temple with an access ramp designed after contemporary Italic models was built above the Punic necropolis during the 3rd-2nd centuries BC (Colavitti 1999:41).

Continuity in the Countryside

Mention has already been made of the problems of applying too rigid a model of latifundistic development to the Sardinian countryside of the Late Republic. Large, slave-based estates probably did not come to dominate the rural areas, but most areas of the island were drawn into the Roman tax and market economy, and as Keith Hopkins has argued the need to pay taxes must have stimulated market activities (Hopkins 1980). Increasingly extensive and intensive archaeological research is providing more evidence of Republican imports into the countryside. A survey in the Sinis back country behind Tharros identified eight sites with mid-late Republican Greco-Italic and Dressel 1 type amphorae and 23 with republican black glazed ware (Tore and Stiglitz 1987).

Other types of archaeological investigations have provided insight into the complex processes at work in the Sardinian rural areas during the early Roman period. Two sites, one village and one nuraghe, illustrate both continuity and change. A little more than 20 km upriver from Bosa on a gentle slope above the Temo river in the area called Sa Tanca 'e Sa Mura-Monteleone Roccadoria a small village was excavated. Occupation started in the 4th or even 5th century BC with a probable nuragic predecessor (Rivo 1985:269-73; Madau 1991a:1001-1009). During the early 2nd century BC it was rebuilt with more Roman style rectangular structures. After a brief abandonment there was a reoccupation that extended from the late 2nd through most of the 1st century BC. Iron and glass slag found in several places showed that it was a small-scale industrial center. While the material culture showed heavy Punic influence, there is nothing to suggest that the inhabitants were not acculturated natives.

Two more traditional nuragic sites illustrate this mixture of internal continuity and outside influence. At the nuraghe Tres Bias in the territory of Tinnura, some 5 km SE of Bosa, occupation was continuous from the nuragic into the early Imperial period. Coins and painted wares of the Carthaginian period were succeeded by cooking wares "in the Punic tradition" of the 3rd-2nd century BC mixed with mid-late Republican amphorae and black-glazed pottery (Madau 1994; Logias and Madau 1998). Nuraghe Losa-Abbasanta, a site that the excavators originally considered to have been abandoned by the end of the Orientalizing period, has produced small quantities of Punic utilitarian wares succeeded by Republican pottery including early 1st century BC amphorae (Tronchetti 1993:111-16).

This continuity of culture in the countryside was reflected in cult practices. At a number of rural shrines religious activity continued from the nuragic through the Punic into the Roman period. That can be seen at a cult place like Sa Dom'e s'Ossu where the large quantities of bones of sacrificed animals were mixed with pottery sherds and coins that extended from the 4th century BC to the 5th century AD (Salvi 1989). However, the rural shrines also show the impact of new arrivals and of new religious forces operating in the Hellenistic and Roman world.

One of the most interesting Roman places of worship was that at Santu Iacci-S Nicolo Gerrei in the mountains northeast of Cagliari (Rowland 2001:108). It started as a nuragic water shrine. Sometime in the early 1st century BC a large bronze altar was erected there by a certain Cleon, a slave belonging to the *societas* of salt workers. His dedication was celebrated in a trilingual inscription in Punic, Greek, and Latin that identified the sanctuary as one dedicated to Eshmun-Merre-Aesculapius. The Punic version of the text named two sufetes, Himilkat and Abdeshmun, presumably from Cagliari. The salt works themselves must have been located along the coast near Cagliari, but the slave Cleon, certainly not of Sardinian origins, sought his cure in the sacred waters of the indigenous sanctuary. The curative traditions of the spring had an even longer life, for the modern titulary saint Santu Iacci is none other than San Giacomo, a patron saint of medicine.

Other nuragic shrines were caught up in the 4th-3rd century emphasis on cult activities related to curative needs. At S. Giuseppe-Iscaniles-Padria, a shrine dedicated to a healing divinity, possibly Melqart-Hercules-Asclepius, was already in operation by the 4th century BC and continued in use until the end of the 3rd century AD (Galli 1994; Campus 1994a). The votive offering dedicated there varied in style and quality from well-finished pieces provided by the elite to the crude dedications of the rural poor. Subjects included human anatomical parts, animal parts, architectural elements, and fruits and flowers. The spring shrine at Sant'Andrea Frius in the Trexenta north of Cagliari had nuragic origins. Cult activity resumed during the 3rd century BC and continued well into the Empire. The votive finds were dominated by body parts and mold-made heads, though some rather simple small masks in clay were also found (Moscati 1993:109-15).

The cult of Ceres continued to unite ethnic groups in the countryside of Sardinia. A major continuum from the Punic to the Roman periods was the collection of grain tribute for export. The need for increased productivity enhanced the importance of deities that protected the harvest. It also created a special role for Ceres. Dozens of Ceres-Demeter sanctuaries have been identified on Sardinia, with their cult activity continuing well into the Roman period (Guido 1993a). One of the largest and most complex of these rustic Ceres sanctuaries was that at the nuragic site of Strumpu-Bagoi-Terreseo-Narcao in the mountains east of Carbonia (Moscati 1992:87-89). The core sanctuary consisted of six altars of varying dates that formed a line in front of a 6 x 3 m cult structure connecting to a smaller shrine which contained an altar, abundant ash deposits and numerous pig teeth. The shrine was rebuilt some time after 15 BC. Apart from a 3rd century BC statuette of Demeter, all the votive objects are post-Augustan and show that worship continued there into the 2nd century AD.

Another Demeter shrine with a long history of worship was that at Nuraghe Lugherras northeast of Tharros. While the nuragic community seems to have been destroyed by the Carthaginians, a new program of

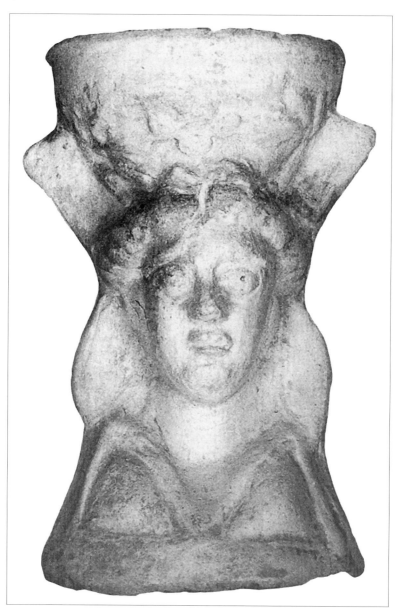

Incense burner in form of female head from Lugherras.

worship developed at the site. Its popularity was evidenced by the 731 votive incense burners in the form of female heads that were found there. They were mold made and of local production, most dating to the 4th-3rd centuries BC. The coins and other votives show that the sanctuary continued in use well into the Roman period (Moscati 1993:37-45).

This first phase of Roman occupation on Sardinia is similar to that found in other parts of the Republican central and western Mediterranean. The conquerors aimed at destroying major elements of resistance and creating an administrative structure that would facilitate the payment of taxes and tribute. Otherwise officially sponsored programs of cultural change were limited. Punic and indigenous cultures show a high level of continuity from the pre-conquest era. To a certain degree this policy continued throughout the whole Roman period, but with the end of the Republic and the formation of the Augustan Empire the Roman presence becomes more visible.

9
The Creation of the Imperial System in Sardinia

Sardinia played a marginal role in the civil wars that destroyed the Republic and led to the triumph of Octavian. It was the scene of no major conflict, though at times the resources of the island and especially the grain proved useful as Rome was cut off from more distant sources of supply. While it was destined to have a secondary place in the new Imperial structure created by Augustus, could not be completely neglected. An increase in evidence that usually comes with the period of the Empire allows us to document change and continuity more clearly.

Augustus inherited a province where many of the interior areas remained only under marginal Roman control. Varro informs us that some fertile lands in Sardinia could not be cultivated because of brigandage, citing as an example an area that seems to have been part of the hinterland of Olbia (Varro *de Re.Rust.* 1.16.2). Livy recorded that the Ilienses were not completely pacified in his own day. Strabo noted that the "mountain tribes live in caves," possibly real caves or possibly a Roman reinterpretation of the function of the nuraghi. He went on to say of the Sardinians, "if they possess any sowable land, they do not sow it conscientiously, but rather plunder the lands of those who do cultivate, whether in their own neighborhood or by sailing against those in the harbor." He provides the following insight into the tactics of the Roman field officers: "since it does not pay to maintain an army continually in plague-ridden regions, the only recourse is to plan certain stratagems. And so, keeping close watch over some one of the barbarian tribes, who hold festivals several days after a raid, they attack them at the time and capture many" (Strabo 5.2.7). The destruction layer detected at the sacred well of S. Vittoria-Serri probably provides an example of such a Roman reprisal (Zucca 1998:74).

Problems of island security persisted well into the reign of Augustus. Dio claimed that as late as AD 6 the Sardinians were not only harassing the lowlands of the island, but were sailing across the Tyrrhenian Sea to attack Italian coastal settlements. While the date of these sea raids is uncertain

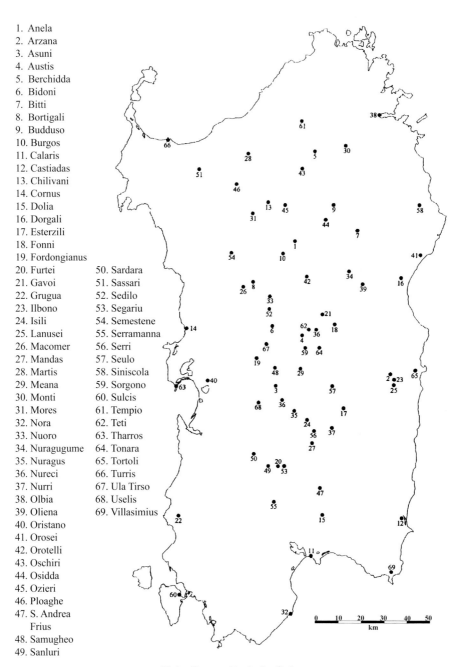

1. Anela
2. Arzana
3. Asuni
4. Austis
5. Berchidda
6. Bidoni
7. Bitti
8. Bortigali
9. Budduso
10. Burgos
11. Calaris
12. Castiadas
13. Chilivani
14. Cornus
15. Dolia
16. Dorgali
17. Esterzili
18. Fonni
19. Fordongianus
20. Furtei
21. Gavoi
22. Grugua
23. Ilbono
24. Isili
25. Lanusei
26. Macomer
27. Mandas
28. Martis
29. Meana
30. Monti
31. Mores
32. Nora
33. Nuoro
34. Nuragugume
35. Nuragus
36. Nureci
37. Nurri
38. Olbia
39. Oliena
40. Oristano
41. Orosei
42. Orotelli
43. Oschiri
44. Osidda
45. Ozieri
46. Ploaghe
47. S. Andrea
    Frius
48. Samugheo
49. Sanluri

50. Sardara
51. Sassari
52. Sedilo
53. Segariu
54. Semestene
55. Serramanna
56. Serri
57. Seulo
58. Siniscola
59. Sorgono
60. Sulcis
61. Tempio
62. Teti
63. Tharros
64. Tonara
65. Tortoli
66. Turris
67. Ula Tirso
68. Uselis
69. Villasimius

Major Roman sites in Sardinia.

it is worth noting that Strabo also referred to the Sardinians taking to the sea (Cassius Dio 55.28.1; Strabo 5.2.7). Eventually the problems became sufficiently serious that Augustus had to remove the island from senatorial control and send in troops to combat the natives (Meloni 1990:139-41). The disturbances lasted for at least three years and probably longer. In AD 13-14 Titus Pomponius Proculus governed with the special rank of equestrian *prolegatus*, an indication that the island was still unsettled (Le Bohec 1990:22).

In AD 19 Emperor Tiberius dispatched to Sardinia 4,000 persons who professed Judaism and other "superstitions" to help suppress the brigandage. If they perished Tacitus observed dismissively *ville damnum* ("little loss"). The derogatory remarks on their possible fate suggest that this was an expendable group (Tacitus *Ann* 2.85.5). These people were probably employed as armed farmers settled on the frontier rather than as regular soldiers. One wonders how effective these forced settlers, probably urban dwellers, would have been as a rural militia. Archaeological indicators for a Jewish presence include a gold ring with a Hebrew inscription found more than a century ago in the territory of Macomer, a lamp with a menorah, and a much-later tombstone with the word *Judaeus* inscribed on it (Rowland 1981:59).

Under the Augustan administrative system Sardinia had its own regular garrison, mainly formed of auxiliary troops, but both the garrison locations and the composition of the units for the Imperial army in Sardegna are poorly documented. Based on Roman place-name etymology the oldest garrison site might be Valentia near modern Nuraghus. Names like Valentia were used for defensive settlements in the 2nd century BC (Dyson 1985:262-63). Military occupation apparently continued at Nuraghus during the Empire. An epitaph of imperial date commemorating a soldier who served seven years in the Roman army was found nearby. Archaeological remains at the site itself range from the early 1st century BC to the 3rd century AD (Rowland 1981:74-76, 146-47).

The archaeological site with the most likely military associations is N. Signora di Castro, whose medieval and modern name seems derived from its use as a Roman *castrum*. Located on a plateau overlooking the modern Lago di Coghinas and the valley of the Riu Mannu di Ozieri and the broad plain to the west, the fort would have controlled a key frontier area and provided protection to the Roman road passing through Ozieri (Rowland 2001:98-99). Early reports on the site mention buildings, inscriptions, lead pipes, and mosaics, but the remains we can see today are few. Recent excavations have uncovered portions of walls and evidence for Imperial and

Byzantine periods of occupation. Inscriptions found in the area document the presence of Sardinian, Aquitanian, and Ligurian soldiers (Le Bohec 1990:66-67; *AE* 1994:795).

Another military garrison might have been located at Sorabile-Fonni. A military diploma dating to 214-17 was found in a nuraghe just to the east of Fonni. Extensive remains discovered in the area have included mosaic floors and a bath. Given the rarity of Roman architecture in the interior that evidence suggests that there was some type of military or administrative center at Fonni. Occupation started at least by the 1st century AD (Meloni 1990:306-07, 311). The site also produced a dedication to Silvanus and possibly Diana set up by Caius Ulpius Severus, *procurator* of Augustus and *praefectus* of the province of Sardinia. The inscription seems to date to the late 2nd or early 3rd centuries (Rowland 2001:100).

Other military inscriptions provide information on possible garrisons in Sardinia. An inscription of an Aquitanian soldier was found at Campu Sa Pattada between Bitti, Budduso, and Osidda, which would have been a good location for a fort, but no remains have been found (Le Bohec 1990:73). In the center of the island at a site called Perda Litterada near modern Austis the tombstone of a horn player serving in a Lusitanian cohort from the Iberian peninsula was discovered. The same site yielded the tombstones of three children, one of them named Castricius. This name with its military associations, reinforces the probability that a garrison was stationed nearby (Rowland 1981:15-16).

Several Sardinian cohorts are known from the Roman auxiliary rosters. The earliest attestation is the epitaph found at Praeneste of a *prefect* of the First Cohort of the Corsi and the *civitates* of Barbaria in Sardinia (*ILS* 2684). A *Cohors I Gemina Sardorum et Corsorum* is documented by the late 80s (Rowland 1978a). Two cohorts of Sardinian Nurritani served in North Africa (Le Bohec 1990:100). The *Cohors II Sardorum* was stationed in Mauretania in the late first or early second century AD (Laporte 1989:37-56). Sardinians were also recruited for the fleet (Nonnis 2001:109-73).

Sardinia has also produced a number of military discharge diplomas, but their scattered locations and the lack of good archaeological contexts limit their use in reconstructing the history of the Roman military on the island. One diploma found at Anela in the interior belonged to Usaris Tornalis *filius Sardus* who served with Legio I Adiutrix (*CIL* 10.7891). He was probably a pensioned soldier returning to his native community. The site at Anela has yielded extensive remains of Roman habitation (Rowland 1981:13). At Seulo, also in the interior, the diploma of a Sardinian ex-sailor was found (*CIL* 16.127). One would not expect a pensioned sailor to be

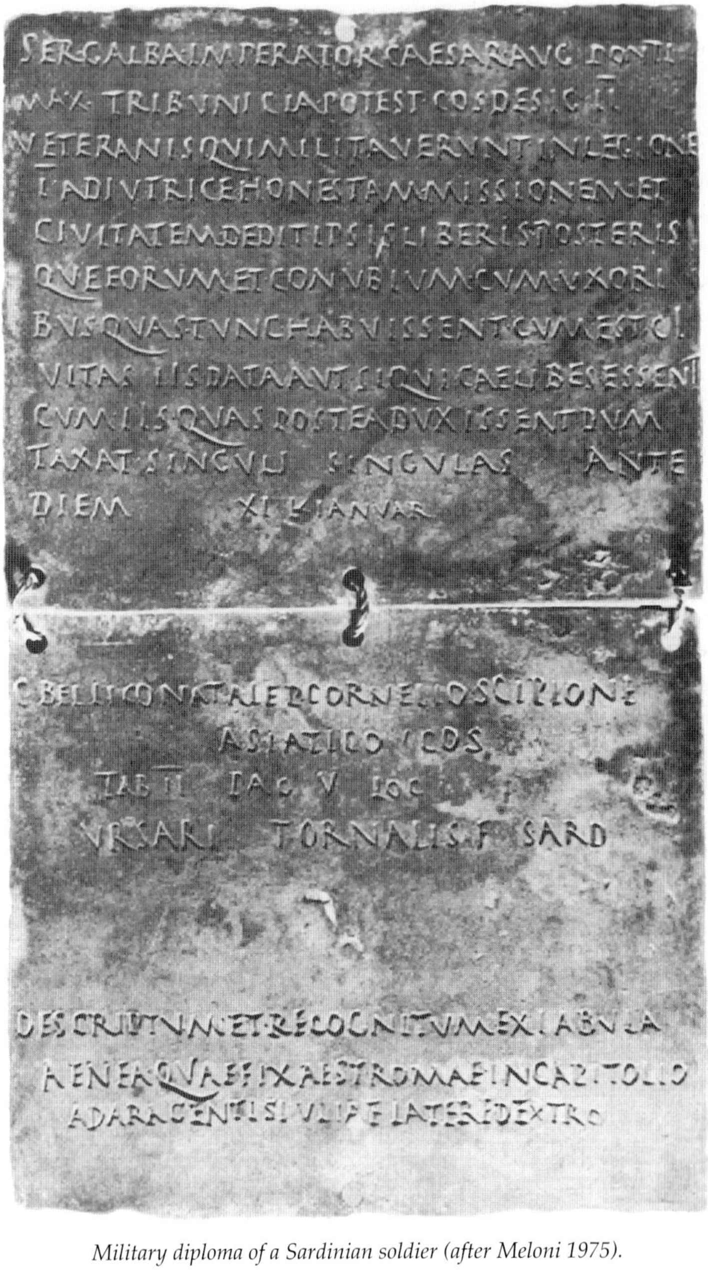

Military diploma of a Sardinian soldier (after Meloni 1975).

living so far from the sea, but he might have been living on land granted to him on retirement. Part of another diploma was found at Sorgono (Rowland 1981:130).

Road Building and Interior Development

One major role of the Roman military was the construction of roads, and those services were much in demand on the island. There is no reason to suppose that the Carthaginians created anything more than a primitive track system based on preexisting indigenous communication routes, but by the time that the Roman road itineraries were composed in the Late Roman Empire the whole island was interconnected by an impressive network of roads (Meloni 1990:317-53; Calzolari 1996). This picture of intensive road building activity is reinforced by the remains of road surfaces and bridges and the numerous finds of milestones. Sardinia has provided one of the most significant collections of milestones from anywhere in the Roman Empire.

The extent of the Roman road system in Sardinia can be compared to those in the other major Mediterranean islands. Corsica had only one road along the east coast and one possible road through the interior. Crete has yielded almost no evidence of interior road development, and that on Cyprus was also very limited. Only Roman Sicily had an interior road development comparable to Sardinia. Those other large islands with poorer road networks than Sardinia had long been the homes of complex indigenous and colonial cultures that required well-developed communications (Talbert 2000). They also had resources in the interior, such as the metals of Cyprus that should have encouraged the Romans to expand their road systems. The most sensible explanation for these differences in road development was that the Romans faced different problems and had diverse policies of interior control in the various islands. Sicily, Crete, and Cyprus did not have a large restless rural population. On Corsica the formidable mountains that dominated so much of the interior and the lack of important resources in those mountains forced the Romans to accept a reality of minimal control outside of the coastal region. Sardinia was too important an island for the Romans to apply the Corsican model of limited domination. The interior had to be penetrated and subdued, if not totally secured. The construction of roads would not only have aided military maneuvers but would also have facilitated the movement of people, goods, and ideas and aided the process of acculturating the interior. They also provided symbolic expressions of Roman

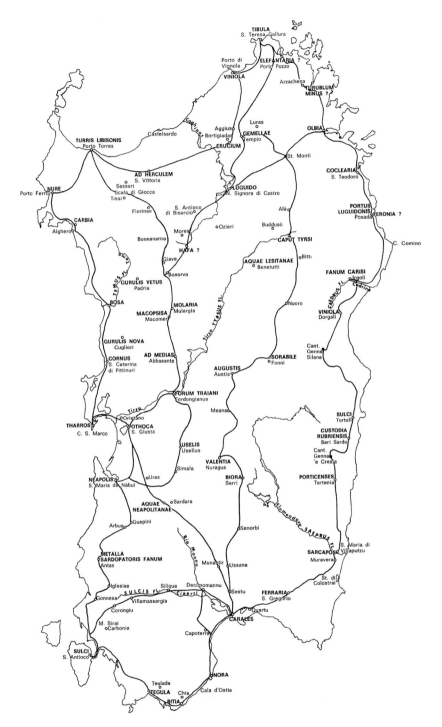

The Roman road network in Sardinia (after Meloni 1975).

power in a landscape dotted with monuments from the era of native independence.

Archaeologists and ancient historians have been relatively success-ful in reconstructing the over-all structure of the Roman road network. Reconstructing the history of its development has not been so easy. Most of the milestones cannot be precisely dated, and the building chronology of structures like bridges and roadbeds is very imprecise. Place names pro-vide some information on route development, but that must be used with caution. Certainly the program started under the Republic, but Augustus played a significant role in its expansion. Austis, located at a key road junction in the center of the island, probably derives its names from an Augustan posting station (Meloni 1990:307; Pittau 1994). A milestone of AD 13-14 was found near Forum Traiani (*ILS* 105). Later dated milestones indicate that the system was kept under repair well into the 4th century and probably beyond (Sotgiu 1988:577).

Romanization of the Coastal Cities

During the course of the Empire the coastal cities gradually acquired the structural and social characteristics of classic Roman urban centers. That can best be appreciated at Tharros, where a bustling port had devel-oped by the High Empire. Its inhabitants were exporters as well as im-porters. Citizens of Tharros are recorded in the *Piazzale degli Corporazioni* at Ostia, and the name of the city, accompanied by a representation of a ship, appears in a *graffito* in the Domus Tiberiana in Rome (Vaananen 1970:70-71, 109-110, nrs. 1-2). The city became a regional production and processing center. The excavations have provided evidence for brick and lamp manufacture. Some of the houses had kilns and presses (Pesce 1966:88-89).

The Imperial city had an aqueduct that fed a reservoir and a com-munal fountain and supplied water for baths. By the end of the Roman period the city had at least three baths, all built during the late 2nd or early 3rd centuries AD and all showing the influence of North African thermal architecture. One had two *caldaria*, a *tepidarium,* and an *apodyp-terium*. Another (the "Convento Vecchio" baths) had an *apodypterium*, a *frigidarium* with two pools, an entranceway *tepidarium*, a *destrictarium* and a *caldarium* (Acquaro and Mezzolani 1996:74-77).

Eight Roman period temples are currently known from the city. In several cases they had been Punic shrines that had been rebuilt under the Romans. The Temple of the Doric Semicolumns was reconstructed

View of the Roman period excavations at Tharros.

once in the late Republic and again in the 3rd century AD. The Semitic Plan Temple reached its final form in the 3rd century AD. The Hellenistic Temple K was also rebuilt under the Empire along with the Temple of Demeter and Kore near the tophet (Acquaro and Mezzolani 1996:73-78: Zucca 1984:54-60). Those religious structures were a testimony both to the continuity of cult from the Punic period and the prosperity that inclusion in the Roman Empire brought to Tharros. Indeed the only truly Roman religious structure at Tharros was the so-called Tetrastyle Temple that might have been the *capitolium* of the city (Zucca 1984:74-75).

The residences in use at Tharros during the Roman period continued to be largely Punic in both plan and construction techniques. They normally consisted of five or six rooms arranged around a courtyard with a well or a cistern. Many had second stories. Finds of stucco, painted walls, mosaics, marble decorations and statuary attest to attempts at domestic elegance (Pesce 1966:88-90).

Since Tharros was an abandoned Roman urban site with little post-classical reoccupation, it has allowed for extensive if often hurried archaeological exploration. Caralis, Turris Libisonis and Olbia were probably more important political and economic centers during the Roman period, but all are now totally or partially covered by modern cities. Excavations in their urban areas have of necessity been more opportunistic and have provided very partial pictures of urban development under the Romans.

The old Punic city of Caralis early assumed an important administrative role in Roman Sardinia. Striking testimony to that is the 2nd century BC theater-temple complex apparently dedicated to Venus located on the modern Via Malta. The design was similar to the elegant theater-temples constructed at places like Praeneste, Tivoli, and Terracina in Latium during the late 2nd to early 1st century BC and testifies to close contacts between the elite of Caralis and that of the mainland (Hanson 1959:32-33; Angiolillo 1986-87). The temple is not the only important monument surviving from Republican Caralis. Near the church of S. Agostino a Republican period bath and dwelling complex were excavated (Mongiu 1989:21; 1995:16).

The stimulus for the construction of such elegant buildings at Cagliari might have come from immigrants like Caius Apsena Pollio who was buried in an expensive tomb decorated with a Doric frieze found underneath a 1st century BC fullers' workshop (Angiolillo 1985; Usai and Zucca 1986:167). The level of Roman culture found in late Republican Caralis is indicated by the career of the singer Tigellius, mentioned several times by Cicero, whose talents won him an appreciative audience in Rome that included Julius Caesar. Caesar found the citizens of Carialis supportive during the Civil War, and after a two-week stay there in June of 46 BC he granted the inhabitants citizenship and made the city a *municipium* (Motzo 1936).

The administrative and religious center of the Roman city developed in the area of the modern Piazza Carmine. The *capitolium*, the municipal basilica, and the *tabularium,* or urban records hall were all located there. An amphitheater with a seating capacity of c. 10,500 was carved into the limestone hill near the present-day botanical gardens. It is usually dated to the 2nd-3rd centuries, but parallels with the amphitheaters at Nimes and Arles suggest an earlier date (Wilson 1980-81:223 n. 8). Caralis received its first aqueduct some time under the High Empire. It must have supplied major public baths and fountains, although such remains have not yet been identified in the modern city. Before the aqueduct was built water was captured and stored in a network of cisterns found throughout the city. Caralis also had a well-developed system of drains. An inscription dates the construction of some of the sewer system to AD 83 (Polastri 2001:18-24).

The Roman elite built impressive dwellings in the city and on its outskirts. The largest and most elegant Roman house found at Carales has received the name Villa of Tigellius after the Caesarian-Augustan period singer, the Sardinian "Apollo" as he was called by a 19th century historian. Even though the house had an opulence appropriate for a personage like

The Roman amphitheater at Cagliari.

Tigellius and was initially built in the 1st century BC, any specific association with the singer is unfounded. The remains unearthed so far consist
of two adjacent blocks and part of a third that appear to belong mainly
to a 2nd-early 3rd century rebuilding phase. One of those blocks housed
part of a bath complex. The remains of at least three other residences with
tetrastyle atria, cisterns, and shops facing the street were found nearby,
decorated with mosaics, painted plaster walls, and stuccoed columns. The
grand polychrome Orpheus mosaic now in Turin along with other mosaics and works of art came from one such building (*Villa di Tigellio* 1981;
Salvi 1993:5-10).

The Imperial city reflected the religious mix typical of the urban
centers of the Roman Empire. Punic worship survived, as did traditional
Greco-Roman cults like those of Mars and Aesculapius. There was at least
one temple of Isis. Several Egyptian statues, including two sphinxes and
images of Isis and Osiris, were found near the amphitheater, and a statue
of a priest of Isis was unearthed at the church of S. Eulalia near the harbor
(Rowland 2001:109, 117).

Cagliari has also produced evidence for several Imperial period cemeteries, though most of their remains have disappeared. The old Punic

Plan of the "House of Tigellius" at Cagliari (after Manconi and Pianu 1981).

necropolis at Tuvixeddu-S. Avendrace continued to be used throughout the Roman period. Several elegant Roman chamber tombs have been discovered there, the most impressive of which was the *heroon-columbarium* called the Grotto of the Viper, the name derived from the reliefs of snakes which decorated the entrance. It belonged to Atilia Pomptilla, wife of Lucius Cassius Philippus and probably the daughter-in-law of the Cassius Longinus who had been exiled to Sardinia by Nero (Zucca 1992; Dadea 1995).

Recent excavations at the cemetery on the Bonaria hill in Cagliari have produced a number of largely intact Roman tombs (Fonzo 1993; Mureddu 1993). Careful scientific analyses have provided considerable information on the funerary rituals and the physical condition of the individuals buried there. Some of the graves contained remains of molluscs and small

18th century drawing of a mosaic depicting Orpheus from the "House of Tigellius" at Cagliari (after L'Africa Romana *1990).*

farm animals, probably surviving from funerary meals. The males tended to be buried face up or have their heads turned to the left with their arms alongside the body. Females were placed face up or turned to the right with the arms folded on their abdomen or turned toward the head. Males averaged 163 cm and females 153.6 in height. Of the 33 individuals whose remains were analyzed 4 died before age 1, 11 between 1 and 20, 4 between 20 and 50, 6 between 50 and 60, and 8 older than 60. More than 40 percent suffered from caries, and damage to various joints was not uncommon.

Turris Libisonis (modern Porto Torres), the major Imperial port on the north coast of Sardinia, appears to have been a new Roman foundation. The few Punic objects found at the site should probably be associated with a small emporion located there, or they may represent trade goods obtained by indigenous settlers. Indicative of the city's Roman origins is the lack of North African names at Turris during the early Imperial period. The Roman *Colonia Iulia ad Turrem Libisonis* possibly was founded as early as 46 BC but more likely is to be associated with the settlement of Antonian veterans of the civil wars between Octavian and Marcus Antonius. The colony was laid out in a regular orthogonal grid with *cardines* and *decumani*. The inscriptions document the standard administrative structure of a High Imperial provincial city (Meloni 1990:259-61, 494-95). It early

A Roman colonnaded street in Porto Torres.

Roman bridge on the Rio Mannu.

became the hub for the Roman road system in the north of the island. The bridge at Turris over the Mannu River appears to date to the early Julio-Claudian period (Maetzke 1963:167-68).

Urban development was rapid. A peristyle building with mosaics located near the bath complex known as the Terme Pallottino seems to date to the 1st century AD. The temple of Fortuna and the basilica with a tribunal that an inscription mentions as being restored after having collapsed through old age in the third century AD probably originated in this early building boom (*CIL* 10.7946; Pallottino 1947:229-31). The city may also have had a theater or an amphitheater (Boninu, Le Glay, and Mastino 1984:23).

The largest surviving Roman monument in modern Porto Torres is the bath complex known as *Palazzo di Re Barbaro*. The baths were originally built in the 1st century AD, but what is visible today dates to renovations of the 3rd and 4th centuries AD (Boninu, Le Glay, and Mastino 1984:12-19). Two other baths are known, the so-called Terme Maetzke of the 2nd century AD and the Terme Pallottino of the late 3rd or early 4th centuries (Boninu, Le Glay, and Mastino 1984:21-22). The baths and the cisterns of the city were fed by an aqueduct whose source was located well outside the city.

The recent discovery of grain warehouses of the late 2nd century AD reminds us of the commercial importance of Turris, the main northern port

Mosaics in offices of shipping agencies from the Piazzale delle Corporazioni at Ostia. The upper represents the merchants and shippers of Cagliari and the lower the shippers of Turris Libisonis.

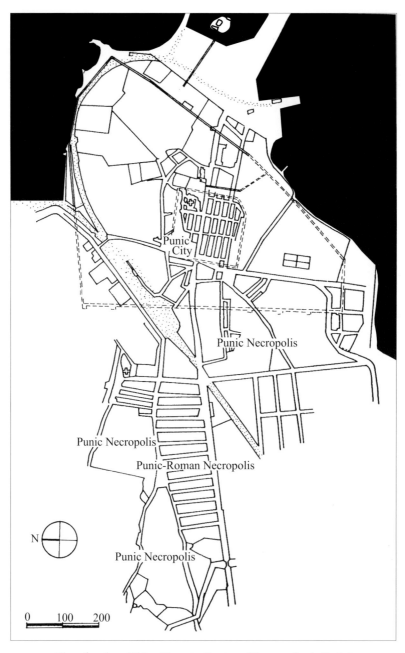

Plan of modern Olbia with major Punic and Roman sites indicated.

of Roman Sardinia. Its commercial character is also indicated by the presence of Turris merchants at the *Piazzale degli Corporazioni* in Ostia (Meiggs 1973:286). The abundant ceramic finds from Torres document the shifting patterns of trade and external contacts of the city. Before the middle years of the 2nd century AD *sigillata* from Gaul and Italy predominated and North African common wares and amphorae were in the minority. By the period AD 150-230 the fine wares were almost all African. African common wares formed about two-thirds of the total ceramic inventory, although African amphorae represent less than one-half of the total found. By the period AD 200-75 almost all of the fine wares were African, and the preponderance of common wares and amphorae were African as well (Villedieu 1984:286-95).

The cosmopolitan flavor of Turris was also reflected in its cults. Traditional Roman religion was represented by the standard priesthoods and by such deities as Fortuna (Rowland 1976:169-70; Rowland 1981:194; Mastino and Vismara 1994:39). The Egyptian deities made their presence known with an altar dedicated to Bubastis dated to AD 35, and dedications to Isis and to Jupiter Ammon. Mithras is attested by an acephalous marble statue of his assistant, Cautopates.

Olbia was the only major port center on the east coast of Sardinia and therefore assumed considerable importance when the Romans took control of the island. Already in 56 BC Quintus Cicero was dispatched there by Pompey to secure the grain supply for Rome. The major east coast road passed through the city and another road ran west from Olbia to link up with other Roman communication routes at the center of the island (Meloni 1990:326-33, 345-50).

Olbia had been one of the latest Carthaginian foundations in Sardinia, and here as elsewhere there was considerable continuity from the Punic to the Roman Republican period. Representative of this was the temple of Melqart-Hercules that had originally been established at the time of the Punic foundation of the city and was rebuilt in the 3rd-2nd centuries BC (D'Oriano 1994).

Along with other major Sardinian centers Olbia enjoyed early imperial prosperity. A 1st century AD inscription commemorating a Cypriot shipper reminds us of Olbia's role in the wider Mediterranean trade (Sotgiu 1988:599, B 85). The baths and aqueduct appear to date to the 1st or early 2nd century AD (Antona et al. 1991:72-73, 85-86). Busts of Nero and Trajan found in the area that has been identified as the *forum* suggest the existence of a *Caesareum* dedicated to the Imperial cult. Another Imperial connection was reflected in a shrine of Ceres dedicated by the freedwoman Acte, the loyal concubine of Nero (Mastino and Ruggieri 1995). Brick stamps attest to the fact that Acte owned estates and workshops in and around Olbia.

Olbia possessed a relatively small hinterland, but in a world where access to water transport was a key to successful marketing the citizens of Olbia were able to make the profitable use of their limited *territorium*. Fourteen villas are known from the area around Olbia and more in the nearby territory of Tempio (Rowland 1981:84-88, 132-34). This is an impressive number for an island where villa development was very limited. One of those was the short-lived working villa at S'Imbalconadu. It was founded around 150-140 BC to produce grain, wine, and oil and to raise stock. Destroyed by fire some time in the late 2nd or early 1st century BC the farmstead does not appear to have been rebuilt (Sanciu 1997).

The Old Punic Centers

The older urban centers of west and southwest Sardinia had retained their traditional Punic character during much of the Republic. They began to change during the Early Empire and by the 3rd century AD had come to resemble most other smaller Roman provincial centers in that part of the Mediterranean.

Nora may have been the original Roman administrative center in Sardinia, but by the time of the Empire it had been supplanted by Caralis. Significantly a lady from Nora, Favonia Vera, donated a house in Caralis for the use of the people of Nora. Presumably it was intended to serve as their base of operations when they were in the provincial capital for public or even private business (*ILS* 5918). Nora did not become an isolated backwater. The first *flamen Augusti perpetuus,* leader in the Imperial cult in Sardinia was Quintus Minucius Pius of Nora, his native town where he served at least three times as *IIIIvir iure dicundo,* one of the college of chief magistrates (*ILS* 45). The city had acquired municipal status by the Early Empire. During the Late Republican or the Augustan period the so-called Temple of Tanit was rebuilt. Several large residences with colonnaded *atria* have also been dated to the Late Republican-Augustan period. Perhaps it was at that time that the Roman street grid was regularized (Tronchetti 2000a:21, 95-96, 184-89).

Most of the major public and private buildings at Nora have been assigned to the High Empire, though for some that dating may be too late. The stone-built Roman theater, with its capacity of 700-1100 people, is today the most prominent monument at the site. It is generally assigned to the mid 2nd century AD, although it may in fact have been built in

The Roman city of Nora with the remains of the theater visible in the center (after Tronchetti 1986).

the early 1st century (Tronchetti 2000a:177-79). What one scholar has described as a fervid restructuring of the city during the late 2nd or early 3rd century led to the construction of the Baths by the Sea, a building of uncertain function east of the forum, a temple from which a lone column survives, the complex north of the Central Baths, the Central Baths, the Small Baths, the House of the Tetrastyle Atrium, another large house to the north, and the *macellum* or *horreum* in the western part of the city (Tronchetti 2000a:22-23, 95-105). We know that the city had an aqueduct, which a 16th century antiquary described as sumptuous. It appears to date

The Roman Theater at Nora.

to a Severan restructuring of the city (Tronchetti 1997:12-13). The site of an amphitheater has been identified, but the remains have not been studied in detail (Rowland 1981:72-73).

Sporadic evidence has emerged for the location of the Roman cemeteries of Nora. They consisted of incineration and inhumation burials of both the Early Imperial and Late Imperial periods. Some of those burials reused earlier Punic *hypogeia* (Tronchetti and Bernardini 1985:52-60). The fertile hinterland around Nora was restricted to the narrow territories of Pula and Sarroch between the mountains and the water and appears to have been intensively cultivated. A number of villas and farmsteads have been identified along with rural hamlets (Tronchetti 1997:7-16). A rural shrine to Demeter-Ceres was discovered at Medau de su Riu Perdosu-S. Margherita di Pula (*Notizie degli Scavi* 1974:506-12).

The large number of inscriptions of Pompeii and Pompeiae at Sulcis provides insight into Late Republican political connections on the island. Because of its traditional ties to Pompey, Sulcis assisted the Pompeian admiral Publius Nasidius and was heavily punished by Caesar. The city quickly recovered and was by the time of Strabo regarded as one of the two most important cities of Sardinia. It became a *municipium* in the Julio-Claudian period, growth partly stimulated by

Sulci's role as the port of embarcation for the mineral resources from the nearby mining areas. A unit of the Imperial fleet was apparently based there. Some tombstones of veterans have been found in its cemeteries (*CIL* 10.7535, 7537).

During the 1st century AD the civic center of Sulcis was embellished by a number of new public and private buildings. Most important was the *Caesareum* with its portrait gallery of Julio-Claudian *divi* (Angiolillo 1975-77). It was probably during the reign of Trajan that the proconsul Caius Asinius Tucurianus financed the paving of a piazza in the city center (*ILS* 5352).

Several new structures including an amphitheater were built during the 2nd century AD (Tronchetti 1995a:113-114). An impressive array of structures, mostly of the 2nd and 3rd centuries AD, has been unearthed along the modern Via Eleanora d'Arborea. They included the *forum*, a basilica, various temples, and numerous floor mosaics probably belonging to the houses of the elite (Tronchetti 1995a:103-116). A temple of Isis and Serapis is also documented (*CIL* 10.7514). A particularly noteworthy discovery was a painted tomb with a bust of the deceased that is now in the museum in Cagliari (Pesce 1962). The remains of villas have been found in the suburbs of the modern city and on the nearby island of S. Pietro (Cossu and Nieddu 1998:36).

Very little of Roman Bithia has been excavated, and we cannot reconstruct a detailed picture of how that small Carthaginian center fared during the Roman period. Continuity of Punic culture was demonstrated by the restructuring of the temple of Bes in the late 2nd or early 3rd century AD. Recently excavated burials suggest a reasonable level of prosperity at least through the 3rd century AD and possibly into the 4th (Tronchetti 1987).

An outlier of Punic urbanization had been the center at Bosa located on the west coast north of Tharros. Although little of Roman Bosa is now visible, structural remains discovered in the past, and the Roman period inscriptions suggest that it was a place of some prosperity during the High Empire (Mastino 1974). An inscription from Picenum on the mainland mentions an *ordo populusque Bosanus* (*EE* 8.227). The city had an *Augusteum* by the second century. At that imperial cult center a certain Quintus Rutilius dedicated silver statuettes of Antoninus Pius, Faustina, Marcus Aurelius, and Lucius Verus (*CIL* 10.7939). The city had large public baths and other notable structures (Rowland 1981:23-24; Zucca 1993a). The important Christian remains testify to the continuing prosperity and importance of Bosa during the later Empire.

Urbanization of the Interior

The late Roman road itineraries, with their notation of many stopping places along the roads, have suggested to some scholars that interior Sardinia attained a relatively high level of urban development, but a detailed analysis of the actual remains found in and around the various sites cited in the itineraries does not support that assumption. In many cases not even the precise location of a place mentioned on an itinerary can be determined, and when it is, the Roman remains on the ground often prove to be disappointing.

Perhaps the most striking contrast between the impression of urban development derived from the epigraphical record and archaeological reality is the case of *Colonia Iulia Augusta Uselis* (Dyson and Rowland 1992). The Latin title of the community implies a colonial foundation of the Augustan period. An inscription of AD 158 found at Cagliari records an agreement of *hospitium* between the named colony and Marus Aristius Balbinus Atinius whom the town coopted as its patron (*ILS* 6107; Meloni 1990:264-65, 496). The arrangements suggest an active community of the High Empire. However, a visit to the modern site of Usellus located on the Roman road southeast of Oristano brings disappointment. In the 19th century there were supposedly significant remains still standing at the site, but nothing is to be seen today except a ruined church and a scatter of potsherds (Rowland and Dyson 1991a:145-70).

More impressive but hardly overwhelming are the ruins at Fordongianus, the Roman Forum Traiani. The original Roman name of the settlement had been *Aquae Hypsitanae*. The role of that settlement as a frontier meeting place has already been discussed. The increased importance of the center as a place of commerce is indicated by the High Imperial designation of Forum Traiani. Forum Traiani became a *municipium* under Diocletian and served as the headquarters for the Roman military in early Byzantine Sardinia (Bonello Lai 1990:29-30; Zucca 1992a; Rowland 2001:139). The most impressive Romans structures surviving at the site today are the ruins of imperial era baths built to tap the still-active thermal springs. Otherwise there is little to see. Earlier reports of an amphitheater and fortifications cannot be corroborated today. Few tombstones or other portable remains have been reported. Certainly Fordongianus does not have the archaeological presence that one would expect of a major provincial center elsewhere in the Roman world (Rowland and Dyson 1998).

A detailed review of the evidence for other supposed urban centers in the interior of Sardinia is beyond the scope of this book. Suffice it to say that the paltry remains at almost all supposed Roman town sites suggest a real-

View of the Roman baths at Fordongianus.

ity of minimal urbanization beyond the coastal zones. Most of the names in the itineraries probably represented little more than posting stations and small market communities (Dyson 1984; Meloni 1990:302-11).

Change and Continuity in the Roman Imperial Countryside

It is only with the Early Empire that the archaeological evidence becomes sufficiently abundant to allow a more detailed reconstruction of the history of rural settlement. The picture that emerges is diverse and complex. In the immediate hinterlands behind the major urban centers and along the important communication routes, especially those close to the coast, remains of a number of large maritime and suburban villas have been discovered. They had elegant residential quarters, bath complexes, and mosaics. In the Campidano a number of villas sites have been found along the rivers and the main Roman roads.

Toward the interior the dominant picture is one of continuity in rural settlement organization from the pre-Roman period. Presumably that meant limited changes in social and economic structures with only superficial Romanization expressed in the acquisition of such items as imported North African ceramics. The Tirso River valley and the hinterland of

Fordongianus have provided almost no evidence for villas or for any other Roman-style rural settlement (Rowland and Dyson 1991). Publication of the remains of the major villas in Sardinia has been sporadic, but the general types are familiar from elsewhere in the Roman Empire. A number of *villae marittimae* are known. Among the most complex appears to have been that at Porto Conte near Alghero. Another coastal villa with mosaic decorations is known from Santa Filicita (Sorso) (Angiolillo 1987a; Cossu and Nieddu 1998:55). Among the villas located more to the interior, that at Siligo near Sassari with its bath buildings later used for a church is among the most impressive (Teatini 1996).

Less archaeological attention has been focused on the productive aspects of the villas, such as wine-and olive- processing complexes, than on the architectural and artistic remains, but some information has emerged. Olive presses have been documented at a number of sites (Mastino 1995). A pottery manufacture of the 1st and 2nd centuries AD has been excavated at the villa of Badde Rebuddu-La Nura (Manconi and Pandolfi 1996).

The art form that best linked the world of the city and that of the high-status villa are the mosaics used to decorate the display rooms of baths and residential areas. The Sardinian mosaics have been well catalogued, and considerable research has been devoted to their stylistic affinities. Not surprisingly in the south of the island the influence of the highly dynamic North African mosaic industry was especially strong, as can be seen in the pavement from the central baths at Nora, the house of the tetrastyle atrium from Nora, and especially in the great Orpheus mosaic from Cagliari (Angiolillo 1973-74). In contrast the mid- imperial mosaics from the northern part of the island display more Ostian and Roman connections in the black and white mosaics from Turris and Olbia (Angiolillo 1981:188-97). During the Late Empire North African influences also appear in the north (Angiolillo 1994).

So strong has been the preconception that the Sardinian countryside was either marginalized or abandoned in the Roman period that few excavations of nuragic settlements with possible Roman period occupations have been undertaken. New evidence from both excavation and survey has forced a modification of the minimalist picture of the development in the countryside during the centuries of Roman occupation. In fact the Roman presence seems to have been quite thick on the ground. A couple of examples must suffice. Excavation of a nuraghe at S'Abba Druche-Bosa located near the coast and the lower Temo River valley on the east coast revealed a Roman period village with an extensive workshop area apparently used for tanning (Satta 1996). One of the towers of the quadrilobate nuraghe S. Pietro-Torpe was used as a storehouse for grain and beans. It

The Severan period Temple of Sardus Pater at Antas.

yielded many containers of cork and wood along with Roman Imperial amphorae. After the tower collapsed the ruins were used for burials that appear to date to the 2nd and 3rd centuries AD. The site continued to be occupied into the 7th century AD (Spanu 1998:125). A small village grew up around the nuraghe Arrubiu-Orroli during the 2nd century AD, and two areas atop the collapsed nuragic structure were developed into wineries (Lo Schiavo and Sanges 1994:69-77).

Systematic surveys and less detailed reports from individual nuragic sites confirm the picture derived from individual site studies. Many of the nuraghi or at least the villages that surrounded them continued to be occupied throughout the Roman period. Roman-glazed ceramics are attested at many sites, but those are usually the only indications of Romanization. In few instances there is evidence of Roman-style construction, but in most cases the native domestic architectural forms appear to have persisted. Tiles are found but not in great numbers, and seem more often associated with burials than buildings. In general the archaeological evidence suggests that a life style characteristic of the nuragic period continued relatively undisturbed. The countryside of Roman Sardinia appears to have been one of the most conservative and unchanged in the Roman Empire (Dyson 1992). Rural religion continued to reflect the complex blend of local and external influences that had characterized it during the Punic period. Some of the Demeter sanctuaries remained in use well

Roman coin depicting Sardus Pater.

down into the Empire. A good example is the rural sanctuary at Narcao near Carbonia (Moscati 1993:77-82), where worship probably began with a spring cult during the nuragic period. Elements of the cult of Demeter began to appear in the 3rd century BC. The numerous, simply made terracotta votives testify to the popularity of the shrine that continued to attract worshippers at least into the 2nd century AD.

One cult whose articulation reflected an effort to bridge Roman ideological needs and the religious traditions of rural Sardinia was that of Sardus Pater. The deity's principal place of worship was an isolated temple location at Antas. As has already been noted the cult place had its origins in the Punic and probably the pre-Punic past. The first Roman reworking of the Punic temple appears to date to the late Republic or the early Augustan period. That cult promotion may have been reflected in the Sardus Pater coins issued around 38 BC by the *praetor* Marcus Atius

Balbus. The imposing structure that exists today dates to the reign of Caracalla, and is a complex blend of Severan and Sardo-Punic architectural forms (Zucca 1989). Under the Romans Sardus Pater acquired a distinctive iconography, including a feather headdress which appears on both the Balbus coins and on the architrave of the sacred well of S. Vittoria-Serri. The appearance of images of Sardus Pater at S. Vittoria shows that the cult extended beyond enclaves of the Romanized coast.

Rural mortuary practice reflected some Roman influences but also strong Punic and indigenous traditions. A number of tile burials with Roman objects have been found. Another indicator of the influence of Roman artistic popular culture in rustic burials is the use of the crude funerary stelae that seem to date to the 1st centuries BC to AD (Rowland 1988:830-32; Moscati 1992). They are designated stele *a specchio* from the image carved on them of a crude round human face with an elongated neck.

Minerals and Mining in Roman Sardinia

It is generally assumed that the Romans extensively exploited the mineral resources of Sardinia and especially those of the Iglesiente region in the southwest of the island. The mines were used as penal colonies, especially for the early Christians, and hence have attracted special attention (Turtas 1999:32-34), but the evidence, especially for the Republic and the early Empire, is rather elusive (Meloni 1990:176-83). This is especially true if the provenances of many of the ingots found in Roman shipwrecks off the coast of Sardinia are not automatically seen as Sardinian but can be attributed to other sources such as Spain (Salvi 1992).

The secure evidence for mining increases with the High and Late Empire. The Late Latin authors Solinus and Sidonius Apollinaris refer to the abundant deposits of silver and iron on Sardinia. Lead ingots inscribed with the name of Hadrian are known from Sardinia. In the *nymphaeum* in the baths at Fordongianus was found an inscription set up by a *procurator metellarum et praediorum* (Rowland 1981:44; Serra and Bacco 1998).

Precise archaeological evidence for the techniques of Roman period mining is less abundant than one would like. Roman lamps have been found in mines at Montevecchio and elsewhere (Rowland 1988:835-37). In the mineral rich Montevecchio a number of Roman period settlements and cemeteries have been discovered. The concentration recalls that of the nuragic period mining and metal working centers. Roman period settlements are also known from other mining areas like S. Lucia-Capoterra and Ballao (Rowland 2001:106-107).

Location of Roman mines in southwestern Sardinia
(after Le Bohec 1992)

10
Sardinia in the Late Empire

The major political and military changes in the wider Mediterranean during the later 4th and 5th centuries had a great impact on Sardinia. The growing insecurity in mainland Italy meant that Sardinia became an increasingly attractive destination for refugees both rich and poor (Turtas 1999:77-78). With the emergence of the Vandal kingdom in North Africa and its assertion of maritime hegemony within the western Mediterranean during 5th century AD the situation on the island again changed significantly. Sardinia remained not only a place of refuge but also was used by the Vandals of exile, especially for heretic clerics. However, it also benefited from regular commercial contact with the Vandals (Rowland 2001:103-104, 126-30, 133-35). The 6th century destruction of the Vandal kingdom by the Byzantine armies led by Belisarius once again brought Sardinia under Roman control. Finally the rise of Islam and the creation of Islamic states on the North African shore in the 8th century changed the fortunes and future direction of the island.

The study of this transitional period has suffered from a combination of too-simplistic historical stereotypes and scholarly neglect. The Later Roman Empire was long regarded as a period of decadence, the Vandals as a Germanic tribe with minimal civilization, and the Byzantines as a retrograde presence whose government on Sardinia resembled that of the later Spanish Bourbons.

Research also suffered from a number of other scholarly limitations. Students of the Late Antique have tended to divide themselves into different subspecialties with insufficient communication among the the various scholarly groups. Christian archaeologists and classical archaeologists generally operate in separate worlds, even though they are conducting research on the same time periods and sometimes on the same social groups. In places like Sardinia excavators have tended to destroy Late Antique and Early Medieval evidence in their search for the remains of earlier periods. Early Christian archaeology on Sardinia still has a very limited agenda, centered mainly on the study of ecclesiastical remains. Early Medieval archaeology hardly exists (Finzi 1982:174-76; Paulis 1983:9-10).

Recently scholarly research in the Late Antique and Early Medieval periods has changed focus, producing more integration of the different categories of evidence both documentary and archaeological and a more sympathetic approach to formerly marginalized groups. The Vandals in North Africa provide an interesting case study for this. The Vandalic kingdom is now seen as relatively sophisticated entity, maintaining a high level of continuity with the Roman political, economic, and cultural systems that had preceded it (Courtois 1955; Pergola 1989). It was in fact probably closer in its social and political structures to the kingdom of Theodoric in Italy than some barbaric tribal regime. Certainly the Vandalic control of the sea spawned piracy and coastal raiding, but it also allowed for continued trade between Sardinia and North Africa, as is documented by the quantities of late African red slip ware found on the island. The transport amphorae unearthed on Sardinia also attest to ongoing trade with other parts of the Empire. This increasing archaeological evidence also compels caution in portraying those centuries as a time of maritime chaos and increasing isolation (Pergola 1989:553-59; Spanu 1998:217-25).

The Establishment of a Christian Community

One of the major changes that took place in Sardinia during the Later Empire was its transformation from a pagan to a Christian society. The earliest references to Christians in Sardinia date to the reign of Commodus, when some Christians were condemned to the island mines. The harsh condition of their internment would have allowed little or no opportunity for proseletyzing except among their fellow convicts (Turtas 1999:32-34). In 235 Pope Pontianus and the presbyter Hippolytus were exiled to Sardinia, where Pontianus suffered martyrdom (Turtas 1999:34). The earliest indigenous Sardinian martyr was Saint Saturno who supposedly died in 303-304 during the persecutions of Diocletian. Although the details of his life and death are few the antiquity of his church at Cagliari would seem to lend credence to the historical reality of his martyrdom (Pani Ermini 1982-84:101-18; Ciomei 1998:157-80; Spanu 2000:51-60). Genuine also seem to have been the martyrdoms of Gavinus at Porto Torres, Luxorius at Fordongianus, and Simplicius at Olbia (Turtas 1999:35-47). The centers mentioned in connection with those martyrs—Olbia, Turris, Forum Traiani, and Calaris—represented the major Roman cities of the island, places where one would expect early Christian communities to develop.

A *graffito* recently discovered in a cistern in Cagliari records a certain Januarius who attached Christian symbols to his name. It is thought to date to the late 3rd or early 4th century. Because the cistern was connected to the amphitheater by an underground gallery and because the walls had stout rings infixed, it is possible that it was used as a prison and that Januarius was a martyr in waiting (Zucca 2000:1124).

A certain number of early Christian mortuary monuments have been discovered in Sardinia. A 3rd-4th century sarcophagus with Christian scenes carved on it was found in Olbia (Pani Ermini 1981:59-61). What appears to be a Christian sarcophagus of the Constantinian period comes from Turris (Pesce 1957:110-13). Another early Christian sarcophagus was discovered at Pirri (Pesce 1957:51-52). The Christian catacomb at Sulcis, the only one in Sardinia officially recognized by the Vatican, developed around reutilized Punic chamber tombs and was in full use from the 4th century (Porru, Serra, and Coroneo 1989:15-26, 30-83; Nieddu 1996). The earliest dated Christian tombstone was set up by a certain Thalassus Pal(atinus) to a 20-year-old named Musa, who died in June 394 (Mastino and Solin 1992).

A Sardinian ecclesiastical structure was in place by 314, when Calaris was represented at the Council of Arles by the bishop Quintasius and the presbyter Ammonius. By the middle of the 4th century the bishop of Calaris ranked as a metropolitan (Jones 1964:2.884; Turtas 1999:92). By 483 five bishops representing Calaris, Forum Traiani, Senafer (probably Cornus), Sulcis, and Turris attended a meeting at Carthage called by the Vandal ruler Hunneric. By the end of the 6th century Sardinia had at least seven bishops (Meloni 1990:293-94; Turtas 1999:71-72). Sardinian Christians also made their marks in the wider world. Eusebius of Vercellae, a Sard by birth, and Lucifer of Calaris acquired international theological reputations as opponents of Arianism. In 354 they were sent by the pope on an embassy to the Emperor Constantius (Turtas 1999:55-71).

Refuge and Invasion

The chaos on land and sea caused by the collapse of Roman power in the west turned Sardinia to a place of refuge. One of the first such disasters was the attack of Alaric and his Visigoths on Rome in AD 410, but others followed. In the wake of the collapse of order on the mainland disparate groups of people arrived on the island, stimulating both religious and social change. The Theodosian Code cited Sardinia as a safe refuge for those "who were driven out by the devastation of the barbarians." The relatively large number of coins issued by Honorius, Arcadius, and Theodosius II that have been found in Sardinia may document that influx of refugees (Rowland 1978a:95; Turtas 1999:77-78).

More serious for Sardinia was the consolidation of Vandalic power in North Africa. The Vandals took to the sea, raiding the coast of Sardinia and threating the island's ability to deliver grain and other products to Rome. The Sardinian grain had once again become important with the transfer of the Egyptian annona to Constantinople. Famines like that reported at Rome in 456 might partly be related to the loss of Sardinian grain (Sirks 1991:163-64). In 452 the patrons of the guild of swine keepers were granted "the authorization to collect the taxes that were furnished to them within the provinces of Sardinia and of which the payments fluctuated on account of the uncertainty of navigation" (*Nov.Val.* 36.1).

Specific attacks by the Vandals are hard to document in the archaeological record. There has been a tendency to associate examples of wall building and destruction debris documented at different sites with the Vandalic threat. Rigorous archaeological analysis does not always support such precise correspondences. For example the 2nd century Baths by the Sea at Nora were converted into a fortification around the mid-5th century. Was it done by the locals to protect themselves against the Vandals or by the Vandals to guard against Gothic or Byzantine attacks? (Tronchetti 1985). The late wall at Porto Torres may date to the Vandalic era, but also could be as late as the Byzantine period (Villadieu 1986:73; Spanu 1998:107-09, 196). The same is true for the walls at Cagliari (Spanu 1998:23-25, 190-91). A thick destruction level at Olbia that had been attributed to a Vandalic attack now appears to be earlier in date (Finzi 1982:374-78; D'Oriano 1996a:357). The recent discovery of a small fleet of sunken ships in Olbia harbor has been associated with Vandalic naval activities, but the scanty archaeological evidence now available suggests that the ships are much earlier in date (A.D.R. 'Un tesoro sotto il lungomare' *Unione Sarda* 25 Settembre 1999).

More recent scholarship has tended to downplay the violence of the Vandals and argue for a more peaceful incorporation of Sardinia into the Vandalic sphere. Indeed a scholar who has studied the Vandalic period in Sardinia has claimed that one day we will "perhaps see in the period of the Vandalic occupation of Sardinia one of the most vital and culturally determinative moments for the medieval period" (Pani Ermini 1985:122). Despite doctrinal differences interaction continued between the Christians on the island and those in North Africa. Sardinian bishops participated in the 484 Council at Carthage (Turtas

1999:71-72). Imported North Africa amphorae and African red slipped pottery document the continued economic contacts between the island and the African shore. Indeed the quantity of African amphorae found on the island has suggested to some that the Vandals privileged Sardinia and Corsica in their wine trade (Carandini, Cracco Ruggini, and Giardina 1993:651).

The Vandalic policy of accommodation was in part a recognition of the long-standing connections between North Africa and Sardinia, born in the Punic period and sustained into the Late Roman Empire. Immigrants from North Africa are attested in the epigraphical record. In other cases North African sounding names like Abeddea, Deusdedit, Quobuldeus, and Deodata appear on the island. The personal names of North African martyrs such as Fortunata, Ianuarius, Perpetua, and Thecla were adopted by Christians on Sardinia (Corda 1999:3-54, 153, 222, 232-34).

Such contacts were also reflected in church architecture and in funerary ritual. The basilica at Cornus has close parallels at Bulla Regia and Sbeitla, while the baptistries at Tharros, Cornus, and S. Giovanni-Nurachi seem to have been influenced by the Christian architecture of North Africa (Testini 1966; R. Serra 1994). Excavations at the Christian cemetery of Cornus have provided information on new funerary rituals coming from Vandal North Africa. The cult place was restructured into an episcopal center with a baptistery, and the custom of a communal liturgical banquet at the tomb was introduced. Hearths were discovered at the tombs along with the remains of molluscs, boar, sheep, and chicken (Giuntella et al. 1985). Near Porto Torres a mosaic tomb Septimia Musa, described as a *bona femina* included the prayer that she be refreshed in the name of Christ (Giuntella, Borgetti, and Stiaffini 1985:41-44). At Sulci one tomb chamber contained a painted, plaster *mensa* and a number of glass bottles, flasks, and cups (Pani Ermini 1995).

Despite a certain level of religious accommodation with the Vandals Sardinia also maintained contacts with the mainland of Italy, and the great majority of the Christian populace remained loyal to Rome. Indeed, during the years of Vandalic hegemony two Sardinians, Hilary (461-68) and Symmachus (498-514) were elected bishop of Rome. Vandal religious policy also served to reinforce orthodoxy is unintended ways. The Vandals exiled orthodox clerics to the island, where they propagandized for the orthodox faith. The most striking example was Fulgentius of Ruspae who was sent to Sardinia in 508-509 and in 517-18. He arrived with more than 200 clerics and bishops. His reception and impact on late antique Caralis are described below (Turtas 1999:86-92).

The Arrival of the Byzantines

The decision made by Justinian to reconstitute the Western Roman Empire meant that Sardinia once again came under the control of Constantinople. Belisarius began an all-out effort to reconquer the island. The task was made easier by divisions between the Vandalic homeland and their troops stationed on Sardinia (Boscolo 1978:27-28). The new Byzantine civil government was established at Caralis and the new military government at Forum Traiani. On April 13, 534 Justinian issued a constitution ordering Belisarius to establish what appear to have been strategic hamlets at key defensive points to ensure limited control of the interior of the island. Forum Traiani established as the headquarters for the Byzantine military administration would fit in well with that strategy (*Cod.Just.* 1.27.2).

The historical division between coast and interior acquired specific administrative form in the early Byzantine period. A fragmentary inscription dated to the reign of the emperor Maurice (582-602) was discovered at S. Nicola-Donori, some 30 km from Cagliari. It lists a series of tariffs that were apparently applied to goods brought from the interior for sale in the capital (Durliat 1982). Some scholars have argued that the inscription documents a formal treaty established between the Byzantine officials and the leaders of the *Barbaricini*, a group that played an important role in the letters of Gregory the Great. However, it maybe nothing more than a *portorium* or interior customs barrier found in many parts of the empire. Whatever the administrative reality behind the inscription it does provide testimony for the persistence of the interior/coastal division so important throughout Sardinian history, but also for ongoing complex interactions between the two regions.

The return of the Romans to Sardinia meant a new civic and religious order as well as social and economic changes. Important insights into developments that followed the reassertion of Byzantine power are provided by the Sardinian letters of Gregory the Great. Many naturally centered on the Christian community of Sardinia, but the fluidity of the military, social, and religious situation on the island meant that the Pope had to concern himself with many problems beyond the religious sphere (Boscolo 1978:37-46).

References to rustic pagans, idolatry, magic, and witchcraft in Gregory's letters show that pre-Christian beliefs still had a strong grip on the island populace, especially in the countryside (Gregory *Epistles* 4.23-27, 9.204; Turtas 1999:108-10, 123-26). Expressions of concerns about lingering paganism had become something of a literary topos among Christian writers by this time, but the fact that Gregory addressed his complaints to the archbishop of Caralis, the great landlords, the governor of the island and even to Constantina Augusta, the wife of the Emperor, shows that he was confronting a real problem of pre-Christian survivals in one of the most conservative countrysides of the Roman Empire.

Many of Gregory's letters focused on administrative concerns and problems with the behavior of members of the Christian community. The church in Sardinia had become large and complex. In one letter to Januarius, bishop of Calaris, Gregory speaks of *xenodochi, presbyteri, clerici, religiosae feminae, sacerdotes, episcopi,* and *monasteria.* Elsewhere we read about a *monasteria ancillarum,* an *abatissa monasterii,* a certain Pompeiana who established a *monasterium* in her own house; *clerici;* various church properties in the countryside, and a number of deacons (Gregory *Epistles* 1.46; 4.9, 46, 59, 81; 3.36; 9.65, 102, 203-204; 11.13; 14.2).

Gregory mentioned ecclesiastical abuses at all levels and of all types in his letters, especially the conflicts between the religious and civic authorities (Gregory *Epistles* 1.47, 5.38, 10.17, 11.7). He also had to serve as an ombusman in defending island interests against the Byzantine administration. In the last year of his papacy Gregory dispatched his administrator of ecclesiastical lands to Constantinople to seek relief for the land-owners of Sardinia. His own clergy was not above reproach. Gregory had to address a complaint that Januarius had ploughed up a neighbor's harvest without permission and then attempted to move boundary stones that marked their respective domains (Gregory *Epistles* 14.2; Turtas 1999:105-106).

The coastal Christian-interior pagan divide continued to concern the Pope, though progress was made in bringing the natives into the fold. In 594 Gregory praised the efforts of the Byzantine Dux Zabardas in converting the *barbaricini* of the interior. Gregory also wrote to a native leader named Hospito, commmending him on his profession of Christianity. These persistent efforts at proselytism appear to have had their effects, for we read in a later letter that many of both the provincials and the barbarians were now celebrating the Christian faith (Gregory *Epistle* 11.12).

The letters also provide a rare insight into the Jewish community on Sardinia. In 599 Gregory censured the Bishop of Caliaris for letting Christians desecrate a synagogue. Attacks by Christians on the Hebrew community in Sardinia remind us of the long history of Judaism in Roman-Byzantine Sardinia (Gregory *Epistles* 9.195; Boscolo 1978:42-43; Urso 1997:70-72). Mention has already been made of the dispatch of Jews by Tiberius to fight banditry on the island. Most of the rest of our evidence for Judaism is mortuary and relatively late. The largest Jewish necropolis

Jewish epitaph in the museum at Sassari.

currently known on Sardinia is that at Sulci (Noy 1993:229-33), probably dating to the 4th-5th century and documenting the presence of a modest-sized Jewish community. There are four inscriptions at one burial complex and a fifth at another. One of the graves belonging to a woman named Beronice had painted a menorah on it, the Latin inscription *in pace* and *shalom* in Hebrew. Another belonging to a man named Juda had an inscribed palm branch and in Hebrew "peace on Israel" and "amen."

Other attestations for a Jewish presence are more scattered. A tombstone from Tharros had the Hebrew inscription 'Tomb of Reubon, son of . . .' on it (BMTharros 48, n. 111). The most common Jewish associated objects are mold-made lamps with a menorah impressed on them, several of those have been found at Turris, Tharros, Sulci, and Cagliari, the last dating to the 4th century AD. Examples have also been found at smaller sites like Cuccurada-Mogoro and Barisoni-Tertenia (Rowland 2001:143).

Urban Life in the Late Empire

In considering the changes that took place in the cities during the Late Antique-Early Medieval period it is worth remembering the shape and limits of Sardinian urbanism even during the Roman period. Most of the coastal cities were survivals from the Punic period, retaining many pre-Roman qualities while adopting some of the amenities of High Imperial urbanism. In the interior even a major administrative center like Forum Traiani was a rather small place, and most of the other communities named in the itineraries little more than way stations and market centers.

Urban life throughout the Empire had been changing profoundly long before the barbarians appeared on the scene. The elites, who had traditionally sustained the cities, faced their own economic and social problems and had to constrict their involvment in urban life. Changes in life style meant that the wealthy turned more to their rural estates. Sumptuous villas were more characteristic of this epoch than new public buildings. The Imperial administration was seriously distracted with other problems and could provide little patronage for urban centers, especially those in the west. The old urban elites weakened or disappeared. In town after town public buildings decayed and civic institutions atrophied (Dyson 1992).

The triumph of Christianity changed the structures and functions of urban life in diverse ways. Many members of the elite had not only embraced Christianity but had become bishops and other church officials. Pagan associated structures like temples, theaters, and baths were closed or neglected, and their associated rituals terminated. At the same time the Christian community developed its own urban ceremonies and created the spaces and structures necessary to carry them out. One should not focus exclusively on the decay of baths and theaters, while neglecting to mention the splendid new churches that were rising in so many communities.

Caralis as the chief Roman city on the island serves as an important barometer to measure these Late Imperial changes. There is evidence of insecurity and the breakdown of urban order. Recent excavations under the church of Saint Eulalia have revealed remains of what appear to be fortifications of the 5th-6th centuries that straddled and blocked the main road leading to the port (Angiolillo et al. 2002:41-47), but there is also recent evidence for the repair of existing public and private buildings between the 4th and the 7th centuries and even the construction of new ones. A particularly interesting set of remains was found on the Via Sauro 750 m west of the central Piazza Carmine. It was a vast, prestigious *domus* with bath that saw several rebuildings before being abandoned not before the 13th century (Mongiu 1995).

Our best sense of the importance of Caralis as a new Christian city comes from the accounts of the North African exile Fulgentius of Ruspae. The Vandals were devout Arians and used Sardinia as a place of exile for orthodox clergy. Fulgentius was sent there first in 508-509 and again in 517-18. On the first occasion he was accompanied by as many as 220 clerics and bishops. The enthusiastic reception he received on his second arrival indicates not only the size of the Christian community at Caralis but also the general vitality of the city.

Fulgentius was welcomed hospitably by Brumasius, Bishop of Caralis, and allowed to build a monastery outside of the city adjacent to the special cult place of S. Saturno. The combination of the shrine of the local martyr and the monastery of the holy exile provided a new Christian focus to the city. The large number of *mausolea* that were built near those holy places testifies to the ritual shift but also to the presence of a prosperous elite. Inscriptions of the pre-Vandalic, Vandalic, and Byzantine periods found in the area of San Saturno during the 17th century provide further testimony to the developing Christian community of Caralis ((Pani Ermini 1982-1984; 1992). Architectural and material culture evidence for Late Imperial occupation at Turris is also abundant. The city had a flourishing Christian community that was by the mid-4th century centered in the southern suburban area. A martyrs' shrine was constructed at the place where later would rise the church of San Gavino (Poli 1997; Spanu 2000:115-40). A recently discovered early Christian tomb from Porto Torres had a mosaic epitaph commemorating the pious couple Septimia Musa and Dionisius (Guillou 1996:243-46). The thermal complex known as the *Palazzo di Re Barbaro* was converted into a religious or a residential/public building in this period. Some time between the late 6th and the early 8th centuries an inscription in Greek was erected over the lintel of the building celebrating a great victory by the consul and Duke Constantinos over the Lombards and other barbarians who had attacked the island by land and sea. While the bath facilities were closed down the building of a fountain in the 5th-6th centuries AD suggests the continued operation of the water supply (Villadeiu 1984:286-95).

Ceramic imports into Turris continued to be abundant and were dominated by North African wares. The supply of African red slip pottery continued down into the 7th century AD. For much of this period North African amphorae are the dominant imported form, but toward the end they diminish to only about 50% of the total with most of the rest coming from the eastern Mediterranean. That follows patterns of pottery imports found elsewhere in Italy and shows that Sardinia was very much linked to wider Mediterranean commercial trends. The discovery of 9th century Byzantine and Arabic coin hoards at Torres documents its ongoing economic vitality at the dawn of the judicate (Turtas 1999:168).

Pottery imports into Olbia begin declining as early as the late 3rd or early 4th centuries AD, appearing to reflect an economic downturn caused by the silting of the harbor. The link with Rome that had contributed to the city's rise during the Late Republic and Early-Mid Empire became less important, when the Imperial capital was transferred to Constantinople. There are relatively few early Christian inscriptions from Olbia, but the city did have an early bishop and two Byzantine castra (Bruschi 1996; Spanu 1998:117-19, 187-88, 196-97).

Tharros provides considerable evidence of both the continuity and change characteristic of this period. Sadly, the reconstruction of developments has been hindered by the poor documentation of Late Antique remains during the hurried postwar excavations. The presence of North African ceramics shows continuing trade with the wider Mediterraean (Serra 1995). We know that one bath complex was turned into a Christian complex in the 5th-6th centuries. As with many cities the new needs of the Christian community produced shifts in urban focus. Near the northern cemetery of the city the church of S. Giovanni Battista in Sinis was established in the late 6th or early 7th centuries. It was destined to become the episcopal seat of Tharros (Spanu 1998:84-85, 89-91).

Excavations at Cornus have provided considerable evidence for the transformation of the still poorly documented Roman city into a Christian community. As early as the 4th century the suburban bath complex was converted into a church. During the 4th-7th centuries a funerary area developed around the church, including a building that was probably an episcopal basilica and a baptistry. Excavations in the cemetery area produced evidence for funerary meals (Giuntella 1999). At some later date the settlement was strengthened by a new fortification system. Occupation at that *castrum* continued into the 8th century, and Cornus itself does not seem to have been abandoned until the 10th century (Zucca 1988a; Spanu 1998:97-98, 195-96).

Nora in contrast presents a pitiful example of urban decline. Sand filtered into the city, and at one point a rude structure was built over one of the streets, testifying to the collapse of the urban grid. Many buildings, including the small baths were abandoned. By the 5th century the theater had fallen into disuse, and habitations were being built into its ruins. Storage and work structures as well as residences reutilized materials from earlier monumental buildings (Tronchetti 2000a:33-66, 147, 180).

All, however, was not in ruins. In the 425-450 period the city's aqueduct was crudely patched, indicating that the city still had need of an external water supply. More important was the construction of an impressive new Christian basilica in the western part of the city. It measured 33x22 m, far larger than the episcopal basilica at Cornus. The addition of such an impressive church indicated not only considerable local resources but also a goodsized Christian congregation (Spanu 1998:44-45; Tronchetti 2000a:173-76).

The only community beyond the coastal zone that showed any significant sign of urban life was Forum Traiani now named Chrysopolis and designated as the military headquarters for the island. There is some archaeological evidence for a military presence during the Late Antique period and some traces of a Byzantine period fortification (Spanu 1998:65-66). A pagan water-cult site and cemetery on the outskirts of the city was transformed probably during the 5th century into a martyrs' shrine and cemetery complex dedicated to the local martyr S. Lussurgiu. That was rebuilt in the 6th century and continued in use thereafter. The late 5th-early 6th century mosaic pavement discovered in the crypt of the church has its best parallels in North Africa. It is tempting to see that as a reflection of the influence of North African Christian exiles. Ceramics and jewelry found at S. Lussurgiu show occupation continuing into the early 8th century (Zucca 1999; Spanu 2000:97-114).

This transitional period also saw the foundation of new communities. The most important of these was the city of Oristano at the junction of the Forum Traiani-Othoca and Tharros-Othoca Roman roads. Recent excavations at the site of the later cathedral have demonstrated an iniital occupation in the 5th-6th century. The Byzantine church of S. Michele in the 12th century became the cathedral of Oristano (Spanu 1998:60-65).

The Countryside in the Late Empire

Survey archaeology and more careful excavations are providing increasing evidence for a continuity of rural occupation into Late Antique-Early Medieval times. Nine of 17 Roman sites in the Villamar area survived into the late Roman and even into the Byzantine periods. Late Imperial occupation has been documented in the region S'Abba Druche-Bosa, just north of the Temo (Paderi 1993; Satta 1996). A farmhouse at Funtana Mura-Sorrabile remained in use into the 5th century, and the village at S. Nicola-Magomadas persisted into the middle of the 6th century. The nearby villa at S. Maltine/S. Giovanni had occupation into the 7th century and possibly beyond. Part of the large village at Nuraghe Cobulas-Milis continued to be inhabited in the 7th century (Cossu and Nieddu 1998:45; Biagini 1998:674-75, 679-82; Santoni et al. 1991: 952-76; B. Serra 1995: 188-93).

Reconstructing the Christianization of the Sardinian countryside is very difficult due both to the complexity of the process and the very

The Roman villa bath converted to a church at Silago.

limited evidence. It does appear that some villas were converted into Christian centers. The so-called basilica at Geremeas was probably part of a villa complex and might date to the 5th century AD. The Christian church at Nostra Signora di Mesumundo-Silago, which probably dates to the 6th-7th century, was incorporated into an abandoned villa. The baths that were often the most substantial structures in villas were often reused for ecclestiastical purposes. The villa baths at San Cromazio-Villaspeciosa were apparently first converted into a church in the 4th century. That building was renovated again in the late 5th-early 6th centuries and was still in use as a cult place and burial center in the 7th century, when the importation of datable pottery ceased (Tronchetti, Pianu et al. 1982). The church at Santa Maria-Villasimius was also constructed in a villa bath structure. It continued in use at least until the 7th century (Tronchetti and Fanni 1982). The *tepidarium* of the rustic baths at San Lorenzo-Ussana was turned into a church, as was the bath at Santa Maria-Vallermosa (Pautasso 1985). The bath of the villa at S. Andrea-Narbolia appears to have been converted into a church in the 5th century. Part of the baths at Santa Filitica-Sorso was converted into a chapel in the 6th century and continued in use until at least the 9th century, for a lead seal of Pope Nicolas I (858-67) was found in the ruins. There was also a small Byzantine village on the site (Cossu and Nieddu 1998:55). The villas in the locality Santu Luxori and Bangius-Barumini experienced a similar transformation by the 5th century (Lilliu and Zucca 1988:21-25).

Varied social and religious processes were probably at work. The villas had stood at the center of large estates and places where the locals were accustomed to assembling on festive occasions. The rural nobility often spearheaded the conversion of the countryside, and their villas became places of retreat, proto-monastic institutions. The career of Paulinus of Nola on the mainland provides a well-documented example, but Sardinia probably had its elite, rustic converts. The baths were well constructed, sturdy, and spacious and therefore suited to Christian assembly. Neglect, the breakdown of the water supply systems, and Christian disapproval of regular bathing certainly contributed to making these structures available for Christian use.

Documenting the spread of rural Christianity outside the elite villa centers is more difficult. The evidence consists of a few ill-dated sacred sites and scattered finds such as the late 3rd-early 4th century Christian lamps from Galtelli and Serramana and a glass vessel representing Christ as orator or law giver from Ittiri (Pani Ermini and Zucca 1989). It can be presumed that we are dealing with a slow process of conversion and that the Sardinia rural areas not located near to administrative or military centers would not have been considered minimally Christian until well into the Middle Ages.

The arrival of the Byzantines in the 6th century AD produced other changes in the Sardinian countryside. The government established fortified garrisons and strategic hamlets at key defensive points. There is definite evidence for a Byzantine military installation at the so-called Castello di Medusa. Pottery and other material of the 7th century document the continued use of the Roman military station at Castro-Oschiri in the Byzantine period (Cavallo 1981; Spanu 1998). Probable Byzantine military settlements have been located at S. Andrea Frius, S. Vittora-Serri and Bora (Rowland 1981:20; Spanu 1998: 181-83; Rowland 2001:101). The medieval castles of Barumele-Ales, Senis, and Laconi may have had Byzantine antecedents (Poisson 1992; Spanu 1998:19-181).

Mortuary evidence also documents this rural military presence during the Byzantine era. At the church of S. Pietro di Sorres-Borutta, not far from Torralba, four iron spear points were found in a tomb. Military equipment including 8 spear points was recovered from Moseddu-Cheremule (Caprara 1988). Burials of the late 8th century at nuraghe Domu Beccia-Uras included metallic objects belonging to the equipment of cavalry and infantry. Military style fibulae have an even wider distribution (Rowland 2001:140).

In the hamlets each colonist was provided with sufficient land to maintain a horse and a family. Indeed the word for these soldier-farmers, *kaballaris,* survived into the next millennium (Paulis 1983:21-25). Equestrian exercises associated with religious festivals, such as the Ardia at the feast of St. Constantine in Sedilo, are particularly common in the towns of interior Sardinia and may derive from those Byzantine settlers (Piras 1966:64-66). The presence of these Byzantine soldier-farmers had other long-lasting influences. The late 7th-early 8th century Byzantine *Farmer's Law* continued with certain modifications to regulate Sardinian rural relations until 1827 (Paulis 1983:30-32; Fois 1990:145-50). A number of the basic agricultural terms preserved in the Sardinian language (as for threshing, vineyard, grape harvest, beeswax, and uncultivated land) derived from Byzantine Greek (Paulis 1983:34-51).

11

Attack, Isolation, and Autonomy

he new Roman Empire that Justinian sought to create in the west did not survive very long. By the 7th century the Longobards had come over the Alps and conquered much of Byzantine Italy. While this weakening of Byzantine power on the mainland had only a limited initial impact on Sardinia, the expansion of Arab land and sea power into the central and then the western Mediterranean during the late 7th and 8th centuries produced major challenges. In 698 Carthage fell to the Muslims, and the North Africa coast so close to the island became once again a hostile shore. The island was now vulnerable to an enemy that came in from the sea. Its position as the bulwark of Byzantine power in an increasingly Islamic Mediterranean was reinforced by the fall of Ceuta on the Strait of Gibraltar (Brett 1978; Rowland 2001:145).

Soon the Arabs began attacking Sardinia. The first recorded Arab raid came in 705 and was directed against Sulcis. Several others are mentioned during the 8th century. Einhard, the historian of Charlemagne's court, records four raids between AD 807 and 813 (Boscolo 1978:55-61). The raids resulted in the destruction of property, the enslavement and transport to North Africa of Sards captured by the Muslims, and the movement of some coastal populations toward the interior.

Islamic sources mention two new communities established in North Africa, both called Sardaniyah, whose populations were presumably composed of captured islanders (Rowland 2001:147-49). However, these attacks gradually tapered off, and after 822 the Arabs left Sardinia in relative peace for nearly a century (Boscolo 1978:61-67).

These incursions have left some traces in the archaeological record. At Tharros an 8th century mass burial has been associated with a Muslim raid, perhaps the incursion of ca. 752-53 when the Muslims were said to have remained for some time and collected tribute. Two vessels found at Tharros with Arabic inscriptions on them might be associated with that occupation (Serra 1998). The destruction of the fortified baths at Nora in the 8th-9th centuries seems to have been the result of an Islamic attack. Burnt levels and broken tombstones around the church of S. Saturno in Cagliari may document an Arab raid on that city (Tronchetti 1985a:80-81).

What was unexpected was that the Muslims, while they continued to raid Sardinia down into the 11th century, made little effort to conquer the island or even use it as a regular launching pad for attacks on the mainland. There is virtually no evidence for long-term Arab settlement in Sardinia. The testimonies of an Arab presence are limited to a few Arab toponymic words, a small body of Arabic inscriptions, and some trade objects and coins (Oman 1970; Marini and Ferru 1993: Rowland 2001:147). Three Cuftic inscriptions have been found on Sardinia at Assemini, Cagliari, and Olbia, but all date to after the main period of Arab attacks. The example from Assemini, a dedication to a certain Maryam, daughter of Atiya al-Sarrag, dates to the 11th century. These documents suggest the presence of small, moderately well-to-do Muslim communities living peacefully in some of the port cities (Oman 1965).

The Moslem hegemony in the central and western Mediterranean had indirect consequences for the island. Once more Sardinia became a place of refuge as administrators, soldiers, ecclesiastics, and civilians fled both the hostile power and the alien religion. While it is uncertain whether Sardinia actually achieved the full status of a Byzantine province or theme, it certainly hosted a considerable number of Byzantine administrators and soldiers. Symbolic of this transfer of governmental power was the presence of an Imperial mint that continued operation in Sardinia down to c. AD 720 (Piras 1966: 100-101). The strong Byzantization of the island was under way. The genetic kinship demonstrated by scientific analysis between the Sardinians and the Greeks finds its best explanation in the combination of Byzantines already present and refugees just arrived (Turtas 1999:140, 144-45).

The most important religious refugee was a holy corpse, the remains of St. Augustine that were transported to Cagliari from North Africa in the late 7th century. His stay on the island was brief. Sometime between 721 and 725 his relics were purchased by the Lombard King Liutprand and shipped to Pavia. While the sale certainly reflected a perceived Muslim threat to the island, it was also an indication of growing Lombard power and the desire on the part of the Byzantine administrators to curry favor with this important mainland power (Hallenbeck 2000).

The Byzantine administrators on Sardinia found themselves increasingly isolated, especially with the expansion of Germanic power on the

Italian peninsula and the Muslim conquest of Sicily that started in 827. They were expected to show at least nominal loyalty to Constantinople, and they did maintain some contacts. A contingent of Sardinians was present at the coronation of Constantine Porphyrogenitus (913-59), an emperor who had a bodyguard of Sardinians (Boscolo 1978:76-77).

Those who governed Sardinia had to display considerable flexibility, imagination, and independence in carrying out policy for their isolated island. Most important was the need to cultivate and placate the emerging powers on the mainland. The sale of the relics of Augustine to Liuprand of Pavia should be seen in that light. With the rise of the Carolingians under Charlemagne and his successors the Sardinians initiated diplomatic overtures to the Franks. In 815 an embassy of Sardinians from Caralis visited the Carolingian court (Casula 1992:159, 550). When the Frankish general Count Bonifatius passed through the island on his way to war in African waters, he found Sardinia to be an *insula amicorum*. Coins of Louis the Pious discovered in various parts of the island testify to economic contact with the Carolingians (Rossi-Sabatini 1935). But the impact of these Frankish contacts should not be exaggerated; Sardinia remained essentially a Byzantine island.

The Religious Struggle Between Byzantium and Rome

The position of the Byzantine administrators on Sardinia was further complicated by the fact that while its people remained devoted to the Greek Orthodox Church, outside pressures pulled the island's rulers toward Rome. The bishops of Rome were gradually imposing their own brand of religious orthodoxy, and the Byzantine emperor lived in an increasingly uneasy relationship with the Pope. The Eastern Church was developing its own set of doctrines and rituals and was itself increasingly divided by doctrinal disputes. Conflicts between a geographical proximity to Rome and a spiritual identity that linked its people to Constantinople created new tensions on the island.

The religious problems worsened over the centuries. The ecclesiastical establishment in Sardinia initially identified with the Roman church. At the Lateran Council of 649 Bishop Deusdedit of Calaris together with Valentinus of Turris and Boethius of Cornus supported the Roman position against eastern- centered monothelitism (Zucca 1985:388-95; Turtas 1999:149-50). An intensifying cultural, linguistic, and doctrinal identity with Byzantium, however, drew the Sardinian clergy increasingly into the orbit of Constantinople. That trend was reflected in such episodes during the mid-7th century as when Euthalios, Bishop of Sulci, wrote his profession of orthodox Roman faith in Greek, and when Citonatus, attending the councils of Constantinople in 680 and 692 also made a declaration adherence to Rome, but signed the documents in Greek (Turtas 1999:149-54).

Events like the Iconoclastic Controversy increased the hostilities between the Byzantine emperor and the pope and raised more problems for the Sardinian Christians. Increasingly they became a Greek rite church, and by the 8th century the island was probably subordinate to the patriarch of Constantinople. The Sardinians, however, also sought to maintain some relations with Rome. There was two Sardinian neighborhoods, *vici Sardorum*, in or near Rome and in Rome a monastery especially associated with Sardinians (Turtas 1999:166; Rowland 2001:145-46). During the middle years of the 9th century, Pope Leo IV (847-55) asked the judex of Sardinia to send a contingent of armed Sardinians, youths or adults to aid him in protecting Rome (Lilliu 1993).

These religious conflicts and compromises worked themselves out on a variety of more mundane levels ranging from the cultivation of certain saints by the ruling elite to the devotions practiced by the rural populace. Representative of the complex interaction between the two ecclesiastical cultures was the education of the early 11th century Saint Giorgio of Suelli. Son of a serf of a noble lady, Greca de Surapen, he had managed to become literate in both Greek and Latin "according to the custom of his people" (Cannas 1976:39, 44-47).

Greek monks played an important part in maintaining Byzantine Christianity on the island. The history of Greek monasticism on Sardinia is difficult to reconstruct, since so many of the rituals, institutions, and even the physical structures of Byzantine monasticism were replaced by Roman practices. The importance of the cults of the Byzantine saints including special veneration for the angels, and the survival of Greek music and art, religious calendars, and liturgical rituals reflects the long-term impact of the teaching of the Greek monks (Rowland 2001:146).

Byzantine religious art and architecture was assuredly more widespread on Sardinia than we realize today. A comprehensive picture of the physical world of the Sardinian Byzantine church is difficult to reconstruct because so many religious centers were rebuilt during later centuries, when Latin Christianity dominated the island, but some structures and parts of structures did survive the influx of Romanesque and Gothic art forms that came with the Pisans and Genoese. Greek crosses and hemispherical domes designed in the Byzantine manner can be seen in churches like San Nicolo di Trulles, San Vero Congiu, and San Giovanni di Assemini. Fragments of Byzantine church decoration reused in later structures provide frustratingly limited insight into former splendors (Boscolo 1987:93-99; Spanu 1998:151-52). Recent research has documented the strong Byzantine influence on the religious architecture in the hinterland of Cagliari. Repair work at the Romanesque church of S. Giorgio (Sant'Iroxi)-Decimoputzu, for instance, has shown that it was built above a Byzantine church (Paulis 1983:274). Other types of Byzantine religious art are also rare. The paucity of Sardinian icons can be attributed either to the iconoclastic conflicts or to their systematic destruction by Latin religious authorities (Boscolo 1987:101-102).

The most powerful testimony to the religious impact of the Byzantine Greeks on the island is the large number of churches and toponyms dedicated to Greek saints. Anastasius appears 13 times, Andreas 33, Barbara 81, Basil 22, Constantine 18, Elias 22, Helena 49, Michael 99, Nicholas 51, and Sophia 9. Such place names are likely to survive, even if the individual churches were rebuilt in post-Byzantine styles. The distribution map of such holy place names shows a considerable overlap with the discovery of archaeological finds of the Byzantine period (Boscolo 1987:105-107).

The Emergence of the Judicate

No event is more closely associated in Sardinia with the long history of island identity than the emergence of the autonomous domains known as the judicate. The judicate is surrounded in Sardinia with romantic traditions of medieval autonomy and independence that recall the English idealization of Magna Carta and yeoman independence. The statue of Eleanora of Arborea that dominates one of the principal squares of Oristano is a testimony to the strength of that particular part of Sardinian historical ideology.

The origin of the *judex* as a political leader in medieval Sardinia was the complex series of political changes that marked the transition of Sardinia from a Byzantine province to a semi-autonomous territory. The title of *provincialis iudex* had been used to designate the governors of the province from at least the time of the Theodosian Code (*Cod.Theod.* 9.1.13). Other terms also appeared in the early Byzantine period. In the inscription at Turris celebrating a victory over the Lombards the commander Constantine described himself as *hypatos* (*Notizie degli Scavi* 1928: 256-59). During the 10th century Constantine Porphyrogenitos used the Greek term *archon* in referring to the governor of Sardinia.

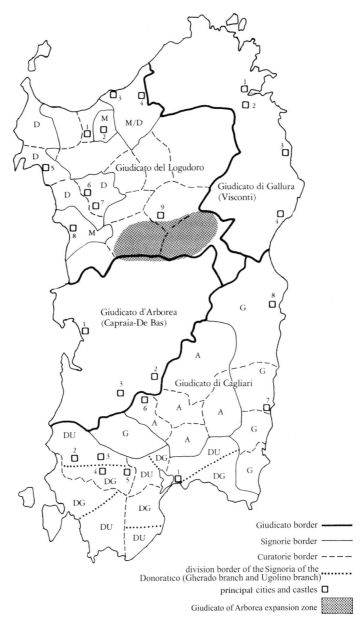

The territories of the Sardinian judicates in the 13th century
(after Conde et al. 1987).

Behind the façade of Byzantine continuity reflected in those titles, however, distance, isolation, and political realities within the island were producing changes. Three interconnected processes reshaped government in Sardinia during the years leading up to the millennium. The first was the consolidation of both civic and military authority in a single official. The second was the growing independence of the officials who vied for the conferral of the Latin title of *judex* by the government in Constantinople. The third was the division of island authority into the four distinct judicates that defined Sardinian government for much of the medieval period.

The question of the time and circumstances of the emergence of the four judicates has been much debated among Sardinian historians. The documents are few, and long-standing claims to supremacy on the part of certain judicates further clouded historical reality. It is known that by 873 Pope John VIII was already referring to *principes Sardiniae* (rulers of Sardinia). A document of 1392-3 claimed that the ruling house of Arborea had existed for 500 years. If accurate that text would support a late 9th-century date for the establishment of that particular judicate dynasty (Milia 1987:2.225).

A system of semi-independent rulers would have provided better local defense for the island in the face of sporadic hit and run attacks of the Arabs. The best time for the start of the process of localization would have been the 8th-9th centuries, when the Muslim conquest of Sicily increased the threat from sea. The gradual division of the island into four judicates had a logical basis in the island's geographical and ethnic-cultural realities and in historical developments going back to the Roman period. Significantly all four had their early capitals in former Roman centers (Casula 1992:193-295; Poisson 1992:312-15). The judicate of Cagliari in the southwest was initially centered at St. Igia, a locality protected by lagoons and swamps. The judicate of Arborea started at Tharros, then moved to S. Giorgio, and by 1070 was centered at Oristano. The judicate of Torres or Logudoro was documented in the 9th century at Porto Torres. Its capital then was transferred to Ardara, nearly 50 km inland and closer to the borders with Gallura and Arborea and eventually to Sassari. In the northeast the judicate of Gallura had its principal center at Civita-Olbia (Rowland 2001:151-52).

The judicates preserved Byzantine rituals, state titles, and instruments of governance such as the seal, emblems, and chancellary formularies (Besta 1908:45-55, 1909:1-14; Boscolo 1978:115, 121-23, 160; Casula 1992:226). During the 11th, 12th and even into the 13th century regal daughters were given Greek-derived names like Giorgia, Elena, Sofia, and

Anastasia. With time, differences in political identity emerged. The northern judicates were closer to Corsica and the mainland and received more Frankish and Italian influences, writing their seals in Latin rather than in Greek. The judicate centered at Cagliari in the south, however, remained much more Greek in character.

Over time their capitals acquired a certain level of cultural and architectural sophistication. The royal palace of Arborea at Oristano, which survived at least in part until 1907, was for its time and place an imposing structure, housing an extended royal family and a considerable retinue. The *judex*, his wife the *judikessa*, their siblings, children, and close relatives as well as the personal armed guard of the *iudex* all lived there (Gaviano 1985:17-27, 57; M. G. Mele 1999:36-40). The importance of a judicial capital was also reflected in the cathedral architecture as S. Igia at Cagliari, a substantial building with a large bishop's palace (Fois 1986:211-12).

The *judices* of Sardinia like so many rulers in Medieval Europe could not dwell permanently in any single city. They and their courts traveled around the judicate, making their power visible, administering justice, controlling their nobility, and attending to the needs of the subjects. The death of one *judex* of Torres *in sa villa de Sorso* shows that they had country estates, which they used to control and exploit the countryside (Artizzu 1995).

As one would expect of rulers who were heirs to the Late Roman-Byzantine system, they created their own bureaucracies, though the conditions of the island meant that they were primitive by Byzantine or even Norman standards (Boscolo 1978:160-61; Casula 1992:167-83). Administrators of the *judex* oversaw both the state property and the ruler's private domain. Officials bore names like *majore de camera, majore de caballos, majore de canes,* and *majore de vinu* that defined their role within the court structure. In each judicate a proto-parliament, the *corona de logu,* also developed, giving some political voice to the local magnates. The major prelates also played a significant role in developing and administering governmental policy as well as in protecting their ecclesiastical interests. Each judicate guarded its own frontiers, looked after its own political and commercial interests, and had its own set of laws.

The territory of each judicate was divided into districts (*curatoria*) overseen by a *curatore*, not infrequently a member of the royal family with administrative and some judicial responsibilities. Each district had its own mini-parliament, the *corona de curadoria* that sent representatives to the proto-parliament of the *corona de logu* (Besta 1909:66-82). The *curatoria* contained a number of villages, each administered by a headman (*majore de villa*). Individual villages often controlled considerable territory, some private and fenced in, some owned in common. That common land was regularly divided among the members of the community according to need. Inhabitants of the villages were organized into *scolca*, consortia of four contiguous villages, headed by a *maiore* and charged with protecting cultivated lands from invasions of animals (Boscolo 1978:162-63).

Judicate society was divided into three classes: free *liberois, liveros, lieros*, some of whom were *mannos* or *majorales*, who were the only ones considered truly free, *collibertos*, and *servos*. Assemblies of larger and smaller groups of notables are also mentioned, gatherings that were grand social occasions providing the opportunity for the exchanges of serfs and property.

Through much of the 10th century and into the early 11th century Sardinia developed on the Byzantine derived judicate model, creating the last distinctive indigenous social and political system in the island's long history. During that time the island enjoyed a period of relative freedom from outside attack, but political and religious developments in the wider Mediterranean began to break that calm and end the isolation. Now under the dynamic leadership of Mugahid Muslim Spain posed new military threats. In 1015 120 boatloads of Spanish Saracens attacked the island, successfully assaulting Cagliari, apparently killing the *judex* Salusio, and capturing many women and children. Mugahid attempted to establish strong points in the south of Sardinia, including the fortress Castro de Mugete. That terrifying presence was short lived, but it had major long-term consequences for the judicates of Sardinia (Boscolo 1978:123-29). The emerging sea powers of Pisa and Genoa feared that the island would become a staging ground for Islamic attacks on the mainland, and they took their own initiatives to keep the Arabs out. In 1016 combined Pisan and Genoese naval forces defeated a Saracen fleet that once again threatened the island (Boscolo 1978:127-29).

The papacy, while concerned about the fate of a Sardinia threatened by Islamic power, was also caught up in the rivalries between Pisa and Genoa. Papal diplomacy was inclined to support Pisa, and some promises were apparently made ceding Sardinia to the Pisans. The Genoese regarded this papal action as against their interests and prepared to resist Pisan claims to the island. The stage was set for major new outside interventions in Sardinia.

12

Italian Power and Local Resistance in High Medieval Sardinia

The shifting alliances on the mainland that would soon change the political landscape of Sardinia were accompanied by increasing religious tensions that led to the final break between Constantinople and Rome. The schism that took place between Rome and Byzantium in 1054 would have enormous consequences for Sardinia. The *judices* felt themselves caught between the Greek religious identifications of the islanders and the pressures brought by the papacy and the increasingly more powerful maritime states on the west coast of the Italian mainland. On the religious front the Papacy gradually but inexorably emerged victorious. The *judices* began to swear allegiance to Rome. Greek monks on the island felt themselves under increasing pressure and in some cases were forced to abandon their monasteries and properties. The *judices* some of those to the Latin church. They also invited the Benedictines to establish Latin monasteries where there had been Greek ones before and to found new ones in different parts of the island. The Benedictine presence led to significant religious, social, and economic transformations in the Sardinian landscape and to conflicts among the various secular and religious forces.

Some of these political and religious transformations can be documented in detail. In 1063 Barisone I de Lacon-Gunale, *judex* of Turris, sent ambassadors to Desiderius, abbot of Montecassino, requesting monks to establish a religious house in his territory (Boscolo 1978:135-37). A dozen set out from Cassino, but they were attacked by the Pisans before they had left Italian waters. Eight survived, returning shaken to their mother house. Apparently the Pisans saw that direct Sardinian overture to Montecassino as a threat to their expanding power base on the island. A second attempt to import Benedictines two years later was more successful. The monks were given what had previously been Greek monastic structures in Silago along with *coloni* and *servi* (*CDS* sec. XI, doc. G). The Benedictine presence was further reinforced in 1065-66 when Torchitorio I of Calaris did penance for an incestuous union and a number of homicides donated six

CIVITAS

Ampurias
Castelgenovese● Viddalba ►
Terranova ►
AMPURIAS
●Tempio
S. Pietro ►
di Simbranos
Torres ►
Sassari● Oschiri
Ploaghe ● ●
●
TORRES Ardara Castra
Bisarciu ► ●Ozieri
BISARCIU **CASTRA**
Sorres **GALTELLI**

BOSA Galtelli●
●Bosa
► Orotelli ►
Bosa **OROTELLI**
Vecchia Ottana●

S. GIUSTA

Oristano
►
Tharros ► ●S. Giusta **ORISTANO** **SUELLI**
►Usellus
●Ales
Terralba **USELLUS**
TERRALBA ●Suelli

DOLIA
CAGLIARI
●San Pantaleo
Iglesias
● Santa Gilla
SULCIS ►Cagliari
Tratalias
►
S. Antioco

► early or
intermediate see
● final see

0   20
├──┼──┤ km

Dioceses and Episcopal seats in Sardinia from the
11th to 13th centuries.

churches to Montecassino for the establishment of monasteries (*CDS* sec. XI, doc. 7).

This process of ecclesiastical transformation was slow and complicated. In 1113, 50 years after the Great Schism, the monastery of S. Nicola di Trullas was donated to the Camaldulensians. Some Greek monks, called *donnos hermitas* still dwelt there and were allowed to remain. The survival of Greek traditions can be seen in relatively minor practices, like different attitudes toward clerical facial hair. Byzantine priests wore beards, a custom that had been condemned in the western church. Despite the fact that the Council of S. Giusta in 1226 repeated the prohibition against beards, church inventories of 1227 mentioned combs for combing the bishop's beard before mass. The bishop in a 14th century relief at S. Serafino-Ghilarza is depicted as bearded (Boscolo 1978:103; Fois 1990:80).

These new Roman monasteries soon waxed wealthy and powerful. The first pioneers from Montecassino were followed in due course by large cohorts of Benedictine monks and nuns. Other orders joined in the exploitation of Sardinia. Victorines from the Abbey of St. Victor in Marseilles are attested in Calaris and Gallura by at least 1090 (Turtas 1992:389-91). Camaldulensians from Tuscany had arrived by the early 12th century, Vallumbrosians also from Tuscany were in Sardinia by 1127 and Cistercians by 1149 (Delogu 1953:137-46; Zanetti 1964:15-21, 1974:37-53). Their tightly structured communities contrasted with the more individualistic monastic traditions of the Byzantine world and proved more effective as forces both for religious conversion and economic development.

The Latinization of the Sardinian church not only affected the monastic orders. The papacy also sought to create more regular diocesan structures on the island. A new diocese was created at Bosa some time before 1062, and that of Sulci was reconstructed between 1061 and 1073. The bishopric of Turris had been elevated to an archbishopric by 1074 (Turtas 1999:186-88). This emphasis on the administrative power of the bishoprics was highlighted by ambitious building programs in their sees, for example, the start of construction at the cathedral of Galtelli in 1090 (Coroneo 1993:79, 84).

The new Sardinian religious establishments soon became major economic forces. It has been estimated that the church and its monasteries ended up by owning 40% of the surface of the island (Cherchi Papa 1974:2.100-08). These ecclesiastical landowners also included institutions from outside the island. The Cathedral of Genoa and especially that of Pisa became major beneficiaries of Sardinian piety (Rossi Sabatino 1935:38; Polonio 1984). Donations to the Pisan and Genoese churches came from a

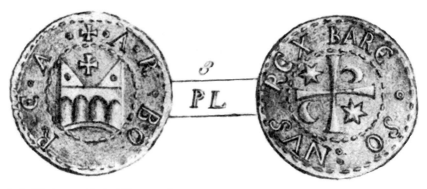

Seal of Barisone with the title rex on it.

variety of sources and for a variety of reasons. In 1082 Mariano, *judex* of Turris granted to the cathedral of S. Maria of Pisa five churches along with their rich properties, stating that the churches of his realm were "vacant and denuded of ecclesiastical doctrine and religion" and his subjects were living "in wicked sin." The desire to cultivate favor among the increasingly powerful Pisans was probably an equally important motive (Artizzu 1974:44-45; Turtas 1999:201-06).

This process of gift giving to Pisan and Genoese ecclesiastical establishments accelerated during the twelfth century. In 1106 the *judex* Torchitorio-Mariane of Calaris donated extensive properties including 40 dependent families to S. Maria de Pisas. The deed of gift provided an exact description of the holdings. Interesting is the use of the Nurak (nuraghe) de Isac as one point of reference. Two years later he added other gifts, including a ship laden with good salt to be sent annually to S. Maria and an exemption from various duties. All of these were thank offerings "for my kingdom and life which I recovered with great honor and victory with the help and assistance of all-powerful God and with the help and assistance also of very noble and brave citizens of Pisa" (Poisson 1996:166-68).

The sequence of events beginning in 1113 that led to the creation of the power base of the S. Maria of Pisa in Gallura was especially melodramatic. The origins lay in domestic politics with the judicate. Padulesa de Gunale, widow of the *judex* Torchitorio de Zori, was forced by her brother, the usurper Ittocore, to flee from the island to the protection of Pisa. She sought to strengthen her position in Pisa by donating a Sardinian village and her portion of the possessions of the church adjacent to it to Santa Maria of Pisa. Villanus, Bishop of Gallura, perhaps feeling under pressure from Pisa, witnessed the document of transfer. To secure his own dubious position in Gallura Ittocore confirmed his sister's gift and added more of his own. He also swore not to attack any Pisans in his territory (Schena 1996:98-102).

The Era of the Genoese and the Pisans

Accumulation of church property by the Pisans and Genoese was just one expression of their increasing involvement on the island. By 1088 Daiberto, Archbishop of Pisa, had become overseer of the church in Sardinia. In 1138 Innocent II granted the archbishop of Pisa primacy over both the diocese of Galtelli and Civita and the kingdom of Turris (Scano 1940:xi; Turtas 1999:214-15). Ecclesiastical influence was coupled to expanding political power as Pisa and Genoa took advantage of the often divided judicates to enhance their influence. By the 12th century they had become the dominant outside presences on the island and were increasingly the determining forces in local politics. Writing in the mid-12th century, the German chronicler Otto of Friesing attributed the failure of an embassy Frederick Barbarosa sent to garner support among the Sardinians to the influence of the Italians, reminding his readers that the "the profits Pisa and Genoa derive from the island of Sardinia" (Otto of Friesing *Gesta Frederici Imperatoris* 4.12).

This enhancement of Italian power derived to a great deal from the self-defeating machinations of the local dynasties. Relations among the judicates had always been tense, and increasingly the Sardinian rulers turned to outsiders for support in their internal dynastic conflicts. The Pisans and Genoese both played the various local powers against each other, while extracting concessions that helped expand their holdings on the island.

The vicissitudes of the ruling dynasties of both Calaris and Turris illustrate the growing mainland presence and the problems that it caused. In 1094 *judex* Turbini of Calaris, trying to curry favor with the Pisans exempted their merchants from customs duties and the local salt tax. The Calaris salt beds were among the most productive in the Mediterranean, and the tax exemption proved immensely profitable to the Pisans. It whetted their appetites, and eventually they achieved total control over the salt beds (Boscolo 1958:66-67, 85).

The dynasty of Turris had even more problems as it tried to weather complex internal politics and balance the two Italian powers[1]. When Costantino I of Turris died, his young son and successor, Gonnario, faced intrigues stemming from the machinations of the Genoese and the power plays of his local rivals, the de Athen family. In desperation he abandoned his homeland and fled to Pisa, where he took up residence in the house of a leading citizen, Cavalleri Ugo Ebriaci. He subsequently married Ebriaci's daughter, Maria, and decided to return to Sardinia to reclaim his judicate. He was accompanied on his quest by his wife, father-in-law, other leading men of Pisa, and by four well-armed Pisan galleys (Rowland 2001:195).

It looked for awhile as if the Pisans would become the controlling external power in Sardinia, but the Genoese were not willing to accept such Pisan domination passively. When Pope Gelasius II in 1118 and Pope Callistus II in 1120 expanded Pisa's privileges in Corsica and Sardinia, the Genoese attacked the port of Pisa itself. A truce was arranged in 1133 that granted Genoa some concessions on the mainland and in Corsica but did not markedly improve their position in Sardinia (Epstein 1996:40-53). The Genoese maintained the pressure and hostilities continued. The prolonged war between Pisa and Genoa finally concluded November 6, 1175 with a treaty that theoretically gave the Genoese a position on the island equal to that of the Pisans. This formal assertion of Genoese equality, however, came too late. The Pisans had established an economic and religious infrastructure on the island that the Genoese could not hope to match. That power reality was reflected in the relatively small portion of Genoa's trade that was conducted with Sardinia, when only in Arborea were they the dominant outside force (Pistarino 1981).

Pisan economic and political power reached its high point in the early 14th century. In 1300 about half of Pisa's total income derived from Sardinia. By one calculation in 1313 Pisa received from Sardinia an income of 100,000 florins against an expense of only 8,804 florins. Additional income also accrued to private individuals, many of whom owned vast estates, some dominated by newly constructed castles (Poisson 1988).

The Reaction of the Judicates

Because of the weaknesses and internal divisions within the judicates Pisan and Genoese interests expanded. Island political struggles and mainland power brokering continually undermined local autonomy in Sardinia as dynastic politics became ever more complex and self-destructive. One further example is illustrative. Costantino-Salusio III, *judex* of Calaris (c. 1163), had three daughters. One married Pietro, brother of Barisone II of Turris, who in time became Pietro-Torchitorio III, *judex* of Calaris. Pietro decided to strengthen his local power by prohibiting the Pisans from trading in his judicate and replacing them with the Genoese. That was not a successful move. In 1187 the Pisans attacked Calaris and expelled both the Genoese and Pietro himself (Petrucci 1986:235-41). Pietro fled to his brother Barisone at Turris, where he soon died. Pietro was replaced in Calaris by the pro-Pisan Oberto (probably Oberto Obertenghi of Massa), who assumed the title of Guglielmo I-Salusio IV de Lacon-Massa.

Similarly complicated power struggles took place in the other judicates. The result was that by 1200 Pisa effectively controlled three of the four judicates. The popes tried without success to counter the expanding power of the Pisans. Pope Honorius III in 1215 demanded that the Pisans abandon the fortress at Cagliari, but the Pisans ignored him. While their hegemony was occasionally threatened by Genoa, the Pisans remained the dominant power on Sardinia, weakening most of the judicates until they disappeared as independent political entities (Casula 1992:210, 250-51, 274-75). Only the arrival of the Catalans and the new national political system that they represented challenged Italian power on the island.

The rulers of Arborea alone managed to retain some independence of action. They accomplished that in part by their more effective use of Genoese support. Again gifts both religious and economic proved important instruments in the international power game. In 1131 Comita III of Arborea donated to San Lorenzo and to the commune of Genoa a church and a village with all of the appurtenances including "half of the mountains in which silver is found in my kingdom." Comita further promised to Genoa that after he acquired the judicate of Turris, he would grant them other possessions, including a quarter of the mountains containing silver in that kingdom. It was a successful short-term strategy, but the alienation to a foreign power of precious metal resources was an ominous development for the future economic health of the judicate (*CDS* sec. XII, doc. 41).

The subsequent history of the Arborese judicate revealed the limitations under which all these Sardinian rulers labored. Comita tried to gain control of the judicate of Turris, but all his attacks were repulsed. His aggression against his neighbor led to his being excommunicated by the Archbishop of Pisa and declared an enemy both of the Pisan people and of the other *judices* (Artizzu 1985:95-96). When Barisone II succeeded his father he decided to open his reign with a grand gesture of peace. His grandfather, Costantino I, had endowed and entrusted to the Camuldosians of S. Zeno in Pisa the monastery adjacent to the Byzantine church of S. Maria di Bonarcao. In 1146-47 Barisone II was ready to dedicate a new church at the site. He arranged that the ceremony be conducted in the presence of Villano, Archbishop of Pisa and his three fellow *judices*. That was the only-known occasion during this period when all four of the *judices* gathered together for such an event (Zanetti 1974:133-54); Coroneo 1993:103-108; 2000a).

The hoped-for peace did not last for long. Barisone, ever wary of the growing power of the Pisans, sought to establish new alliances through dynastic marriages outside the island. He repudiated his marriage to Pellegrina de Lacon in order to wed Agalbursa, daughter of Pons de Cervera, Viscount of Bas, niece of Ramon Berenguer IV, count of Barcelona and more importantly an ally of the German emperor, Frederick Barbarossa. The Catalans took advantage of this new alliance to establish a foothold in Arborea, assuming offices in the judicial administration and gradually accumulating vast estates in the territory (Rowland 2001:161).

Barisone in the end did succeed in extending his power across the island, and by 1164 he had proclaimed himself king of Sardinia. This was very much a pyrrhic victory, since his ambitions led to extensive borrowing from the Genoese. Because of that debt Barison was forced to grant Genoa and its citizens ever greater concessions, some of those at the expense of Pisa and the holdings of the Pisans in his judicate. Moreover, his overtures to Frederick Barbarossa bore their own bitter fruit, as Sardinia was sucked into the mainland struggles between Guelphs and Ghibellines. Ironically for Barisone that further reinforced the positions of the Pisans. In return for Pisan cash grants and naval support Barbarossa made the entire island of Sardinia their fiefdom. Pope Alexander III, enraged that Frederick had so disposed of territory that he regarded as his own property, turned his support to Genoa (Turtas 1999:256-57). That switch in papal position did not halt the weakening local power position on Sardinia.

Barisone's debt to the Genoese caused him increasing problems, and he was even briefly held hostage at Genoa. He was eventually allowed to return to his kingdom, but his title was reduced to King of Arborea. He was forced to provide pledges to satisfy his debts to Genoa and to concede land in Oristano to accommodate the needs of the Genoese merchants. Genoese pottery found in the excavations at the cathedral of Oristano reflects that closer commercial association (Depalmas 1995).

Barisone spent his last years trying to balance the rival claims of Pisa, Genoa, and Catalonia. His son and successor, Pietro I de Lacon Serra, continued that difficult struggle. To counter the influence of the Catalan faction in the entourage of his stepmother and that of his father's Genoese creditors and of the Genoese settled in Oristano, he took a Pisan wife and in 1187 made a donation to the cathedral at Pisa (Heer 1987:243).

The most serious new threat came from the Catalans. Ugone de Bas, the nephew of Barisone's Catalan widow, laid claim to the kingdom of Arborea. The Genoese, desirous of recovering money owed them by Arborea, mediated between the two parties. In 1192 an accord was reached between Ugone and Pietro whereby the two shared power. The period 1192-1353 saw Arborea survive as the only judicate still functioning as an independent state. Its rulers continued to play one external power against another, but increasingly Catalonia cast its shadow over Arborea and the rest of Sardinia.

The next critical moment for Catalonia, Arborea, and for Sardinia in general came in 1297 when Boniface VIII issued the bulls *Redemptor mundi* and *Super rege et regina*, which formally created a new Kingdom of Sardinia and Corsica and granted it in perpetual fief to the Catalan ruler Jaime II, King of Aragon and Valenza and Count of Barcelona (Abulafia 1994:234-52). Jaime was thus provided with a major justification to invade the island and lay claim to his kingdom. Jaime did not take precipitous action, spending more than two decades making careful preparations that included recruiting support among the Sardinian clergy. On June 13, 1323, he disembarked his invasion force at Palma di Sulcis in southwest Sardinia.

A long struggle followed (Simbula 1993:69-90). Jaime initially moved against the Pisan strongholds. Cagliari, Sassari, and the Gallura all fell into Catalan hands. In 1354 after a major naval victory over the Genoese his forces seized Alghero and began the Catalanization of that city. Remnants of that policy survive today, especially in the local dialect. The Iberian forces were not destined to achieve a quick and easy domination of the island, however, and the *judex* of Arborea was to have one more period of glory.

While the rulers of the judicates were engaged in their often mutually destructive rivalries a new social, political, and cultural order was emerging in Sardinia. An important role in this transformative process was played by new nobility. During the 12th century individual Pisan and Genoese families had established footholds in Sardinia. By the 13th century they had become major social, political, and economic forces (Day 1984:167-71). A good example was the Dorias of Genoa. As early as 1102 they had established castles in the north at such places as Alghero, Castelgenoese (now Castelsardo), and Casteldoria (Carta Raspi 1933:86-94). They also began intermarrying with the local ruling elite. Andrea Doria married Susanna, daughter of Barisone II, *judex* of Turris, around 1180. He then used that family alliance to persuade his father-in-law to support Genoa against the

Pisans. Another mainland family, the Malaspina, first arrived in Sardinia in 1016 and by the early 1100s had created a power base in the northwest of the island. They built castles like that at Serraville, positioned to dominate Bosa and the lower Temo Valley (Carta Raspi 1933:95-99; Fois 1981).

The rise of these new feudal families from the mainland was partly balanced by the emergence of Sassari as a communal city (Orlandi 1985:72-87; Castellaccio 1996a:136-228). Earlier in the Middle Ages Sassari had been an obscure village. By the High Middle Ages it had become a community increasingly animated by the ideals of civic liberty promoted by its new mercantile bourgeoise. In 1235-36 Sassari proclaimed its independence as a free commune, but Sardinia had few such cities, and the communal movement so important on the mainland never set deep roots.

More significant for both cultural and economic developments on the island was the growing power of the monastic establishments. The Benedictines by now had an extensive network of houses and a fully developed economic infrastructure. They had from the beginnig been expected to promote mainland church Latin culture on Sardinia. The first failed monastic expedition from Monte Cassino had included books in its baggage. A 1280 inventory from the monastery of S. Nicola di Trullas suggests that many of those books would have been liturgical works, such as Bibles, homilaries, passions, antiphonaries, sermons, missals, letters, psalteries, and manuals. An inventory of the property of the cathedral in S. Igia shows that in addition to liturgical texts the canons also possessed medical and scholastic works (Cossu Pinna 1986; Turtas 1999:231-32).

The degree to which the Benedictines and other orders were able to create an educated local clergy is open to debate. Some Sardinians became priors of their own monasteries, suggesting that they had received some Latin-based education in their own houses. In 1182 when Barisone of Arborea donated the church of S. Nicola di Gurgo to the Benedictines of Monte Cassino, he had to ask specifically for literate monks who would be capable of working in the chancellary and becoming bishops and other high ecclesiastical officials (CDS sec. XII, doc. 110).

The Benedictines were not alone in extending their presence on the island. The Victorines acquired extensive properties in Sardinia. They were responsible for the building or reconstructing more than two dozen churches in the south. Major projects included the church of S. Saturno at Cagliari and of S. Antioco in Sulcis. Victorine churches such as S. Maria-Utia, S. Platano-Villaspeciosa, and S. Maria di Sibiola-Serdonia remain among the most important monuments of Romanesque architecture in Sardinia (Boscolo 1958:117-19).

The Victorines could not escape being caught up in the complex power politics of medieval Sardinia. The Pisans drove the Victorines from their monastery in the Bagnaria area of Cagliari, replacing them with their own favored clerical order, the Hospitallers of the Misericordia (Boscolo 1958:86-90). The Victorines, aided by Pope Urban IV and the local archbishop, moved to reclaim their possessions, but they were driven off by force of arms. In the end they were restored to their monastery, if not to all of their endowments.

The Vallumbrosians and the Camaldulensians were closely allied to one another and to the interests of Pisa. In areas like the fertile hinterland of Turris in northern Sardinia the Vallumbrosians worked energetically to bring new land into cultivation and to develop irrigation systems, waterworks, and mills (Fois 1990:121-32). Vallumbrosian houses were concentrated in the northern portions of the island, where their properties came to form "an almost unitary monastic principality." However, Pietro of Arborea as part of his pro-Pisan policy also endowed them with some churches and properties in his judicate (Zanetti 1964:49-61).

The most important Camaldulensian foundation in Sardinia was the abbey of the Holy Trinity at Saccargia-Codrongianus. It was consecrated in 1116 by the *judex* of Turris in thanksgiving for the birth of an heir. The surviving remains of the abbey, with their striking black and white stone facings, represent a marvelous combination of Lombard, Byzantine, Tuscan, Tyrrhenian, and even possibly Islamic elements (Delogu 1953:77-78, 155-57; Coroneo 1993:137-44).

The Camaldulensians were also noteworthy among the monastic orders for their exploitation of the interior of the island. In 1139 the bishop of Ortoli granted to them the church of S. Pietro de Oddini. The clerics of that church came over time came to control a number of rural centers and villages where "the assiduous labor of the monks . . . attracted the wandering shepherds to a stable domicile and taught them the peaceful labors of agriculture" (Zanetti 1974:123-29).

The Cistercians arrived in Sardinia later than the other orders and departed sooner. There as elsewhere they were sought out for their skills in rural development. In 1149 Gonnario of Turris invited the first group to his kingdom. Half a century later his grandson, Comita, followed with another request that Clairvaux send more monks. He granted them the church of S. Maria di Paulis-Ittiri with a domain of 10,000 hectares, 300 *serbos*, 10,000 sheep and 300 horses (*CDS* sec. XIII, doc. 5).

The Cistercians were always great builders, although only fragments survive of what were once some of the architectural masterpieces

Abbey of the Holy Trinity at Saccargia-Codrongianus.

of Sardinia. Their first establishment in the judicate of Turris was at St. Maria de Corte, Cabuabbas-Sindia a monastery founded in 1149 (Delogu 1953:137-40). Today only parts of the transept, choir, apse, and sacristy as well as two chapels remain of what was once a 60-m long, three-naved church with accompanying monastic structure. Even these sad remains convey some sense of the quality of Cistercian architecture on the island.

Cistercian power and prosperity did not last for long. Predatory neighbors, the arrival of the Aragonese, unrest in the countryside, the Black Death, and climatic deterioration all contributed to their decline as a monastic force in Sardinia. St. Maria di Paulis, for instance, found its possessions systematically raided by families like the Doria (Meloni 1990). Two of the five Cistercian establishments on the island had been abandoned by the late 14th century and S. Maria de Corte was vacated by 1458.

The economic and social impact of the monastic orders can best be appreciated from a study of the monastic registers called *condaghi* (from the Greek *kontakion*). Three survive from Logudoro (S. Pietro di Silki, S. Nicola di Trullas, and S. Michele di Salvennor) and one from Arborea (S. Maria di Bonarcado). Another *condaghe* was discovered in an archive in Pisa (Rowland 2001:170-79). Dated to 1190 it is a record of the donations made by Barisone II di Lacon, *judex* of Turris, to the Hospital of S. Leonardo di Bosove that was affiliated with S. Leonardo di Stagno in Pisa.

The *condaghi* provide a detailed picture of transactions in the areas where ecclesiastical properties were located, but the sample is uneven. No parts of Calaris and Gallura are covered by the documents that survive and only limited portions of Turris and Arborea. They present a geographically restricted world about which generalizations must be made with caution. For example, when a year of famine is mentioned in two documents we cannot be sure if it was merely a local or regional phenomenon or something that had wider implications for the island.

There are other limits to the evidence provided by the *condaghi*. Some well known elite families appear frequently in their pages, others only sporadically. The important de Gital clan is documented only rarely, and their recorded donations were not impressive. In the non-condaghi donation records of another church, however, Furatu de Gital and his wife are mentioned as giving to the church extensive estates, 40 serfs, 12 liturgical books and about 1,700 animals (*CDS* sec. XII, doc 15-16).

The *condaghi* document acquisition of property by donation, sale or exchange, various acts related to serfs, and litigations. The exquisite detail they can provide is seen in the record of the exchanges between the monastery of S. Nicola di Trullas and a certain Dorbeco Furca: "I [the abbot] traded with him vineyard for vineyard. He gave me the vineyard in the valley of Nuce, I gave him the vineyard of S. Marcu in the valley de Suberciu. Being equally content we traded vineyards and fruit, and because he had more fruit than I, I gave him a piece of mutton" (*CSNT* 26).

The *condaghi* also provide intimate insights into the mentalite and social actions of medieval Sardinians. Such a window into the past is provided by the complex history of the benefactions of a certain Comita d'Iscanu (*CSPS* 152-53, 161, 181, 228, 358-59). Comita, thinking that he had arrived at the moment of death, donated a vineyard to the church. He temporarily recovered, but soon found himself again in what seemed to be another prolonged death agony. That new crisis pressured him to make still more donations to the church. First he deeded everything he possessed in Silki: lands, vineyards, and serfs' labors. Still lingering on the point of death, he upped his donations, adding his garden and a spring with groves of nut trees and mulberries. Yet another crisis brought more gifts of lands, vineyards, and gardens as well as the decision to become a monk. His mother, donna Vittoria de Iscanu, brought him to the monastery saying, "if God and S. Pietro heal my son, S. Pietro will have as reward my uncultivated land of Presnaki and all the fruit trees that are there, both mine and those belonging to my brothers." Her pious plea was granted, for the last entry related to Comita declared, "God and S. Pietro healed him and she donated both her uncultivated land and fruit trees."

The appearance of Donna Vittoria, taking the situation in hand and convincing her brothers to donate their share of what was presumably common patrimony to secure the health of their nephew, provides important insight into the place of women in medieval Sardinia. In the extant *condaghi* women are shown as acting autonomously, possessing and disposing of property on their own account. Women of all classes and conditions donated, bought, and sold property. They were frequently noted as proprietors, and they initiated litigation. Often their mutual approval (*a boluntade de pari*) was necessary for property transactions. Calculations from the condaghi indicate that some 20-25% of the property in rural Sardinia was controlled by women. It is to be expected that rich and powerful women (called *donna* in the documents) would appear more frequently in the documents of the church. However, the poor and non-noble females, including serfs, are also mentioned as having made gifts. For instance, Maria Canba donated an abandoned vineyard in order to finance masses for her daughter who had been taken away to Pisa (*CSNT* 76).

The law did stipulate that a woman, married or not, could not make a testament without her father (or lacking him some other male relative) serving witnesses. The father or the other relatives were apparently there more to observe the transactions than to control the outcome. The important point was that women had property and could make wills.

The law provided other testamentary protections for women. Both husbands and wives had to leave half of their property to their surviving spouse. A husband could not independently dispose of property inherited from either of her parents. While a wife could not participate in a contractual act or affect a sale without the authorization of her husband, a widow was free to dispose of property (Di Tucci 1915).

David Herlihy has demonstrated that in certain regions of medieval Europe women at certain times had more control over property than has generally been recognized (Herlihy 1962). It would seem that Sardinian women were even more independent than their contemporaries on the continent. That autonomy extended beyond the sphere of property transactions. Women are mentioned as engaged in commercial transactions. They also had freedom of movement. In 1211 a woman named Furada of her own free will followed her lover to Genoa and there bore him a daughter (Boscolo 1957a:xxiv).

The *condaghi* also present a picture of social and economic complexity on medieval Sardinia greater than has sometimes been assumed by historians. This can be appreciated from the information on sales and donations listed in the *condaghi*. Some of the individuals involved were clearly great landlords, but a fair number of small landowners also appear. Serfs' donations could also be substantial. When Terico Melone, a serf, died childless, his properties included large tracts of lands and vineyards.

The churches were able to consolidate the small holdings of pious peasants. They benefited from the continual transferal of property from secular to church estates and were often able to consolidate the small holdings of pious peasants. A certain Gottifriedo at the time of his death in 1253 donated to the church 4 entire farms, a quarter of 3 others, a quarter of 13 *saltos* of land, 2 vineyards, 2 meadows, and three quarters of a lagoon and the stream that flowed into it. They were scattered around the Oristanese from Cabras to Guspini and from Sardara to Neapolis. The result of this ongoing donative process was the creation of ecclesiastical latifundia, extensive land-holdings spread over wide areas of rural Sardinia. In 1218 the diocese of Sulci possessed 14 churches and all of the lands, vineyards, and serfs that belonged to them plus 13 villages and five *saltos*. By 1365 the archdiocese of Calaris controlled 296 fields in grain or barley, 45 vineyards, 11 gardens and 12 *saltos* scattered over the territory of 38 villages (Turtas 1999:283-85). This long succession of pious donations led to the church owning some 40% of the land in Sardinia. The alienation to the church of this much territory eventually weakened Sardinian secular society, especially as the locals competed with the increasingly large numbers of immigrant landowners from Pisa, Genoa, and Catalonia.

The *condaghi* also provide important insights into two of the most important social structures in medieval Sardinia, the family and the village. Two of the condaghi contain detailed information about the children born to serf couples. Demographers have reconstructed 84 offspring cohorts in one ranging in size from 1 to 7 children. The total number of children documented was 280, or 3.3 children for each parental couple. Striking is the fact that 140 of the children listed were females, yielding a sex ratio of precisely 100. Twenty families had 3 or more male children, but only 2 of these twenty had no daughter (Rowland 1982a). Females children are well represented in the sample

There were 69 offspring cohorts in the other document. There is a total of 226 children or 3.3 per parental couple, the same as in the first sample. However, here there were only 97 female children, yielding a sex ratio of 133. Five of the 19 families with 3 or more sons had no daughters, while the rest had an average of 1.3 daughters each (Rowland 1982a:119-20).

It is certainly possible that some of these differences are due to the limitations of the data. However, one important difference exists between the territories documented in these two *condaghi*. While both churches held varied agricultural lands, the possessions of S. Maria di Bonarcado included the territory of modern Austis and Neoneli situated in the uplands of the interior at 555-737 m. Four of the texts provide specific data for Austis and 2 others give more general data for Barbagia. The sex ratios are especially interesting. In the Austis texts there are 69 male offspring and 39 females, a sex ratio of 177. Combining Austis and Barbaria, there are 93 males and 56 females, a sex ratio of 166. Two-thirds of the male-only offspring cohorts in the entire *condaghi* are from these two upland zones. One has to wonder whether such differences in the upland zones where pastoralism was predominant were the result either of female infanticide or the sale of surplus girls to slave traders (Rowland 1982a:120-21).

Clearly the village remained at the heart of social organization in medieval Sardinia, but even with the evidence from the *condaghi* we are not in a position to talk in detail about the realities of village life. While the location of many villages can be determined, we can as yet say relatively little about their physical or socioeconomic structures. They seem generally to have been open, unprotected by walls. The houses were mudbrick or stone huts, generally no more than one story high and built directly on the ground without foundations. They rarely employed plaster or mortar or had a tile roof (Day 1973; Terrosu Asole 1975; Artizzu 1995a:25-34).

Although Medieval archaeology in Sardinia is a discipline still in its infancy, it is beginning to provide some information to complement our literary sources. The preliminary reports of the well-conducted excavations at the village of Geridu near the church of S. Andrea at Sorso show the potential of archaeological information (Milanese 2001). The archaeologists found remains of a Roman village on the site, but no apparent continuity between antiquity and the medieval community. The medieval village covered about 14 hectares. The houses varied in size from 30-43 to 66 m^2 of useable space. Their interiors were divided into a stall and a cooking-living area. The latter had a hearth in one corner and the amphorae used for storing beans and grain in another. Roofs were made of wooden beams and tile. The floors were of beaten earth. Sherds of Tuscan, Ligurian, Campanian, Catalan, and Islamic pottery were recovered, documenting varied contacts with the wider Mediterranean world. In addition to grains the diet included the expected sheep and goat, beef, and to a lesser extent pig, horse, and deer, with small amounts of chickens, birds, rabbits, and molluscs. Occupation at the village extended into the early 15th century, when the combined impact of plague and political insecurity led to its abandonment.

Research by Medieval archaeologists in Sardinia on both the domestic and imported ceramics is beginning to provide a more complex picture of the productive capacities of the rural world and of the trading networks that linked these medieval Sardinian villages. They have identified a so-called judical ware, a painted pottery mainly in the form of jugs and casseroles that was produced in Sardinia, primarily in the south. More than half of the sites that have so far yielded this pottery are located in the Cagliari area (Dadea 1995a).

The village of Santu Jaccu on the shore of Stagno Pauli 'e Sali at the boundary of Cabras and Nurachi was a small agglomeration of single-roomed mudbrick huts with reed roofs. Notwithstanding the relative poverty of the site, the archaeologists recovered along with the judical wares large amounts of imported pottery including Ligurian, Pisan, North African, Iberian, and south Italian wares (Dadea 1998). Excavations at the village of Bia 'e Palma yielded a large number of locally made wares as well as late 13th or early 14th century archaic maiolica (Salvi 1987). Indigenous ceramic production was also represented by the so-called proto-judical vases found at nuraghe Adoni-Villanovatulo.

Reports on Medieval burials are becoming more common and more informative, although Sardinian Medieval mortuary archaeology is still relatively underdeveloped. Christian religious practice limited the quantity of grave goods, so the information derived from burial studies archaeology will never match that from settlement archaeology. Grave goods, if present at all, were limited to small amounts of locally made pottery, copper rings and buttons, and the occasional iron weapon[2]. The extra-island world was represented by such items as the lead pilgrimage souvenir found in a 12th century burial in Silargus or the 12th-13th century Piedmont coin found in a burial at the church of Ss. Proto, Gavino, and Gianuario-Muros (Serra and Coroneo 1989:236-41).

As we reach the 13th and 14th centuries, the documentation on the economy improves, especially as it relates to external trade. The general picture is one of a basic core-periphery economy with Sardinia providing raw materials for overseas productive enterprises. Agro-pastoral activities that yielded grain and sheep products were central to the island export economy (Deliperi 1935; Tangheroni 1973:107-26). In the words of David Herlihy, "the opening up of the central Mediterranean, especially Sardinia and North Africa, brought the first of two revolutions to the fur industry: the wide use of the lamb pelt. In the 13th century . . . lamb pelts . . . storm the market" (Herlihy 1958:148-49). Sardinian wool was used extensively in blanket manufacturing at Pisa, appearing more frequently in Genoese markets after 1250. Sardinian cheese was also much appreciated at Genoa, Lucca, Florence, and Pisa. Cow and deerskins were also exported, as was salted meat (Manca 1974).

Agricultural products also played a role in the external trading economy. Grain, barley, dried fruit, honey, cork, wine, and wax were all exported, much of it coming from estates belonging to continental and ecclesiastical establishments. Exports of cotton and linen are mentioned in the Medieval sources (Artizzu 1965; Day 1984). By 1288 Pisa was exporting 3,000 tons of salt from Sardinia, and in 1349-50 the Catalans shipped out more than 2000 tons. By the late 13th century coral was being mined and dispatched to Marseilles to be converted into jewelry (Bautier 1968; Balletto 1997).

This core-periphery economy based heavily on the supply of raw materials meant that imports into the island were mainly humble objects for daily use, including finished cloth products, household items in metal, pottery, dyes, soaps, spices, sugar, wine, and oil (Tangheroni 1985:97-103, 141-46). In 1237 a certain Sardo of Rivalta went from Genoa on an island sales trip loaded with 2,000 ceramic bowls, which had cost him 10 lire (*Documenti inediti Liguri* nr. 77). Most of these traders did not rise even to the level of itinerant merchants. An example of such a wandering salesman was Fulcherio di Andrea who received pottery worth 80 Genoese lire to sell throughout Sardinia (Day 1984:141; Marini and Ferru 1993:21-24).

Mention should also be made of the slave trade that impacted the island in a variety of ways. Islamic raiders carried off a large number of Sardinians, but Christians also dealt in slaves, including their own co-religionists. While it is impossible to know generally how widespread Christian slave trading was, the practice was certainly not negligible. It has been estimated that slaves comprised as much as 10% of the population of Genoa in the early 13th century (Verlinden 1977:2.446). It appears that the slave trade preyed predominantly on women, valuable as servants and concubines for the affluent of Pisa and Genoa. One of the earliest references to Pisans in the condaghi is to a Pteru de Sune of Sassari, who had seized a young woman and sold her to the Pisans. However, male slaves are also found, employed as day laborers and in trades requiring heavy physical work (Verlinden 1977:2.427-450). Muslims were also enslaved. Their presence on Sardinia is reflected in names like Sarakina, Sarakinu, and Sarakinelle. The Islamic traveler Ibn Jobair (1145-1217), who visited the island in 1183, found about 80 of his co-religionists for sale near Capo San Marco-Tharros (Ibn Jobair 1952:27).

Gradually the foreign merchant community in Sardinia expanded and organized itself. From the small beginnings of a few merchants visiting Sardinia's ports, more and more merchants, bankers, and artisans settled on the island. They normally congregated in their own quarters of a city and patronized their own churches. Some succeeded in using Sardinia as a trampoline for success in the wider Mediterraean. With time these extra-territorial communities at centers like Turris, Cagliari, and Oristano organized themselves as autonomous entities on the model of their home-cities, becoming virtually independent of the states in which they resided. They had their own consuls, representatives, laws and courts operating under the protection of the local *judex* (Poisson 1995). A major turning point in the evolution of these merchant communities came in the 1200s when the mainland communes imposed their own governance over the merchants of the ports. They were now managed by consuls sent from Pisa or Genoa with full civil and criminal jurisdiction over their fellow citizens (D'Arienzo 1984).

Sardinia's Last Hurrah

This long story of independent Sardinia opened with the image of the statue of Eleanora of Arborea that dominates the piazza in Oristano that bears her name. It was a 19th century creation, combining Medieval nostalgia with local Sardinian political aspirations. It will now close with her story.

In Sardinia it becomes difficult to distinguish the legendary Eleanora from the historical ruler (Turchi 1984:176-88; Mattone 1995). In 1392 she issued the *Carta de Logu*, the legal code that remained in effect in Sardinia until 1827. She became in certain respects the Joan of Arc of Sardinia, a woman who personifies the Romantic nationalism of the island. Her *Carta* acquired some of the historical significance of England's *Magna Carta*.

The reality behind Eleanora's reign is complex, but her history is central to the last years of Sardinian independence. She was the daughter of Mariano II and the wife of Brancaleone Doria. Her brother, Mariano IV of Arborea, had decided to resist the invading army of Aragon. He had considerable success in driving back the Aragonese. With his death in 1376 his son, Ugone III, continued the war but was killed in an uprising at Oristano in 1383. His sister, Eleanora, then chose to govern in the name of her young son Frederico. She remained a major force in Sardinian politics until her death from the plague in 1402. At her death Arborea controlled much of the island, with only small pockets around Alghero and Cagliari remaining loyal to Aragon. The judicate of Arboria survived only a few years after her death, the dynasty being replaced in 1410 by the podesta Leonardo Cubello. The succeeding decades saw the Aragonese reassert their power on the island. In 1470 Leonardo Alagon, marchese di Oristano, raised the final banner of resistance. He and his forces were defeated by the Spanish on the field of Macomer June 16, 1478.

With the hopes of an autonomous Sardinia having perished on the field of Macomer, our story can come to an end. From that point onward foreign powers would control Sardinia. That foreign domination would first be political and social. Then, with the 19th century and such acts as the division of the communal land and the cutting of the ancient forests it became economic as well. An authentic, indigenous folk culture survived in the rural areas, but to a large degree native Sardinia would be defined by negatives, its passive, stubborn resistance to these outside forces.

What is striking is how long the Sardinians had managed to maintain their distinctive cultural dialogue with the outside world. The other large islands of the Mediterranean were not so lucky. Sicily has had a long and complex history, but almost all of it has been shaped by outside groups. Sicels and Sicans disappeared early in Antiquity. On Cyprus the indigenous history extended later, but even there outside forces were shaping the history of the island by the Roman period. On Crete there is a longer, stronger indigenous history, but few would attribute to it great creativity and independence beyond the archaic period of the 6th century BC.

Sardinia instead retained elements of island cultural autonomy and even *de facto* political independence from early prehistoric times to the end of the judicates. We have argued for a long prehistory shaped mainly by insular developments and relatively little by the outside invasions so beloved of earlier generations of archaeolgists. Neither Phoenicians nor Carthaginians ever succeeded in fully conquering the island, and even Rome was less transformational in its assertion of power in Sardinia than elsewhere in the Empire. The weakness and rivalries of external powers gave Sardinia a high degree of maneuvering room and independence throughout much of the Middle Ages. Only with the rise of new powers like Aragon and Piedmont did the era of Sardinian autonomy really end. What survived was a folk society represented by language, dress, and customs, but one increasingly marginalized in the more remote geographical regions of the island. Slowly in the 19th and 20th centuries the educated elite of the island articulated a new consciousness of the island's unique history.

Bibliography

Abulafia, D. 1993. *Commerce and Conquest in the Mediterranean 1100-1500.*Aldershot, Hampshire: Variorum.

— 1994. *A Mediterranean Emporium.* Cambridge: Cambridge University Press.

Acquaro, E. 1974. Il tipo del toro nelle monete puniche di Sardegna e la politica barcide in occidente. *Rivista di Studi Fenici* 2:105-107.

— 1989. Il tofet di Tharros: note di lettura. *Quaderni della Soprintenza Archeologica di Cagliari e Oristano* 6, suppl:13-22.

Acquaro, E., M. E. Aubet, and M. H. Fantar 1993. *Insediamenti fenici nel mediterranro occidentale.* Rome: Libreria dello Stato,Istituto poligrafico e Zecca dello Stato.

Acquaro, E., and A. Mezzolani 1996. *Tharros.* Rome: Libreria dello Stato, Istituto poligrafico e Zecca dello Stato.

ADR. 1999. Un tesoro sotto il lungomare. *Unione Sarda* 25 Settembre 1999.

AE. *L'Annee Epigraphique.*

Agus, P. 1983. Il Bes di Bithia. *Rivista dei Studi Fenici* 11:41-47.

Anati, E. 1984. *I sardi. La Sardegna dal paleolitico all' eta romana.* Milan: Jaca Book.

Angiolillo, S. 1973-74. Il mosaico di Orfeo al Museo di Torino.*Studi Sardi* 23:181-89.

— 1975-77. Una galleria di ritratti giulio-claudi da Sulci. *Studi Sardi* 24:157-70.

— 1981. *Mosaici antichi in Italia. Sardinia.* Rome: Istituto poligrafico e Zecca dello Stato.

— 1985. A proposito di un monumento con fregio dorico rinvenuto a Cagliari. In *Studi in onore di Giovanni Lilliu per il suo settantesimo compleanno,* 99-110. Cagliari: n. p.

— 1986-87. Il teatro-tempio di Via Malta a Cagliari: una proposta di lettura. *Annali della Facolta-Perugia* 29:57-81.

— 1987. *L'arte romana in Sardegna.* Milan: Jaca Book.

— 1987a. Modelli africani nella Sardegna di età romana: il mosacio di Santa Filitica a Sorso. *L'Africa Romana* 4:603-14.

—1994. Ricezione e rielaborazione di modelli africani nel mosaico di età romana in Sardegna. In *Rapporti tra Sardegna e Tunisia dell' eta antica all eta moderna,* 47-57. Cagliari: Università.

—2000. Le fasi romane della necropoli di Tuvixeddu. In *Tuvixeddu. La necropolis occidentale di Karales. Atti della tavola rotunda internazionale,* 18-26. Cagliari: Edizioni della Torre.

Angiolillo, S. 2002. *Cagliari, le Radici di Marina.* Cagliari: Scuola Sarda.

Angioni, G., and A. Sanna, eds. 1996. *L'architettura popolare in Italia. Sardegna,* 2nd ed. Rome-Bari: Laterza.

Angius, V., comp. 1833-56. Articles on Sardinia in G. Casalis. In *Dizionario geografico, storico, statis-*

tico, commerciale degli Stati di S.M. il Re di Sardegna, passim. Torino: G. Maspero.

Antona, A., ed. 1991. *Olbia e il suo territorio*. Ozieri: Edizioni Il Torchietto.

Antona Ruju, A., and M. L. Ferrarese Ceruti 1992. *Il nuraghe Albucciu e I monumenti di Arzachena*. Sassari: C. Delfino editore.

Antonaccio, C. 1995. *An Archaeology of Ancestors*. Latham, MD: Rowman & Littlefield.

Artizzu, F. 1965. Agricoltura e pastorizia nella Sardegna pisana. In *Fra il passato e l'avvenire. Saggi storici sull'agricoltura in onore di Antonio Segna*, 71-84. Padova: CEDAM.

— 1973 Il testamento di Gottifredo di Pietro d'Arborea. In *Pisani e Catalani nella Sardegna mediovale*, 25-38. Padova: CEDAM.

—1974. *L'Opera di Santa Maria di Pisa e la Sardegna*. Padova: CEDAM.

—1985. *La Sardegna pisana e genovese*. Sassari: Chiarella.

—1995. I giorni di giustizia (Festività religiose e corone giudicali). In *Societa e istituzioni nella Sardegna medioevale* 35-44. Cagliari: Deputazione di storia patria per la Sardegna.

— 1995a. Sulla casa sarda nel medioevo. In *Societa a istituzioni nella Sardegna medioevale*, 25-44. Cagliari: Deputazione di storia patria per la Sardegna.

Assorgia, A. 1998. *Alberto Lamarmora e il progresso delle conoscenze geologiche e minerarie in Sardegna nell'ottocento*. Cagliari: C.U.E.C.

Aste, M. 1990. *Grazia Deledda: Ethnic Novelist*. Potomac, MD: Scripta Humanistica.

Atzeni, C., ed. 1998. Compendio delle caratteristiche chimiche, metallografiche e isotopiche dei reperti metallurgici di Baccu Simeone-Villanovaforru. *Quaderni della Soprintendenza Archeologica di Cagliari e Oristano* 15:150-71.

Atzeni, E. 1959-61. I villaggi preistorici di San Gemiliano di Sestu e di Monte Ollàdiri di Monastir presso Cagliari e le ceramiche della "facies" di Monte Claro. *Studi Sardi* 17:1-216.

— 1979-80. Menhirs antropomorfi e statue-menhirs della Sardegna. *Annali del Museo Civico di La Spezia* 2:9-64.

—1992. Reperti neolitici dall'Oristanese. In *Sardinia antique. Studi in onore di Piero Meloni in occasione del suo settantisimo Compleanno*, 35-62. Cagliari: Della Torre.

Aubet, M. E. 1993. *The Phoenicians and the West*. Cambridge: Cambridge University Press.

Baffico, S. and G. Rossi 1988. Il nuraghe S. Antine di Torralba. Gli scavi e i materiali. In *Il Nuraghe Santu Antine nel Logudoro-Meilogu*, ed. A. Moravetti, 61-184. Sassari: C. Delfino.

Bagella, S. 1998. Corridor nuraghi: territorial aspects. In *Papers* from the EAA Third Annual Meeting at Ravenna 1997: v. III *Sardinia*, ed. A. Moravetti, 113-36. Oxford: Archaeopress.

Balletto, L. 1997. Pescatori di corallo marsigliesi in Sardegnanel XIII secolo. In *Pesca e pescatori*, 35-39. Milan: Leonardo arte.

Balmuth, M., ed. 1986. *Studies in Sardinian Archaeology II: Sardinia in the Mediterranean*. Ann Arbor, MI: Univeristy of Michigan Press.

Balmuth, M., and R. J. Rowland, eds. 1984. *Studies in Sardinian Archaeology*. Ann Arbor, MI: University of Michigan Press.

Barbanera, M. 1998. *L'archeologia degli italiani. Ranuccio Bianchi Bandinelli*. Milan: Skiro.

Barnett, R. D., and C. Mendelson 1987. *Tharros, A Catalogue of Material in the British Museum from Phoenician and other Tombs at Tharros, Sardinia*. London: Published for the Trustees of the British Museum by British Museum Publications.

Barnett, W. K. 1990. Small Scale Transport of Early Neolithic Pottery in the West Mediterranean. *Antiquity* 64:859-65.

Barreca, F. 1974. *La Sardegna fenicia e punica.* Sassari: Chiarella.

— 1978. Le fortificazioni fenicio-puniche in Sardegna. In *Atti del primo convegno italiano sul Vicino Oriente antico*, 115-38. Rome: Centro per le Antichità e la Storia dell'Arte del Vicino Oriente.

—1983. L'archeologia fenicio-punica in Sardegna. In *Atti del I congresso internazionale di studi fenici e punici (Roma 1979)*, 291-310. Rome: Consiglio nazionale delle ricerche.

—1986. *La civiltà fenicio-punica in Sardegna.* Sassari: C. Delfino.

—1986a. Phoenicians in Sardinia: The Bronze Figurines. *Studies in Sardinia Archaeology* 2:91-110.

Bartoloni, P. 1973. Gli amuleti punici del Tophet di Sulcis. *Rivista di Studi Fenici* 1:181-203.

— 1981. Contributo alla cronologia delle necropoli fenicie e puniche di Sardegna. *Rivista di Studi Fenici* 9 Suppl:1-32.

—1983. *Studi sulla ceramica fenicia e punica di Sardegna.* Rome: Consiglio nazionale delle ricerche.

—1997. Un sarcofago antropoide filisteo da Neapolis (Oristano-Sardegna). *Rivista dei Studi Fenici* 25:97-103.

—1998. L'insediamento fenicio-punico di Bithia. In *Phoinikes B SHRDN. I fenici in Sardegna*, 80-83, 254-63. Oristano: S'Alvure.

—1998a. Monte Sirai. In *Phoinikes B SHRDN. I fenici in Sardegna* 85-90. Oristano: S'Alvure.

Bartoloni, P., and L. A. Marras 1989. Materiali ceramici di età romano-repubblicana recuperati in mare (Villasimius). *Quaderni della soprintendenza archeologica di Cagliari e Oristano* 6:185-97.

Basoli P., and A. Foschi Nieddu 1991. Il sistema insediativo nuragico nel Monte Acuto-analisi preliminare dei fattori geomorfologici esocio-economici. In *Arte militare e architettura nuragica. Nuragic Architecture in Its Military and Socio-economic Context. Proceedings of the First International Colloquium on Nuragic Architecture*, ed. Barbro Santillo Frizell, 23-40. Stockholm: Svenska Institutet i Rom.

Bautier, R. H. 1968. Le sel de Sardaigne et l'activité portuaire de Cagliari, M. Mollat. In *Le Rôle du Sel dans l'Histoire*, 203-25. Paris: Presses universitaires de France.

Bernardini, P. 1991. *Micenei e Fenici. Considerazioni sull'età precoloniale in Sardegna.* Rome: Istituto per l'Oriente C.A. Nallino.

— 1993. Considerazioni sui rapporti tra la Sardegna, Cipro e l'area egeo-orientale nell'età del bronzo. *Quaderni della soprintendenza archeologica di Cagliari e Oristano* 10:37-38.

—1993a. La Sardegna e i Fenici. Appunti sulla colonizzazione. *Rivista di Studi Fenici* 21:29-81.

—2000. I fenici nel Sulcis: la necropoli di San Giorgio di Portoscuso e l'insediamento del Cronicario di Sant' Antioco. In *La ceramica fenicia di Sardegna. Dati, problematiche,confronti. Atti del primo congresso internazionale sulcitan*, 29-62. Rome: Consiglio nazionale delle ricerche.

Bernardini, P., P. G. Spanu, and Raimondo Zucca 1999. *Mache. La battaglia del Mare Sardonio, Catalogo della mostra Oristano Antiquarium arborense, ottobre 1998-ottobre 1999.* Cagliari: La memoria storica; Oristano: Mythos iniziative.

Besta, E. 1908, 1909. *La Sardegna medioevale*, 2 vols. Palermo: A. Reber.

Biagini, M. 1998. Archeologia del territorio nell' *Ager Bosanus:* ricognizioni di superficie nel comune Di Magomadas (Nuoro). *L' Africa Romana* 12:667-93.

Binford, L. 1972. *An Archaeological Perspective.* New York: Seminar Press.

Bittichesu, C. 1998. La tomba di giganti di Barrancu Mannu (Santadi, Cagliari). In *Papers from the EAA Third Annual Meeting at Ravenna, 1997 v. III: Sardinia*, ed. A. Moravetti, 137-44. Oxford: Archaeopress.

Blake, E. 1997. Strategic symbolism: miniature nuraghi of Sardinia. *Journal of Mediterranean Archaeology* 10:151-64.

— 1997a. Negotiating Nuraghi: Settlement and the Construction of Ethnicity in Roman Sardinia. In *TRAC 96: Proceedings of the Sixth Annual Theoretical Roman Archaeology Conference*, 113-19. Oxford: Oxbow.

—2001. Constructing a Nuragic Locale: The Spatial Relationship between Tombs and Towers in Bronze Age Sardinia. *American Journal of Archaeology* 105,2:145-61.

Blasco Ferrer, E. 1984. *Storia linguistica della Sardegna*. Tübingen: M. Niemeyer.

Bondì, S. F. 1987. Monte Sirai 1988. Lo scavo nel tofet (campagne 1984 e 1985). *Rivista di Studi Fenici* 15:179-90.

— 1990. La cultura punica nella Sardegna romana: un fenomeno di sopravvivenza? *L' Africa Romana* 7:457-64.

Boninu, A., M. Le Glay, and A. Mastino 1984. *Turris Libisonis colonia Iulia*. Sassari: Edizioni Gallizzi.

Boscolo, A. 1957. Introduzione. In *Documenti inediti sui traffici commerciali tra la Liguria e la Sardegna nel secolo XIII*, ed. N. Calvini, E. Putzulo, and V. Zucchi, IX-XXXII. Padova: CEDAM.

— 1958. *L'abbazia di San Vittore, Pisa e la Sardegna*. Padova: CEDAM.

— 1978. *La Sardegna bizantina e alto-giudicale*. Sassari: Chiarella.

Bray, W. 1963. The Ozieri Culture of Sardinia. *Rivista di Studi Preistorichi* 18:158-62.

Brett, M. 1978. The Arab Conquest and the Rise of Islam in N. Africa. In *Cambridge History of Africa* 2:490-555.

Brizzi, G. 1989. *Carcopino, Cartagine e altri scritti*. Sassari: Università degli studi, Dipartimento di storia.

Broadbank, C. 2006. The Origins and Early Development of Mediterranean Maritime Activity. *Journal of Mediterranean Archaeology* 19:199-230

Broughton, T. R. S. 1951. *The Magistrates of the Roman Republic*. Cleveland, OH: Published for the American Philological Association by Case Western Reserve University Press.

Bruschi, T. 1996. Un saggio di scavo sull'acropoli di Olbia. In *Da Olbia a Olbia 2500 anni di storia di una citta mediterranea. Atti del convegno internazionale di Studi Olbia 1994*, eds. A. Mastino and P. Ruggeri, 341-52. Sassari: Chiarella-Sassari.

Bunimovitz, S., and R. Barkai 1996. Ancient Bones and Modern Myths: Ninth Millenium BC Hippopotamus Hunters at Akrotiri *Aetokremnos* Cyprus. *Journal of Mediterranean Archaeology* 9:85-96.

Calzolari, M. 1996. Introduzione allo studio della rete stradale dell'Italia romana:l'Itinerarium Antonini. *Memorie della Accademia dei Lincei* 9.7.4.

Campus, A., ed. 1994. *Padria-I*. Rome: Bonsignori.

Cannas, V. M. 1976. *San Giorgio di Suelli*. Cagliari: Editrice sarda Fossataro.

Caprara, R. 1988. L'età altomedievale nel territorio del Logudoro-Meilogu. In *Il nuraghe S. Antine*, 399-432. Sassari: C. Delfino.

Carandini, A., and A. Giardina 1993. Momigliano, Aldo Schiavone, and L. Cracco Ruggini. In

Storia di Roma 3,2. Torino: Einaudi.

Carta Raspi, R. 1933. *Castelli medioevali di Sardegna.* Cagliari: Edizioni della Fondazione Il Nuraghe.

Castaldi, E. 1969. Tombe di giganti nel Sassarese. *Origini* 3:119-43.

— 1999. *Sa Sedda de Biriai.* Rome: Quasar.

Castellaccio, A. 1996. *Sassari medievale.* Sassari: C. Delfino.

Casula, F. C. 1992. *La Storia di Sardegna.* Sassari: C. Delfino.

Cavallo, G. I. 1981. Il castello della Medusa. Un antico "castrum" Bizantino. *Archeologia Sarda* 67-85.

CDS. P. Tola, ed. 1861-68. *Codex diplomaticus Sardiniae.* Turin: Royal Printing House. E Regio typographeo.

Cecchini, S. M. 1969. *I ritrovamenti fenici e punici in Sardegna.* Rome: Consiglio nazionale delle ricerche.

Champion, T. 1984. *Prehistoric Europe.* London: Academic Press.

Cherchi Paba, F. 1974. *Evoluzione storica dell'attività industriale agricola caccia e pesca in Sardegna.* Cagliari: Sotto gli auspici della Regione autonoma sarda, Assessorato allindustria e commercio.

Cherry, J. F. 1990. The First Colonization of the Mediterranean Islands: A Review of Recent Research. *Journal of Mediterranean Archaeology* 3:145-221.

— 1992. Palaeolithic Sardinians? Some Questions of Evidence and Method. In *Sardinia in the Mediterranean: A Footprint in the Sea*, eds. R. H. Tykot and T. K. Andrews, 19-45. Sheffield: Sheffield Academic Press.

Ciomei, P. F. 1998. *Gli antichi martiri della Sardegna,* 3rd ed. Sassari: Poddighe.

Clarke, D. 1968. *Analytical Archaeology.* London: Methuen.

Cline, E. H. 1994. *Sailing the Wine-Dark Sea. International Trade and the Late Bronze Age Aegean.* Oxford: BAR.

Cocco, D., and L. Usai 1988. Un monumento preistorico nel territorio di Cornus. In *Ampsicora e il territorio di Cornus. Atti del II convegno sull' archeologia romana a altomedievale nell'Oristanese*, 13-24. Taranto: Scorpione.

Colavitti, A. M. 1999. *La presenza dei negotiatores italici nella Sardegna di età romana.* Oristano: S'Alvure.

Contu, E. 1952-54. Ipogei eneolitici di Ponte Secco e Marinaru presso Sassari. *Studi Sardi* 12,13:54-63.

— 1965. Nuovi petroglifi schematici della Sardegna. *Bollettino di Paletnologia Italiana* 74:69-122.

— 1988. *Il nuraghe S. Antine.* Sassari: C. Delfino.

— 1997. *Sardegna preistorica e nuragica,* 2 vols. Sassari: Chiarella.

— 1999. Pozzi sacri. Ipotesi ricostrutttive. *SACER* 6:125-48.

— 2000. *L'Altare preistorico di Monte d'Accoddi.* Sassari: C. Delfino.

Corda, A. M. 1999. *Le iscrizioni cristiane della Sardegna anteriori al VII secolo.* Città del Vaticano: Pontificio Istituto di Archeologia Cristiana.

Cornell, T. J. 1995. *The Beginnings of Rome.* London: Routledge.

Coroneo, R. 1993. *Architettura romanica dalla metà del mille al primo '300.* Nuoro: Ilisso.

— 2000. L'irradiazione delle maestranze della *ecclesia nuova* di Santa Maria di Bonarcado nel giudicato di Arborea. In *Giudicato d'Arborea e Marchesato di Oristano. Proiezioni mediterranee e aspetti di storia locale*, ed. G. Mele, 463-85. Oristano: ISTAR.

Corridore, F. 1902. *Storia documentata della popolazione Sardegna (1479-1901).* Torino: C. Clausen.

Cossu, C., and G. Nieddu. 1998. *Terme e ville extraurbane della Sardegna romana*. Oristano: S'Alvure.

Cossu Pinna, G. 1986. Inventari degli argenti, libri e arredi sacri delle chiese di Santa Gilla, San Pietro Santa Maria di Cluso. *S. Igia capitale giudicale*, 249-60. Pisa: Ets Editrice.

Courtois, C. 1955. *Les Vandales e l'Afrique*. Paris: Arts et métiers graphiques.

Cross, F. M. 1984. Phoenicians in the West: The Early Epigraphic Evidence. In *Studies in Sardinian Archaeology*, eds. M. Balmuth and R. J. Rowland, 53-65. Ann Arbor, MI: University of Michigan Press.

CSMB. 1982. *Il Condaghe di S. Maria di Bonarcado, ristampa del testo di E. Besta riveduto da M. Virdis*. Oristano: Carrias.

CSMS. R. 1997. *Il Condaghe di S. Michele di Salvennor*, a cura di V. Tetti. Sassari: Giuseppi Dessi.

CSPS. 1900. G. Bonazzi. *Il condeghe di San Pietro di Silki*. Sassari: Giuseppi Dessi.

Cunliffe, B. 1978. *Iron Age Communities in Britain*. London: Routledge & Kegan Paul.

Dadea, M. 1995. Ancora a proposito della "Grotta della Vipera." *Quaderni d'epigrafia* 2:45-53.

— 1995a. Ceramiche giudicali dipinte dall'areale cagliaritano. In *La ceramica racconta la storia. Atti del convegno La ceramica artistica, d'uso e da costruzione nell Oristanese dal neolitico a giorni nostril*, 245-58. Oristano: S'Alvure.

— 1998. Ceramiche giudicali dal villaggio abbandonato di Santu Jaccu. In *La ceramica racconta la storia. Atti del 20 convegno di stidu. La ceramica nel Sinis dai neolitica ai giorni nostri*, 437-63. Oristano: S'Alvure.

D'Arienzo, L. 1984. Influenze pisane e genovesi nella legislazione statuaria dei comuni medievali della Sardegna. In *Genova, Pisa e il Mediterraneo tra due e trecento*, 453-69. Genova: La Società.

Day, J. 1973. *Villaggi abbandonati in Sardegna dal trecento al settecento:inventario*. Paris: CNRS.

— 1984. La Sardegna e i suoi dominatori dal secolo XI al secolo XIV, John Day, Bruno Anatra, Lucetta Scaraffia. *La Sardegna medievale e moderna*, 3-186. Torino: UTET.

Deliperi, A. C. 1935. Aspetti della vita economica della Sardegna nel secolo XII. *Mediterranea* 9:34-46.

Delogu, R. 1953. *L'architettura del Medioevo in Sardegna*. Rome: Libreria dello Stato.

Depalmas, A. 1995. Materiali dall'area della Chiesa di Santa Maria, Cattedrale di Oristano. In *La ceramica racconta la storia. Atti del convegno 'La ceramica artistica, d'uso e da costruzionenell' Oristanese dal neolitico ai giorni nostril* 1:225-28.Oristano: S'Alvure.

Depalmas, A., and M. G. Melis. 1989. La cultura di Monte Claro: considerazioni e aspetti tipologici. *Antichità Sarde* 2:5-62.

Desantis, P., and F. Lo Schiavo. 1982. Rinvenimento di bronzi nuragici a Costa Nighedda (Oliena,Nuoro). *Rivista di Studi Preistorichi* 37:287-91.

Di Tucci, R. 1915. La vedova nel diritto e nell'economia di Sardegna. *Rivista Italiana di Sociologia* 19:183-96.

Dominguez, A.J. 2002. Greeks in Iberia: Colonialism without Colonization. In *The Archaeology of Colonialism*, eds. C. L. Lyons and J. K. Papadopoulos, 65-95. Los Angeles, CA: Getty Research Institute.

Donati, A., and R. Zucca. 1992. *L'ipogeo di San Salvatore*. Sassari: C. Delfino editore.

D'Oriano, R. 1985. Contributo al problema di Pheronia polis. *Nuovo Bollettino Archeologico Sardo* 2:229-47.

— 1994. Un santuario di Melqart-Ercole ad Olbia. *L' Africa Romana* 10:937-48.

— 1996. Prime evidenze su Olbia arcaica. In *Da Olbia ad Olbia. 2500 anni di storia di una cita mediterranea*, eds. A. Mastino and P. Ruggeri, 37-48. Sassari: Chiarella-Sassari.

— 1996a. Olbia. Su Cuguttu 1992: lo scavo. In *Da Olbia ad Olbia. 2500 anni di storia di una citta mediterreanea*, eds. A. Mastino and P. Ruggeri, 357-58. Sassari: Chiarella-Sassari.

Drews, R. 1993. *The End of the Bronze Age*. Princeton, NJ: Princeton University Press.

Durliat, J. 1982. Taxes sur l'entrée des marchandises dans la cité de Carales-Cagliari à l'époque byzantine (582-602). *Dumbarton Oaks Papers* 36:1-14.

Dyson, S. L. 1984. *The Roman Villas of Buccino*. Oxford: BAR.

— 1985. *The Creation of the Roman Frontier*. Princeton, NJ: Princeton University Press.

— 1992. *Community and Society in Roman Italy*. Baltimore, MD: Johns Hopkins University Press.

Dyson, S. L., and R. J. Rowland, Jr. 1988. Survey Archaeology in the Territory of Bauladu. Preliminary Notice. *Quaderni della soprintendenza archeologica di Cagliari e Oristano* 5:129-40.

— 1992. Survey Archaeology in West-Central Sardinia: The 1991 Season. *Quaderni della soprintendenza archeologica di Cagliari e Oritano* 9:177-96.

— 1992a. Survey and Settlement Reconstruction in West-Central Sardinia. *American Journal of Archaeology* 96:203-24.

Emerson, T.A. 1997. *Cahokia and the Archaeology of Power*. Tuscaloosa, AL: University of Alabama Press.

Epstein, S. A. 1996. *Genoa and the Genoese, 958-1528*. Chapel Hill, NC: University of North Carolina Press.

EE. *Ephemeris Epigraph.*

Fadda, A. F. 1985. Il villaggio. In *Civilta nuragica*, eds. F. Barreca, F. Lo Schiavo, and E. Arslan, 111-31. Milan: Electo.

— 1995. Ricerca e tesarurizzazione delle offerte negli edifici culturali della Sardegna nuragica. Nota preliminare. In *Settlement and Economy in Italy 1500 BC-AD 1500*, ed. N. Christie, 112-16. Oxford: Oxbow.

Fagan, B. 1999. *Floods, Famines and Emperors: El Niño and the Fate of Civilizations*. New York: Basic Books.

— 2000. *The Little Ice Age: How Climate Changed History*. New York: Basic Books.

Fantar, M. H. 1973. A propos d'Ashtart en Mediterranée occidentale.*Rivista di studi fenici* 1:19-29.

Fedele, F. 1983. Tharros: Anthropology of the Tophet and Palaeoecology of a Punic Town. In *Atti del I congresso internazionale di studi fenici e punici*, 637-50. Rome: Consiglio nazionale delle ricerche.

Ferrarese Ceruti, M. L. 1968. Tombe in Tafoni della Gallura. *Bollettino di paletnologia italiana* 77:93-165.

— 1982. Il complesso nuragico di Antigori (Sarroch, CA). In *Magna Grecia e mondo miceneo: atti del ventiduesimo Convegno di studi sulla Magna Grecia: Taranto, 7-11 ottobre 1982*, 1071-74. Taranto: Istituto per la storia e l'archeologia della Magna Grecia.

— 1985. Un bronzetto nuragico da Ossi (Sassari). In *Studi in onore di G. Lilliu per il suo settantesimo compleanno*, 51-59. Cagliari: n. p.

Ferrarese Ceruti, M. L., L. Vagnetti, and F. Lo Schiavo 1987. Minoici, micenei e ciprioti in Sardegna alla luce delle più recenti scoperte. In *Studies in Sardinian Archaeology* v.3, 7-34. Oxford: BAR.

Ferreli, O. 1999. Monumenti del Gennargentu. *Studi Ogliastrini* 5:36-38.

Filigheddu, P. 1996. Un sigillo fenicio da Olbìa. In *Da Olbia ad Olbia 2500 anni di una citta mediter-*

ranea, eds. A. Mastino and P. Ruggeri, 115-28. Sassari: Chiarella-Sassari.

Finocchi, S. 2000. Nora: anfore fenicie dai recuperi subacquei. In *La ceramica fenicia di Sardegna. Dati problematiche, confronti. Atti del rpimo congresso internazionale sulcitano. Sant'Antioco 1997*, 163-73. Rome: Consiglio nazionale delle ricerche.

Finzi, C. 1982. *Le città sepolte della Sardegna*. Rome: Newton Compton.

Fois, B. 1981. Annotazioni sulla viabilità nell'Arborea giudicaleattraverso il Condaghe di Santa Maria di Bonarcado ed altre testimonianze. *Archivio Storico Sardo* 32:27-64.

— 1990. *Territorio e paesaggio agrario nella Sardegna medioevale*. Pisa: ETS.

Fonzo, O. 1993. I reperti osteologici umani. *Quaderni didattici* 5:19-21.

Foschi Nieddu, A. 1998. Una fase Ozieri dell'età del Rame nella tomba I di Janna Ventosa (Nuoro). In *Sardinian and Aegean Chronology*, eds. M. Balmuth and R. Tykot, 273-83. Oxford: Oxbow.

Fuos, J. 1780. *Nachrichten aus Sardinien von der gegenwärtigen Verfassung dieser Insel*. Leipzig: S. L. Crusius. Galeazzi, D. 1986. Gli ex-voto di Bithia: una interpretazione storico-medica. *Rivista di studi feniche* 14:185-89.

— 1991. Le figurine votive di Bithia tra paleo-patologia e paleo-antropologia. In *Atti del II congresso internazionale di studi fenici e punici 1987*, 875-87. Rome: Consiglio nazionaledelle ricerche.

Galli, F. 1991. *Padria: il museo e il territorio*. Sassari: C. Delfino.

— 1994. Lo scavo. *Padria-I*, ed. A. Campus, 17-21. Rome: Bonsignori.

Gallin, L. 1989. Architectural Attributes and Inter-Site Variation. A Case Study: the Sardinian Nuraghi, Ph.D. Dissertation, UCLA.

Gallin, L., and O. Fonzo 1992. Vertebrate Faunal Remains at the Nuragic Village of Santa Barbara, Bauladu (OR). In *Sardinia in the Mediterranean: A Footprint in the Sea*, eds. R. Tykot and T. Andrews, 287-95. Sheffield: Sheffield Academic Press.

Gallin, L., and R. Tykot 1993. Metallurgical Activities at the Nuragic Village of Santa Barbara (Bauladu), Sardinia. *Journal of Field Archaeology* 20:335-45.

Garbati, G. 1999. Sid e Melqart tra Antas e Olbia. *Rivista di studi fenici* 27:151-66.

Garbini, G. 1966. Documenti artistici a Monte Sirai. In *Monte Sirai III*, 107-126. Rome: Istituto di studi del Vicino Oriente Università di Roma.

Gaviano, P. 1985. *La bifora in dispensa. Ricerca sulla struttura urbana di Oristano medioevale*. Oristano: S'Alvure.

Gemelli, F. 1776. *Rifiorimento della Sardegna proposto nel miglioramento di sua agricoltura*. Torino: Presso G. Briolo.

Germanà, F. 1995. *L'uomo in Sardegna dal paleolitico all'età Nuragica*. Sassari: C. Delfino.

Giardino, C. 1987. Sfruttamento minerario e metallurgia nella Sardegna protostorica. In *Studies in Sardinian Archaeology*, M. Balmuth, ed. 3:189-22. Oxford: BAR.

— 1992. Nuragic Sardinia and the Mediterranean: Metallurgy and Maritime Traffic. In *Sardinia in the Mediterranean: A Footprint in the Sea*, eds. R. Tykot and T. Andrews, 304-17. Sheffield: Sheffield Academic Press.

Gibson, D. B., and M. N. Geselowitz 1988. *Tribe and Polity in Late Prehistoric Europe*. New York: Plenum Press.

Giuntella, A. M., G. Borghetti, and D. Stiaffini. 1985. *Mensae e riti funerari in Sardegna. La testimonianza di Cornus*. Taranto: Scorpione.

Gras, M. 1972. A propos de la "bataille d'Alalia." *Latomus* 31:698-716.

— 1985. *Trafics tyrrhéniens archaïques*. Rome: BEFAR.

Guidi, A. 1988. *Storia della paletnologia*. Rome-Bari: Laterza.

Guido, F. 1993. Monete. In *Genna Maria II.1. Il deposito votivo delmastio e del Cortile*, ed. C. Lilliu, 125-59. Cagliari: Università degli studi di Cagliari, Catterdra di antichità Sarde; Villanovaforru: Parco museo archeologico.

Guilaine, J. 1994. *La mer partagée. La Méditerranée avant l'écriture, 7000-2000 avant Jésus-Christ*. Paris: Hachette.

Guillou, A. 1996. *Recueil des inscriptions grecques médiévales d'Italie*. Rome: École française de Rome.

Hallenbeck, J. T. 2000. *The transferal of the Relics of St. Augustine of Hippo from Sardinia to Pavia in the Early Middle Ages*. Studies in the Bible and Early Christianity 41. New York: Mellen Press.

Hanson, J. A. 1959. *Roman Theater Temples*. Princeton, NJ: Princeton University Press.

Heer, J. 1987. Pisani e Genovesi nella Sardegna mediovale: villa politica e sociale (x-xv secolo). In *Storia dei Sardi e della Sardegna: vol. 2: il medioevo dai giudicati agli arganonesi*, ed. M. Guidetti, 231-50. Milan: Jaca Book.

Herlihy, D. 1962. Land, Family and Women in Continental Europe 701-1200. *Traditio* 18:89-120.

Herzfeld, M. 1991. *A Place in History*. Princeton, NJ: Princeton University Press.

Hodder, I. 1958. *Reading the Past*. Cambridge: Cambridge University Press.

Hofmeijer, G. K. 1997. *Late Pleistocene Deer Fossils from Corbeddu Cave. Implications for Human Colonization of the Island of Sardinia*. Oxford: BAR.

Holloway, R. R. 2001. Nuragic Tower Models and Ancestral Memory. *Memoirs of the American Academy in Rome* 46:1-10.

Hopkins, K. 1980. Taxes and Trade in the Roman Empire. *Journal of Roman Studies* 70:101-25

Horden, P., and N. Purcell 2000. *The Corrupting Sea. A Study of Mediterranean History*. Oxford: Blackwell.

Hubschmid, J. 1953. *Sardische Studien. Das mediterrane Substrat des Sardischen, seine Beziehung zum berberischen und baskischen sowie zum eurafrikanischen und hispano-Kaukasischen Substrat der romanischen Sprachen*. Bern: A. Francke.

Ibn Jobair 1952. *The Travels of Ibn Jubayr*. London: Jonathan Cape.

Ichnussa. 1981. *La Sardegna dalle origini all'età classica*, ed. E. Atzeni. Milan: Libri Scheiwiller.

ILLRP. *Inscriptiones Latinae Liberae Rei Publicae*. Florence: La Nuova Italia.

Jones, A. H. M. 1964. *The Later Roman Empire*. Oxford: Blackwell.

Knapp, A. B. 1990. Ethnicity, Entrepreneurship and Exchange: Mediterranean Inter-island Relations in the late Bronze Age. *Annual of the British School at Athens* 85:115-53.

Køllund, M. 1996. Sea and Sardinia. *Hamburger Beiträge zur Archäologie* 19,20:201-204.

La Marmora, A. 1868. *Itinerario dell'isola di Sardegna*. Cagliari: Caserta.

Lamb, H. H. 1981. An Approach to the Study of the Development of Climate and its Impact on Human Affairs. In *Climate and History*, eds. T. L. Wigley, M. J. Ingram, and G. Farmer, 291-309. Cambridge: Cambridge University Press.

Lanternari, V. 1954-55. Il culto dei morti e della fecondità-fertilità nella paletnologia della Sardegna alla luce del folklore sardo e dell'etnologia. *Bollettino di paletnologia italiana* 1:17-19.

Laporte, J. P. 1989. *Rapidum. Le camp de la cohorte des Sardes en Maurétanie Césarienne*. Sassari:

Dipartimento di Storia Università degli Studi di Sassari.

Lazrus, P. K. 1999. Farmers or Pastoralists in Sardinian Prehistory? Settlement and Environment. In *Social Dynamics of the Prehistoric Central Mediterranean*, eds. R. Tykot, J. Morter, and J. E. Robb, 123-35. London: Accordia Research Institute.

Le Bohec, Y. 1990. *La Sardaigne et l'armée romaine sous le Haut-Empire*. Sassari: C. Delfino.

— 1992. Notes sur les mines di Sardaigne à l'époque romaine. Sardinia Antica: in onore di Piero Meloni in occasione del suo settentesimo compleanno, 255-64. Cagliari: Edizioni della Torre.

Le Lannou, M. 1979. *Pastori e contadini di Sardegna*, translation by M. Brigaglia of *Pâtres et Paysans de la Sardaigne* (Tours, 1941). Cagliari: Edizioni Della Torre.

Leighton, R. 1989. Antiquarianism and Prehistory in West Mediterranean Islands. *The Antiquaries Journal* 69:183-204.

— 2001. *Sicily before History*. Ithaca, NY: Cornell University Press.

Leon Leurquin, J. 1996. *Atlas préhistorique et protohistorique de la Sardaigne*, fascicule 2. Paris: L'Harmattan.

— 1997. *Atlas préhistorique et protohistorique de la Sardaigne* fascicule 3. Paris: L'Harmattan.

Levi, D. 1952. La necropoli di Anghelu Ruju e la civiltà eneolitica della Sardegna. *Studi Sardi* 10,11:5-51.

Lewthwaite, J. 1986. Nuragic Foundations: An Alternate Model of Development in Sardinian Prehistory ca. 2500-1500 BC. *Studies in Sardinian Archaeology III*, 57-74. Oxford: BAR.

Lilliu, G. 1952-54. Il nuraghe di Barumini e la stratigrafia Nuragica. *Studi Sardi* 12,13:90-469.

— 1962. Storiografia nuragica del secolo XIV al 1840. *Archivio storico sardo* 28:257-76.

— 1966. *Sculture della Sardegna nuragica*. Cagliari: Edizioni La Zattera.

— 1967. *La civiltà dei Sardi dal neolitico all'età dei nuraghi*. Torino: ERI.

— 1975. *Questioni di Sardegna*. Cagliari: Editrice sarda Fossataro.

— 1984. *La civilta nuragica*. Sassari: C. Delfino.

— 1988. *La civilta dei Sardi dal paleolitico all'età dei nuraghi*. Torino: Nuova ERI.

— 1992. Ancora una riflessione sulle guerre cartaginesi per la conquista della Sardegna. *Rendiconti della academia dei Lincei* 9,3.1:17-35.

— 1993. Milizie in Sardegna durante l'eta bizantina. In *Sardegna Mediterraneo e Atlantico tra Medioevo ed eta moderna. Studi storici in memoria di Alberto Boscolo a cura di L' D'Arienzo*105-35. Rome: Bulzoni.

— 1995. *Storia e problemi della Sardegna negli scritti giornalistici di Giovanni Lilliu, a cura di A. Moravetti*. Sassari: C. Delfino.

— 1997. La grande statuaria nella Sardegna nuragica. *Atti della Accademia Nazionale dei Lincei, Classe di Scienze Morali Storiche e Filologiche* 9.9.3:281-385.

— 1998a. Luoghi di culto e monumenti "pagani" convertiti in sedi della religione cristiana. In *Studi in onore di Pietro Alberti*, 41-60. Cagliari: Edizioni della Torre.

— 1999. *Arte e religione della Sardegna prenuragica: idoletti ceramiche, oggetti d'ornamento*. Sassari: C. Delfino.

Lilliu, G., and R. Zucca 1988. *Su Nuraxi di Barumini*. Sassari: C. Delfino.

Logias, N., and M. Madau 1998. Tres Bias (Tinnura-NU). Campagna archeologica 1995-1996. *L'Africa Romana* 12:657-66.

Lo Schiavo, F. 1994. Bronzi nuragici nelle tombe della prima età del ferro di Pontecagnano. In *La Presenza etrusca nella Campania meridionale*, 61-82. Florence: Leo S. Olschki.

— 1996. Olbia: orientamenti della ricerca archeologica. In *Da Olbia ad Olbia 2500 anni di storia di una citta mediterranea*, eds. A. Mastino and P. Ruggeri, 29-36. Sassari: Chiarella-Sassari.

— 1998a. Zur Herstellung und Distribution bronzezeitlicher Metallgegenstände im nuraghischen Sardinien. In *Mensch und Umwelt in der Bronzezeit Europas*, ed. B. Hänsel, 193-216. Kiel: Oetker-Voges Verlag.

— 1999. I lingotti *oxhide* nel Mediterraneo ed in Europa centrale, con appendici di Ubaldo Badas, Franco Campus Valentina Leonelli. In *EPI PONTON PLAXOMENOI. Simposio italiano di Studi egei dedicato a Luigi Bernabò Brea e Giovanni Pugliese Carratelli, Rome, 18-20 febbraio 1998*, 499-518. Rome: Scuola archeologica italiana di Atene.

Lo Schiavo, F., and R. D'Oriano 1990. La Sardegna sulle rotte dell'occidente. In *La Magna Grecia e il lontano occidente: Atti del ventinovesimo convegno di studi sulla Magna Grecia, Taranto 6-11 ottobre 1989*, 99-161. Taranto: Istituto per la storia e l'archeologia della Magna Grecia.

Lo Schiavo, F., and M. Sanges 1994. *Il nuraghe Arrubiu di Orrolì*. Sassari: C. Delfino.

MacKendrick, P. 1972. *Roman France*. New York: St. Martin's Press.

Madau, M. 1994. Presenze puniche e romano-repubblicane in Planargia. *L' Africa Romana* 10:961-72.

Maetzke, G. 1963. Architettura romana in Sardegna. In *Atti XII Congresso di storia dell'architettura*, 155-69. Rome: Centro di studi per la storia dell'architettura.

Manca, C. 1974. La lana di Sardegna: cenni sulla produzione e sulla distribuzione nei secoli XIII-XVIII, M. Spallanzani, ed. In *La lana come materia prima*, ed. M. Spallanzani, 169-74. Florence: Olschki.

Manconi, F. 1982. La fame, la povertà e la morte. In *Opere e giorni: Contadini e pastori nella Sardegna Tradizionale*, eds. F. Manconi and G. Angioni, 50-68. Cagliari: Silvana.

Manconi, F. and A. Pandolfi 1996. Località Badde Rebuddu, scavo di un impiano per la produzione fittile. *L'Africa Romana* 11:873- 90.

Manfredi, L. I. 1995. *Monete puniche. Repertorio epigrafico e numismatico delle leggende puniche*. Rome: Istituto poligrafico e Zecca dello Stato; Libreria dello Stato.

Manganaro, G. 1994. Massalia-Sardegna-Sicilia: la rotta commerciale in epoca ellenistica. In *Le Ravitaillement en blé de Rome et des centres urbains des débuts de la république jusq'au haut empire*, 261-65. Naples: Centre Jean Bérard.

Manunza, M. R. 1998. Scavo della tomba I di Is Calitas (Soleminis CA). Relazione preliminare. *Quaderni della sopritendenza archeologia di Cagliari e Oristano* 15:59-105.

Marasco, G. 1988. *Economia, commercio e politica nel Mediterraneo fra il III e il II secolo a. C.* Florence: Dipartimento di storia.

Marini, M., and M. L. Ferru 1993. *Storia della ceramica in Sardegna. Produzione locale e importazione dal medioevo al primo Novecento*. Cagliari: Tema.

— 1998. *Le ceramiche del convento di Santa Chiara. Storia dell'artigianato a Oristano*. Cagliari: Sole.

Marrocu, L., ed. 1997. *Le Carte d'Arborea. Falsi e falsari nella Sardegna del XIX secolo*. Cagliari: AM & D.

Mastino, A. 1974. Le origini di Bosa. In *Il IX centenario della cattedrale di San. Pietro di Bosa*, 108-12. Sassari: Gallizi.

— 1993. Analfabetismo e resistenza: geografia epigrafica della Sardegna. Faenza: Fratelli Lega

Editori.

— 1995. La produzione ed il commercio dell Olio nella Sardegna antica. *Olio sacroe profane. tradizioni olearie in Sardegna e Corsica*, eds. M. Atzori and A. Vodret, 60-76. Sassari: Edes.

— 2002. Ettore Pais a la Sardegna romana. In *Aspetti della stiografia di Ettore Pais*, ed. L. Polverini, 249-300. Naples: Edizioni scientifiche italine.

Mastino, A., and P. Ruggeri 1995. Claudia Augusti liberta Acta, la liberta amata da Nerone ad Olbia. *Latomus* 54:513-44.

Mastino, A., and H. Solin 1992. Supplemento epigrafico turritano II. *In Sardinia antique. Studi in onore di Piero Meloni*, 361-72.Cagliari: Edizioni della Torre.

Mastino, A., and C. Vismara 1994. *Turris Libisonis*. Sassari: C. Delfino.

Mattingly, D. J., ed. 1997. *Dialogues in Roman Imperialism*. Portsmouth, RI: JRA.

Mattone, A. 1980. La Sardegna e il mare. Insularita e isolamento. *Quaderni Sardi di Storia* 1:20-42.

Meiggs, R. 1973. *Roman Ostia*. Oxford: Clarendon Press.

Mele, M.G. 1999. *Orsitano giudicale. Topografia e insediamento*. Cagliari: Consiglio nazionale delle ricerche, Istituto sui rapporti italo-iberici.

Meloni, P. 1947. La cronologia della campagne di Malco. *Studi Sardi* 7:107-13.

— 1990. *La Sardegna romana,* 2nd ed. Sassari: Chiarella.

Michels, J. W., and G. S. Webster 1987. *Studies in Nuragic Archaeology*. Oxford: BAR.

Milanese, M. 2001. *Geridu. Archeologia e storia di un villaggio medievale in Sardegna*. Sassari: C. Delfino.

Milia, G. 1987. La civilta giudicale. *Storia dei Sardi e della Sardegna v.II: il medioevo dai guidicati agli Aragones*, ed. I. M. Guidetti, 193-230. Milan: Jaca Book.

Minutula, M. A. 1976-77. Originali greci provenienti dal tempio di Antas. *Dialoghi di Archeologia* 9,10:399-438.

Momigliano, N. 1999. *Duncan MacKenzie*. London: Institute of Classical Studies, School of Advanced Study, University of London.

Mongiu, A. M. 1989. Il quartiere tra mito, archeologia e progetto Urbano. In *Cagliari, Quartieri storici. Marina*, 13-22. Milan: Silvaza editoriale.

— 1995. Stampace: un quartiere tra polis e chora. In *CagliariQuartieri storici. Stampace*, 13-22. Milan: Silvana editoriale. *Monumenti Antichi*. Accademia nazionale dei Lincei; Reale Accademia d'Italia. Milan: Ulrico Hoepli.

Moravetti, A. 1980. Riparo sotto roccia con petroglifi in località Frattale (Oliena-Nuoro). *XXII Riunione* 199-221.

— 1992. *Il complesso nuragico di Palmavera*. Sassari: C. Delfino.

— 2000. *Il complesso prenuragico di Monte Baranta*. Sassari:C. Delfino.

—, ed. 1988. *Il nuraghe S. Antine nel Logudoro-Meilogu*. Sassari: C. Delfino.

Moscati, S. 1968. Statuette puniche da Narbolia. *Rendiconti della Accademia dei Lincei* 8,23:197-203.

— 1989. *L'ancora d'argento. Colonie e commerci fenici tra Oriente e Occident*. Milan: Jaca Book.

— 1992. Tra Cartaginesi e Romani. Artigianato in Sardegna dal IV secolo a. C. al II d. C. In *Memorie dell' Accademia dei Lincei* 9.3.1. Rome: Accademia nazionale dei Lincei.

— 1992a. *Le stele puniche in Italia*. Rome: Libreria dello Stato Istituto poligrafico e Zecca dello Stato.

— 1993. *Il tramonto di Cartagine*. Torino: Società editrice internazionale.

— 1995. *Italia punica*. Milan: Rusconi.

Moscati, S., P. Bartolini, and S. F. Bondì 1997. *La penetrazione fenicia e punica in Sardegna. Trent'anni dopo, Memorie dell' Accademia dei Lincei* 9.9.1. Rome: Accademia nazionale dei Lincei.

Motzo, B. R. 1936. Cesare e la Sardegna. *Sardegna romana*, 25-49. Rome: Istituto di studi romani.

Mureddu, D. 1993. La necropoli di Bonaria. *Quaderni didattici* 5:17-21.

Nieddu, A. M. 1996. La pittura paleocristiana in Sardegna: nuove Acquisizioni. *Rivista di Archeologia Cristiana* 72:266-70.

Nonnis, G. L. 2001. *Marinai sardi nella flotta di Roma antica*. Cagliari: T & A.

Noy, D. 1993. *Jewish Inscriptions of Western Europe* 1. Cambridge: Cambridge University Press.

Oggiano, I. 1993. Nora II. Lo scavo. *Quaderno della Soprintendenza Archeologica di Cagliari e Oristano* 10:101-14.

Oman, G. 1965. Iscrizioni arabe di Sardegna. In *Atti del I congresso internazionale di studi nord-africani*, 213-27. Cagliari: Stab. tip. edit. G. Fossataro.

— 1970. Vestiges arabes de Sardaigne. In *Congresso internazionale di studi nord-africani*, 175-84. Cagliari: Della Torre.

Orlandi, G. F. 1985. *Thathari. Pietra su pietra. Sassari dalle origini al XIII secolo*. Chiarella, Sassari: G. F. Orlandi.

Otto of Freising. *Ottonis et Rahewini Gesta Friderici I impertoris* ed. G. Waitz. Hanover: Hahn Publishers.

Paderi, M. C. 1982. La necropoli di Bidd'e Cresia e le tombe. Puniche. *Ricerche archeologiche nel territorio di Sanluri*, 49- 51.

— 1993. Materiali di età romana e bizantina dal territorio di Villamar. In *Villamar, una communita, la sua storia*, 107-16. Dolianova: Grafica del Parteolla.

Paderi, M. C., G. Ugas, and A. Siddu 1993. Ricerche nell'abitato di Mara. Notizia preliminare sull'area della necropoli punica di San Pietro. In *Villamar, una communita, la sua storia*, 123-43. Dolianova: Grafica del Parteolla.

Pais, E. 1881. *Sardegna prima del dominio romano*. Rome: Salviucci.

— 1923. *Storia della Sardegna e della Corsica durante il dominio romano*. Rome: A. Nardecchia.

Pallottino, M. 1947. Rassegna sulle scoperte e sugli scavi avvenuti in Sardegna negli anni 1941-1942. *Studi Sardi* 7:227-32.

Panedda, D. 1953. *Olbia nel periodo punico e romano*. Rome: n. p.

Pani Ermini, L. 1981. *Museo Archeologico Nazionale di Cagliari. Catalogo dei materiali Paleocristiani e altomedievali*, with M. Marinone. Rome: n. p.

— 1982-84. Ricerche nel complesso di S. Saturno a Cagliari. *Rendiconti della Pontificia Accademia di Archeologia* 55-56:101-18.

— 1992. Contributo alla conoscenza del suburbia cagliaritano "iuxta basilicam sancti martyris saturnini." In *Sardinia antiqua. Studi in onore di Piero Meloni*, 477-90. Cagliari: Edizioni della Torre.

— 1995. Le citta sarde nell'altomedioevo: una ricerca in atto. In *Materiali per una topografia urbana. V convegno sull'archeologia tardoromana e medievale in Sardegna*, 366-67. Oristano: S'Alvure.

Pani Ermini, L., and R. Zucca 1989. L'età paleocristiana e altomedievale-la produzione artigianale e l'epigrafia. In *Il museo archeologico nazionale di Cagliari*, ed. V. Santoni, 247-86. Sassari:

Banco di Sardegna.

Pardi, G. 1925. *La Sardegna e la sua popolazione attraverso i Secoli*. Cagliari: Il Nuraghe.

Patton, M. 1996. *Islands in Time*. London: Routledge.

Paulis, G. 1983. *Lingua e cultura nella Sardegna bizantina*.Sassari: Asfodelo.

— 1996. Saggio introduttivo. In *La vita rustica della Sardegna riflessa nella lingua*, ed. M. L. Wagner, 7-46. Nuoro: Ilisso.

Pautasso, A. 1985. Edifici termali sub ed extra urbani nelle provincie di Cagliari e Oristano. *Nuovo Bollettino Archeologico Sardo* 207-14.

Pergola, P. 1989. Economia e religione nella Sardegna vandala: nuovi dati da studi e scavi recenti. *L' Africa Romana* 6:553-60.

Perles, C. 1992. Systems of exchange and organization of production in Neolithic Greece. *Journal of Mediterranean Archaeology* 5:115-64.

Perra, C. 1998. *L'architettura templare fenicia e punica di Sardegna: il problema delle origini orientali*. Oristano: S'Alvure.

Perra, M. 1997. *SARDO, SARDINIA, SARDEGNA. Le antiche testimonianze letterarie di Carattere etnografico, socio-economiconaturalistico e geografico sulla Sardegna e iSardi, dai primordi sino al VII sec. d. C.*, 3 vols. Oristano: S'Alvure.

— 1997a. From Deserted Ruins: An Interpretation of Nuragic Sardini. *Europaea, Journal of the Europeanists Society* 3,2:90-95.

Pesce, G. 1957. *Sarcofagi romani di Sardegna*. Rome: L'Erma di Bretschneider.

— 1965. *Le statuette puniche di Bithia*. Rome: Centro di studi semitici, Istituto di studi del vicino Oriente, Università.

— 1966. *Tharros*. Cagliari: Editrice Sarda Flli Fossataro.

— 1972. *Nora. Guida agli scavi*. Cagliari: Editrice Sarda Fossataro.

Petrucci, S. 1986. Tra S. Igia e Castel di Castro di Cagliari: insediamenti, politica, società pisana nella prima metà del XIII secolo. In *S. Igia capitale giudicale*, 235-41. Pisa: Ets Editrice.

Piga A., and M. A. Porcu 1990. Flora e fauna della Sardegna antica. *L' Africa Romana* 7:569-98.

Pinza, G. 1901. Monumenti primitivi della Sardegna. *Monumenti Antichi* 11:5-280.

Piras, P. G. 1966. *Aspetti della Sardegna bizantina*. Cagliari: T.E.F.

Pistarino, G. 1981. Genova e la Sardegna nel secolo XII. In *La Sardegna nel mondo mediterraneo. Atti del primo convegno internazionale di studi geografico-storico*, ed. M Brigaglia, 64-74; 109-23. Sassari: Gallizzi.

Pittau, M. 1994. Due toponomi sardi di mansioni romane: Austis e Meana. *L'Italia dialettale: rivista. di dialettologia italiana* 27:287-89.

Plaisant, M. L. 1970. *Martin Carillo e le sue relazioni sulla Sardegna*. Cagliari: Edizioni della Torre.

Poisson, J. M. 1988. L'érection de châteaux dans la Sardaigne pisane (XIIIe siècle) et ses conséquences sur la réorganisation du réseau des habitats. *Chateau Gaillard* 14:351-66.

— 1992. Châteaus, frontières et naissance des judicats en Sardaigne. In *Castrum 4. Frontière et peuplement dans le monde méditerranéen au Moyen Age*, 310-12. Madrid: Casa de Velázquez.

— 1995. Formes urbaines de la colonisation pisane en Sardaigne (XIIIe-XIVe siècle). In *Coloniser au Moyen Age*, 42-46. Paris: A. Colin.

Polastri, M. 2001. *Cagliari: viaggio nella città sotterranea*. Cagliari: Edizioni Sole.

Poli, F. 1997. *La basilica di San Gavino a Porto Torres. La storia e le vicende architettoniche*. Sassari: Chiarella.

Polonio, V. 1984. Patrimonio e investimenti del capitolo di San Lorenzo di Genova nei secoli XII-XIV. In *Genova, Pisa e il Mediterraneo tra due e trecento*, 231-81. Genova: La Società.

Pulacchini, D. 1998. *Il museo archeologico di Dorgali*. Sassari: C. Delfino.

Regoli, P. 1991. *I bruciaprofoumi a testa femminile dal nuraghe Lugherras (Paulilatino)*. Rome: II Università degli studi di Roma. Dipartimento di storia.

Renfrew, C. 1976. *Before Civilization*. Harmondsworth: Penguin.

Ribichini, S. 1989. Il sacrificio di fanciulli nel mondo punico: testimonianze e problemi. *Quaderni della soprintendenza archeologica di Cagliari e Oristano* 6 Suppl.:45-66.

Rickman, G. 1980. *The Corn Supply of Ancient Rome*. Oxford: Clarendon Press.

Ridley, R. 1976. Ettore Pais. *Helikon* 15-16

Rossi Sabatini, G. 1935. *L'espansione di Pisa nel mediterraneo fino alla Meloria*. Florence: G. C. Sansoni.

Rowland, R. J., Jr. 1978. Numismatics and the Military History of Sardinia. In *Limes: Akten des XI Internationalen Limeskongresses*. Budapest: Akadémiai Kiadó.

— 1981. *I ritrovamenti romani in Sardegna*. Rome: L'Erma di Bretschneider.

— 1982. Beyond the Frontier in Punic Sardinia. *American Journal of Ancient History* 7:20-39.

— 1982a. The Sardinian Condaghi: Neglected Evidence for Medieval Sex Ratios. *Florilegium* 4 = I Condaghi sardi: testimonianza dimenticata sui rapporti numerici fra i sessi nel Medioevo. *QB* 11:118-20.

— 1985. The Roman Invasion of Sardinia. In *Papers in Italian Archaeology IV, The Cambridge Conference*, eds. C. Malone and S. Stoddard, 107—12. Oxford: BAR.

— 1987. Faunal Remains of Prehistoric Sardinia: The Current State of the Evidence. In *Studies in Nuragic Archaeology*, eds. J. Michels and G. Webster, 147-61. Oxford: BAR.

— 1988. The Archaeology of Roman Sardinia: a Selected Typological Inventory. In *Aufstieg und Niedergang der romische Welt* II.11.1: 740-875. Berlin: W. de Gruyter.

— 1988a. Preliminary Etymological Observations on the Romanization of Sardinia. *Annali della Facolta-Cagliari* 45:243-47.

— 1990. The Production of Grain in Roman Sardinia. *Mediterranean History Review* 5:14-20.

— 1991. Contadini-guerrieri: an alternative hypothesis of Sardinian cultural evolution in the nuragic period. In *Arte militare e architettura nuragica*, ed. B. Frizell, 87-117. Stockholm: Svenska Institutet i Rom; Distributor, P. Aström.

— 1999. The Sojourn of the Body of St. Augustine in Sardinia. In *Augustine in Iconography. History and Legend*, eds. J. C. Schnaubelt and F. Van Fleteren, 189-98. New York: P. Lang.

— 2001. *The Periphery in the Center: Sardinia in the Ancient and Medieval Worlds*. Oxford: Archaeopress.

Rowland, R. J., Jr., and S. L. Dyson 1991. Survey Archaeology in Sardinia. In *Roman Landscapes: Archaeological Survey in the Mediterranean region*, ed. G. Barker, 54-61. Archaeological monographs of the British School at Rome 2. London: British School at Rome.

— 1991a. Survey Archeology around Colonia Julia Augusta Uselis (Usellus). First preliminary report. *Quaderni della soprintendenza archeologica di Cagliari e Oristano* 8:145-70.

— 1999. Notes on some Roman-period Pottery from West-Central Sardinia. *Quaderni della soprint-*

endza archaeological di Cagliari e Oristano 16:223-37.

Rowlands, M., M. Larsens, and K. Kristiansen 1987. *Centre and Periphery in the Ancient World.* Cambridge: Cambridge University Press.

Runnels, C., and P. M. Murray 2001. *Greece before History.* Palo Alto CA: Stanford University Press.

Saba, A. 1999. Le statue-menhir di Isili (NU). *Studi Sardi* 32:111-64.

Salvi, D. 1989. *Testimonianze archeologiche.* Dolianova: Associazone archeologica parteollese.

— 1992. Le massae plumbeae di Mal di Ventre. *L'Africa Romana* 9:661-72.

— 1993. La villa di Tigellio. *Quaderni didattici* 5:5-10.

— 2000. Tuvixeddu. Vicende di una necropolis. In *Tuvixeddu: La* necropolis occidentale di Karales. Atti della tavola rotunda *internazionale,* 139-202. Cagliari: Edizioni della Torre.

Sanciu, A. 1997. *Una fattoria d'età romana nell'agro di Olbia.* Sassari Boomerang.

Sandars, N. K. 1978. *The Sea Peoples. Warriors of the ancient Mediterranean, 1250-1150 BC.* London: Thames & Hudson.

Santoni, V. 1976. Nota preliminare sulla tipologia dele grotticelle artificiali funerary in Sardegna. *Archivio Storico Sardo* 30:3-46.

— 1989b. Cuccuru-S'Arriu-Cabras. Il sito di cultura San Michele di Ozieri. Dati preliminary. In *La cultura di Ozieri. Problematiche e nuove acquisizioni,* ed. L. Campus. Ozieri: Edizioni Il Torchietto.

— 1993. L'architettura e la produzione materiale nuragica. In *Nuraghe Losa di Abbasanta I,* 15-20; 47-48. Cagliari: Stef.

Santoni, V., *et al.* 1982. Cabras-Cuccuru s'Arriu-Nota preliminare di scavo. *Rivista di Studi Feniche* 10:102-27.

Santoni, V., and S. Sebis 1984. Il complesso nuragico "Madonna del Rimedio" (Oristano). *Nuovo Bollettino Archeologico Sardo* 1: 97-114.

Santoni, V., P. B. Serra, F. Guido, O. Fonzo. 1991. Il nuraghe Cobulas di Milis- Oristano: preesistenze e riuso. *L' Africa Romana* 8:952-76.

Satta, M. C. 1996. *S'Abba Druche: un insediamento rustico a poche iglia da Bosa Vetus.* Bosa: Tip. San Giuseppe.

Scano, D. 1940. *Codice diplomatico delle relazioni fra la Santa Sede e la Sardegna.* Cagliari: Arti grafiche b.c.t.

Schena, O. 1996. Civita e il giudicato di Gallura nella documentazione sarda medioevale. In *Da Olbia ad Olbia. 2500 anni di storia di una citta mediterranea,* eds. A. Mastino and P. Ruggeri, 98-102. Sassari: Chiarella-Sassari.

Scott, J. 1990. *Domination and the Arts of Resistance.* New Haven, CT: Yale University Press.

Schüle, W. 1993. Mammals, Vegetation and the Initial Human Settlement of the Mediterranean Islands: A Palaeoecological Approach. *Journal of Biogeography* 20:399-411.

Serra, R. B. 1995. Campidano maggiore di Oristano: ceramiche di produzione locale e d'importazione e altri materiali d'uso nel periodo tardoromano e altomedievale. In *La ceramcia racconta la storia. Atti del convegno 'La ceramica artistica, d'uso e da costruzione nell'Oristano dal neolitico ai giorni nostril,* 188-93. Oristano: S'Alvure.

— 1998. Ceramiche d'uso e prodotti dell'industria artistica minore del Sinis. In *La ceramica racconta la storia. Atti del 2. convegno di studi. La ceramica nel Sinis dal neolitico ai nostril giorni*

Oristano-Cabras, 343-45. Cagliari: Condaghes.

Serra, P. B., and G. Bacco 1998. Forum Traiani: il contesto termale e l'indagine archeologica di scavo. *L'Africa Romana* 12:1213-55.

Serra, P. B., R. Coroneo, and R. Serra 1989. San Giuliano di Selargius (Cagliari). *Quaderni della Soprintendenza Archeologica di Cagliari e Oristano* 6:227-59.

Serra, R. 1994. Cornus e Africa: Riscontri tipoloigici fra il complesso basilicale di Columbarie e le architetture cristiane d'Africa. In *Rapporti tra Sardegna e Tunisia dall' eta antica all' eta moderna*, 63-68. Cagliari: Università.

Sirks, B. 1991. *Food for Rome.* Amsterdam: Gieben.

Sismondo Ridgway, B. 1986. Mediterranean Comparanda for the Statues from Monte Prama. In *Studies in Sardinian Archaeology*, ed. M. Balmuth, 61-72. Oxford: BAR.

Smith, C., and J. Serrati, eds. 2000. *Sicily from Aeneas to Augustus.* Edinburgh: Edinburgh University Press.

Solmi, A. 1917. *Studi storici sulle istituzioni della Sardegna nel medio evo.* Cagliari: Presso la Società storica sarda.

Sondaar, P. Y., and M. Sanges. 1984. First Report on a Palaeolithic Culture in Sardinia. In *The Deya Conference of Prehistory. Early Settlement in the Western Mediterranean Islands and their Peripheral Areas,* 29-59. Oxford: BAR.

— 1993. Il popolamento della Sardegna nel tardo Pleistocene: nuova acquisizione di un fossile umano dalla Grotta Corbeddu. *Rivista di Scienze Preistoriche* 45:243-51.

— 1995. The Human Colonization of Sardinia: A Late-Pleistocene Human Fossil from Corbeddu Cave. In Comptes Rendues-Academie des Sciences. Earth & Planetary Sciences. Série II, Sciences de la terre et des planets, 145-50. Paris: CNRS.

Sotgiu, G. 1961. *Iscrizioni latine della Sardegna v. 1.* Padova: CEDAM.

— 1968. *Iscrizioni latine della Sardegna v. 2.1.* Padova: CEDAM.

Spano, G. 1867. *Memoria sopra i nuraghi di Sardinia,* 3rd ed. Cagliari: Tipografia Archivescovile.

Spanu, P. G. 1998. *La Sardegna bizantina tra VI e VII secolo.* Oristano: S'Alvure.

— 2000. *Martyria Sardiniae. I santuari dei martiri sardi.* Oristano: S'Alvure.

Spiga, G. 1981. Il castello di Montefore della Nurra attraverso la lettura di un'epigrafe medio-evale. In *Miscellanea di studi medioevali sardo-catalani.* Cagliari: Edizioni della Torre.

Stiglitz, A. 1999. *La necropoli punica di Cagliari. Tuvixeddu, un colle e la sua memoria.* Cagliari: Janus.

Stos-Gale, Z. A., and N. H. Gale 1992. New Light on the Provenience of the Copper Oxhide Ingots Found on Sardinia. In *Sardinia in the Mediterranean: A Footprint in the Sea*, eds. R.H. Tykot and T. K. Andrews, 317-46. Sheffield: Sheffield Academic Press.

Stos-Gale, Z. A., N. H. Gale 1998. The Copper and Tin Ingots of the Late Bronze Age Mediterranean: New Scientific Evidence. In *The Fourth International Conference on the Beginning of the Use of Metals and Alloys*, 115-26. Shimane, Japan: BUMA-IV Organizing Committee; Sendai: Japan Institute of Metals.

Talbert, R. 2000. *Barrington Atlas of the Greek and Roman World.* Princeton, NJ: Princeton University Press.

Tanda, G., A. Mura, and G. Pittui. 1999. Analisi archeometriche su ceramiche di cultura Abealzu e Filigosa. In *Archeologia delle isole del mediterraneo occidentale, a cura di G. Tanda,* 161-81.

Rome: L'Erma di Bretschneider.

Tangheroni, M. 1973. *Politica, commercio, agricoltura a Pisa nel Trecento, Pisa. 1985 La citta dell'argento.* Naples: Pacini.

Teatini, A. 1996. Alcune osservazioni sulla primitiva forma architettonica della chiesa di Nostra Signora di Mesumundu a Siligo (Sassari). *SACER* 3:119-49.

Terrosu Asole, A. 1965. Note sulla dimora rurale in Sardegna, *Fra il passato e l'avvenire. Saggi storici sull'agricoltura sarda in onore di Antonio Segni,* 81-144. Padova: A. Milani.

Testini, P. 1966. Il battistero di Tharros. *XIII congresso Architettura,* 181-99. Roma: Centro di Studi per la Storia dell'Architettura.

Tore, G. 1991. Ricerche fenicio-puniche nel Sinis (OR-Sardegna).In *Atti del II Congresso Internazionale di Studi Fenici e Punici,* 1263-69. Rome: Consiglio nazionale delle ricerche.

Tore, G., and A. Stiglitz 1987. Gli insediamenti fenicio-punici nel Sinis settentrionale e nelle zone contermini (ricerche archeologiche 1979-1987). *Quaderni della Soprintendenza Archeologica per le Provincie di Cagliari e Oristano* 4,1:161-74.

Torelli, M. 1981. Colonizzazioni etrusche e latine di epoca arcaica: un esempio. In *Gli Etruschi e Roma. Atti dell'incontro di studi in onore di Massimo Pallottino.* Rome: G. Bretschneider.

Torrence, R. 1986. *Production and Exchange of Stone Tools.* Cambridge: Cambridge University Press.

Trigger, B. G. 1989. *A History of Archaeological Thought.* Cambridge: Cambridge University Press

Tronchetti, C. 1979. Per la cronologia del tophet di Sant'Antioco. *Rivista di Studi Fenichi* 7:201-205.

— 1985. Le terme a mare. In *Nora. Recenti studi e scoperte* 15-20. Pula: Amministrazione comunale.

— 1986. Nuragic Statuary from Monte Prama. In *Studies in Sardinian Archaeology,* 41-59. Ann Arbor, MI: University of Michigan Press.

— 1987. Bithia I: la tomba 49 della necropoli romana. *Quaderni della Soprintenza Archeologica per le Provincie di Cagliari e Oristano* 4,2:15-20.

— 1988. *I Sardi. Traffici, relazioni, ideologie nella Sardegna arcaica.* Milan: Longanesi.

— 1990. *Cagliari fenicia e punica.* Sassari: Chiarella.

— 1993. Le ceramiche di età storica: puniche, romane repubblicane e di prima età imperiale. *Quaderni della Soprintendenza Archeologica per le Provincie di Caglairi e Oristano* 10 Suppl:111-16.

— 1995. Per la topografia di Sulci Romana. In *Materiali per una topografia urbana: status questionis e nuove acquisizioni. V convegno sull' archeologia tardoromana e medievale in Sardegna(1988),* 1103-1116. Orotano: Carrias.

— 1997. *Nora e il suo territorio in epoca romana.* Sassari: Ed. Poddighe.

— 2000. Importazioni e imitazioni nella Sardegna fenicia. In *La ceramica fenicia di Sardegna. Dati, problematiche, confronti. Atti del primo congresso internazionale sulcitano 1997,* 349-50. Rome: Consiglio nazionale delle ricerche.

— 2000a, ed. *Ricerche su Nora-I (anni 1990-1998.* Cagliari: Soprintendenza archeologica per le province di Cagliari e Oristano.

Tronchetti, C., and A. Fanni 1982. Santa Maria. In *Villasimius: prime testimonzianze archeologiche nel territorio,* 80-84. Cagliari: Tip. Gazz. pop.

Tronchetti, C., and P. van Dommelen 2005. Entangled Objects and Hybrid Practices: Colonial Contacts and Elite Connections at Monte Prama, Sardinia. *Journal of Mediterranean Archaeology* 18: 183-208.

Tronchetti, C., and P. Bernardini 1985. La necropoli romana. In *Nora. Recenti studi e scoperti*, 52-60. Pula: Amministrazione comunale. Tronchetti, C., and G. Pianu 1982. Villaspeciosa (CA). *Archeologia Mediavale* 9:382-409.

Tronchetti, C., F. Mallegni, and F. Bartoli 1991. Gli inumati di Monte Prama. *Quaderni della Soprintendenz Archeologica per le Provincie di Cagliari e Oristano* 8:119-32.

Trump, D. 1984. The Bonu Ighinu Project and the Sardinian Neolithic. In *Studies in Sardinian Archaeology*, eds. M. S. Balmuth and R. J. Rowland, 1-22. Ann Arbor, MI: University of Michigan Press.

— 1990. *Nuraghe Noeddos and the Bonu Ighinu Valley. Excavation and Survey in Sardinia*. Oxford: Oxbow.

— 1998. Grotta di Su Coloru, Laerru (Sassari). *Paleo-express* 2: 7-8.

Trump, D., A. Foschi, and M. Levine 1983. *La grotta Filiestru a Bonu Ighinu Mara (SS)*. Sassari: Dessi.

Turchi, D. 1984. *Leggende e racconti populari della Sardegna*. Rome:Newton Compton.

Turtas, R. 1992. Gregorio VII e la Sardegna (1073-1085). *Riviste di stori delle chiese in Italia* 46:375-97.

Turtas, R. 1999. *Storia della chiesa in Sardegna dalle origini al Duemila*. Rome: Città Nuova.

Tykot, R. H. 1994. Radiocarbon Dating and Absolute Chronology in Sardinia and Corsica. In *Radiocarbon Dating and Italian Prehistory*, eds. London R. Skeates and R. Whitehouse, 115-45. London: British School at Rome; Accordia Research Centre.

— 1996. Obsidian Procurement and Distribution in the Central and Western Mediterranean. *Journal of Mediterranean Archeology* 9: 39-82.

— 2001. Chemical Fingerprinting and Source Tracing of Obsidian: The Central Mediterranean Trade in Black Gold. *Accounts of Chemical Research* 35:618-37.

Uberti, M. L. 1973. *Le figurine fittili di Bithia*. Rome: Consiglio Nazionale delle Ricerche.

Ugas, G. 1987. Indagini ed interventi di scavo lungo la SS. 131 tra il km. 15 e il km. 32. Breve notizia. *Quaderni della Soprintendenza Archeologica di Cagliari e Oristano* 4,1:117-28.

— 1990. *La tomba dei guerrieri di Decimoputzu*. Cagliari: Edizioni della Torre.

Ugas, G., G. Lai, and L. Usai 1985. L'insediamento prenuragico di Su Coddu (Selargius-Ca). Notizia preliminare sulle campagne di scavo 1981-1984. *Nuovo Bollettino Archeologico Sardo* 2:7-40.

Ugas, G., and G. Lucia 1987. Primi scavi nel sepolcreto nuragico di Antas. *La Sardegna nel Mediterraneo tra il secondo e il primo millenio a. C.* In *Atti del II convegno di studi Selargius-Cagliari 1987*, 255-77. Cagliari: Edizioni delle Torre.

Ugas, G., and M. C. Paderi 1990. Persistenza rituali e culturali in età punica e romana. *L'Africa Romana* 8:475-86.

Urso, C. 1997. *Storia, società ed economia in Sardegna e Corsica: la testimonianza di Gregorio Magno*. Catania: CULC.

Usai, A. 1987. Tomba megalitica in località "Mitza 'e Fidi" Donori (Cagliari). *Quaderni della Soprintenza Archeologica per le Provincie di Cagliari e Oristano* 4,1:59-66.

— 1998. Scavi nelle tombe di giganti di Tanca 'e Suei e di Tanca 'e Perdu Cossu (Norbello, OR). *Quaderni della Soprintendenza Archeologica per le Provincie di Cagliari e Oristano* 15:32-38.

Usai, E. 1995. Materiali dell'età del ferro in Marmilla. In *La Sardegna nel Mediterraneo tra il secondo e il primo millenio a.C. Atti del II convegno di studi. Selargius-Cagliari 1987.*Cagliari:

Amministrazione provinciale di Cagliari, Assessorato alla cultura.

Usai, E., and R. Zucca 1986. Testamonianze archeologiche nell'area di S. Gilla dal periodo punico all' Epoca altomedievale Contributo alla ricostruzione della topografia di Carales. In *S. Igia capitale giudicale*, 158-72. Pisa: Ets Editrice.

Vaänänen V. 1970. *Graffiti del Palatino. II. Domus Tiberiana*. Helsinki: Institutum Romanum Finlandiae.

Van Andel, T. H., and C. Runnels 1987. *Beyond the Acropolis*. Palo Alto, CA: Stanford University Press.

Van Dommelen, P. 1996-97. Colonial Constructs: Colonialism and Archaeology in the Mediterranean. *World Archaeology* 28:305-23.

— 1997. Some Reflections on Urbanization in a Colonial Context: West Central Sardinia in the 7th to 5th centuries BC. In *Urbanization in the Mediterranean in the 9th to 6th Centuries BC, Acta Hyperborea* 7:243-48. Copenhagen: Museum Tusculanum Press.

— 1998. *On Colonial Grounds*. Leiden: Faculty of Archaeology, University of Leiden.

Verlinden, C. 1977. *L'esclavage dans l'Europe médiévale*. Brugge: De Tempel.

Vigne, J. D. 1992. Zooarchaeology and the Biogeographical History of the Mammals of Corsica and Sardinia since the Last Ice Age. *Mammal Review* 22:870-96.

— 1996. Did Man Provoke Extinctions of Endemic Large Mammals on the Mediterranean Islands? The View from Corsica. *Journal of Mediterranean Archaeology* 9:117-20

Villa di Tigellio 1981. *La villa di Tigellio: Mostra degli scaviCagliari 24 ott.-14 nov. 1981*. Cagliari: Stef.

Villedieu, F. 1984. *Turris Libisonis. Fouille d'un site romain tardif à Porto Torres, Sardaigne*. Oxford: BAR.

Watrous, L. V. 1992. *Kommos III*. Princeton, NJ: Princeton University Press.

Webster, G. S. 1996. *A Prehistory of Sardinia 2300-500 BC*. Sheffield: Sheffield Academic Press.

— 2001. *Duos Nuraghes. A Bronze Age Settlement in Sardinia, volume 1, The Interpretive Archaeology*. Oxford: BAR.

Webster, G. S., and M. Webster 1998. The Duos Nuraghes Project in Sardinia: 1985-1996 Interim Report. *Journal of Field Archaeology* 25:183-201.

Webster, M. R. 1997. An Early History of Sardinia 1000 BC-AD 1000: Literary and Epigraphical Evidence. *The Ancient World* 28:3-23.

Whittle, A. 1996. *Europe in the Neolithic*. Cambridge: Cambridge University Press.

Willey, G., and J. Sabloff 1980. *A History of American Archaeology*. San Francisco, CA: W. H. Freeman.

Wilson, R. J. A. 1980-81. Sardinia and Sicily during the Roman Empire. *Kokalos* 26,27:219-42.

Zanetti, G. 1964. *I Vallombrosani in Sardegna*. Sassari: Gallizzi.

—1974. *I Camaldolesi in Sardegna*. Cagliari: Editrice sarda Fossataro.

Zertal, A. 1997. The Sites of el-Ahwat and Mt. Carmel: The Archaeological Evidence. In *International Colloquium, West and East: Connections between the Western and Eastern Mediterranean in the End of the Late Bronze and the Beginning of the Iron Age: New Evidence*, Haifa, 10-12 December 1997:27-40.

— 1998. *First International Congress on the Archaeology of the Ancient Near East*, Rome, 18-23 May 1998. Rome: Università degli studi di Roma "La Sapienza," Dipartimento di scienze storiche archeologiche e antropologiche dell'antichità.

Zucca, R. 1984. *Tharros*. Nuoro: Poligrafica Solinas.

— 1985. *Nurachi. Storia di una ecclesia*. Oristano: Editrice S'Alvure.

— 1986. Cornus e la rivolta del 215 a.C. in Sardegna. *L'Africa Romana* 3:363-95.

— 1987. *Neapolis e il suo territorio*. Oristano: S'Alvure.

— 1988. *Il santuario nuragico di S. Vittoria di Serri*. Sassari: C. Delfino.

— 1988a. Osservazioni sulla storia e sulla topografia di Cornus. In *Ampsicora e il territorio di Cornus. Atti del II convegno sull' archeologia romana e altomedievale nell' Oristanese (Caglieri 1985)*, 43-44. Taranto: Scorpione.

— 1989. *Il tempio di Antas*. Sassari: C. Delfino.

— 1992. *Il complesso epigrafico rupestre della Grotta delle Vipere. Rupes Loquentes, Iscrizioni ruprestri di eta romana in Italia Roma, Bomarzo 1989*. Rome: Istituto italiano per la storia antica.

— 1993a. Profilo storico di una città fluviale dell'antichità. In *Archeologie e ambiente naturale. Prospettive di cooperazione tra le autonomie locali nel sud dell' Europa*. Sassari: Industria grafica.

— 1997. Le scoperte archeologiche e le Carte d'Arborea. In *Le Carte d'Arborea. Falsi e Falsari nella Sardegna del XIX secoloed*. L. Marrocu. Cagliari: AM & D.

— 1998. L'insediamento fenicio di Othoca. *Phoinikes B Shrdn. I Fenici in Sardegna, nuovi acquisizioni*. Oristano: S'Alvure.

— 1998a. La necropoli settentrionale di Tharros. *Phoinikes B. Shrdn. I Fenici in Sardegna, nuovi acquisizioni*. Rome: Oristano: S'Alvure.

— 1998b. *Antiquarium arborense*. Sassari: C. Delfino.

— 1999. Marytrium Luxurii. *La Sardegna paleocristiana tra Eusebio e Gregorio Magno. Atti del convegno nazionale di studi. Cagliari 1996*, 94-97. Cagliari: Pontificia Facoltà teologica della Sardegna.

— 2000. Inscriptiones parietariae Sardiniae. In *Epigraphai: miscellanea epigrafica in onore di Lidio Gasperini*, a cura di G. Paci, 119-1132. Tivoli: Tripigref.

Index